Three-Layer
Chocolate Cake
(page 247)

# BIG BOOK OF
# COUNTRY BAKING

*Over 400 sweet & savory recipes for every meal of the day*

# Our Story

**B**ack in 1984, we were next-door neighbors raising our families in the little town of Delaware, Ohio. Two moms with small children, we were looking for a way to do what we loved and stay home with the kids too. We had always shared a love of home cooking and making memories with family & friends and so, after many a conversation over the backyard fence, **Gooseberry Patch** was born.

We put together our first catalog at our kitchen tables, enlisting the help of our loved ones wherever we could. From that very first mailing, we found an immediate connection with many of our customers, and it wasn't long before we began receiving letters, photos and recipes from these new friends. In 1992, we put together our very first cookbook, compiled from hundreds of these recipes, and the rest, as they say, is history.

Hard to believe it's been over 25 years since those kitchen-table days! From that original little **Gooseberry Patch** family, we've grown to include an amazing group of creative folks who love cooking, decorating and creating as much as we do. Today, we're best known for our homestyle, family-friendly cookbooks, now recognized as national bestsellers.

One thing's for sure, we couldn't have done it without our friends all across the country. Each year, we're honored to turn thousands of your recipes into our collectible cookbooks. Our hope is that each book captures the stories and heart of all of you who have shared with us. Whether you've been with us since the beginning or are just discovering us, welcome to the **Gooseberry Patch** family!

## Your friends at Gooseberry Patch

### We couldn't make our best-selling cookbooks without YOU!

Each of our books is filled with recipes from cooks just like you, gathered from kitchens all across the country.

Share your tried & true recipes with us on our website and you could be selected for an upcoming cookbook. If your recipe is included, you'll receive a FREE copy of the cookbook when it's published!

## www.gooseberrypatch.com

### We'd love to add YOU to our Circle of Friends!

Get free recipes, crafts, giveaways and so much more when you join our email club...join us online at all the spots below for even more goodies!

## Dear Friend,

When you think of life in the country, do you think of baking? Does it bring to mind warm breads, bubbly casseroles, and hearty potpies? Can you just smell the fruity cobblers and chocolatey cakes in the oven? Baking is one of our favorite activities, so we've put together this brand-new recipe collection of our best baked recipes...from breakfast to dinner to sweets.

There's nothing better than waking up to the smell of freshly baked treats, so start your morning off right with Peach Cobbler Muffins (page 11). For dinner, you'll be surprised to find out how many delicious entrées you can bake, such as Buttermilk Baked Chicken (page 105) or Tamale Pot Pie (page 165) for a fun twist on the usual all-in-one dish.

In addition to yummy breakfast treats and dinner entrées, we're also sharing plenty of sides, casseroles, one-dish meals, a whole chapter dedicated to all kinds of breads and some scrumptious sweets. From Chocolate Pound Cake (page 271) to Heavenly Key Lime Pie (page 296), we have an array of cakes, cupcakes, pies and cobblers worthy of a blue ribbon. And for some giftable goodies (or just to enjoy yourself), whip up a batch of Chocolate Fudge Cookies (page 318) or Brown Sugar Brownies (page 340).

So go ahead and preheat the oven...we've also included menus to help you plan your entire meal, as well as helpful kitchen tips. Whether you're making a weeknight dinner for the family or hosting a gathering of friends, we know you will find what you're looking for in this cookbook.

## From our kitchen to yours,

## Jo Ann & Vickie

Mocha Muffins
(page 12)

Tuscan Pork Loin
(page 99)

Green Bean Bundles
(page 213)

Comforting Southern Cake
(page 262)

# contents

Our Story ................................4
*How Gooseberry Patch got started*

Cozy Breakfast & Brunch....................8
*Morning favorites to start the day off right*

Heartwarming Breads, Rolls
& Biscuits..............................46
*Sweet & savory delights to enjoy with
any meal*

Best Baked Entrées .....................84
*Must-have main dishes for every occasion*

Potluck-Perfect Casseroles...........128
*Comforting recipes for easy, at-home meals
or for sharing*

Family-Style One-Dish Dinners.....162
*Simple suppers for any night of the week*

Hot & Bubbly Sides...........................202
*Delicious baked side dishes to complete
your meal*

Favorite Cakes & Cupcakes........242
*Yummy baked goods to ensure every meal
has a sweet ending*

Homestyle Pies & Cobblers......280
*These tasty treats are comfort food at its finest*

Warm from the Oven...........................314
*Satisfy your sweet tooth with scrumptious
cookies, bars & treats*

Menus for all Occasions ..............356
*Twelve menus for all year 'round*

Index ................................363
*Find any recipe...fast*

Mocha Muffins (page 12)

Supreme Caramel Apple Rolls (page 19)

Crab, Corn & Pepper Frittata (page 37)

Pumpkin Biscotti (page 44)

# COZY BREAKFAST & BRUNCH

*Morning favorites to start the day off right*

Peach Cobbler
Muffins

# Peach Cobbler Muffins

*My most requested muffins...I hope you like them as much as my family & friends do! Everyone loves them so much, they disappear right away whenever I make them to share.*

3 c. all-purpose flour
1 c. sugar
1½ T. baking soda
½ t. salt
¾ c. butter, diced
1¾ c. milk
16-oz. can peaches, drained and chopped

Mix flour, sugar, baking soda and salt in a large bowl. Cut in butter with a pastry blender or fork until crumbly. Add milk and peaches; stir just until moistened. Fill greased or paper-lined muffin cups ⅔ full. Spoon Topping onto muffins. Bake at 400 degrees for about 20 minutes, until golden and a toothpick inserted in the center comes out clean. Turn out and cool slightly on a wire rack; serve warm or cold. Makes 2 dozen.

## Topping:
4 T. butter, diced
4 T. sugar
1 t. cinnamon

Mix all ingredients together with a pastry blender or fork in a small bowl until crumbly.

*Bonnie Allard*
*Santa Rosa, CA*

# Brown Sugar Muffins

*I have 14 grandchildren, and when they come for breakfast at my house, they all love to eat these yummy muffins!*

1 c. quick-cooking oats, uncooked
¾ c. brown sugar, packed
½ c. milk
¼ c. butter, melted and slightly cooled
1 egg, beaten
1 c. all-purpose flour
½ c. chopped walnuts
2 t. baking powder

Mix oats, brown sugar and milk in a large bowl; let stand for 5 minutes. Add butter and egg; blend well. Stir in remaining ingredients just until moistened. Fill greased muffin cups ⅔ full. Bake at 400 degrees for 15 to 20 minutes, until a toothpick inserted in center comes out clean. Makes one dozen.

*Doris Carrig*
*Miami, FL*

## get creative

Muffins just seem sweeter served from a create-your-own farmhouse-style muffin stand. Use household cement, found at hardware stores, to secure the bottom of a jadite teacup to the center bottom of a vintage plate. Let cement dry according to the manufacturer's instructions. When completely dry, arrange muffins on the plate and then top with a glass cake stand lid.

## Chocolatey Banana Muffins

2 c. all-purpose flour
⅓ c. sugar
2 T. baking cocoa
1 T. baking powder
1 c. bananas, mashed
⅔ c. oil
1 egg
1 c. semi-sweet chocolate chips

Stir together flour, sugar, cocoa and baking powder in a bowl. Combine bananas, oil and egg in a separate bowl; beat with an electric mixer at medium speed until blended. Gradually add flour mixture to banana mixture, stirring just until blended. Fold in chocolate chips; fill paper-lined muffin cups ¾ full. Bake at 425 degrees for 15 to 20 minutes, until a toothpick inserted in center comes out clean; remove from pan and cool completely on a wire rack. Makes one dozen.

*Diana Pindell*
*Wooster, OH*

## Grandma Retha's Rhubarb Muffins

1 c. brown sugar, packed
1 egg, beaten
1 c. buttermilk
½ c. oil
2 t. vanilla extract
1½ c. rhubarb, diced
Optional: ½ c. chopped walnuts
2½ c. all-purpose flour
1 t. baking powder
1 t. baking soda
½ t. salt
1 t. butter, melted
½ c. sugar
1 t. cinnamon

Combine brown sugar, egg, buttermilk, oil and vanilla in a large bowl; mix well. Stir in rhubarb and nuts, if desired. Combine flour, baking powder, baking soda and salt in a separate bowl; stir dry ingredients into rhubarb mixture. Fill greased muffin cups ⅔ full. Stir together melted butter, sugar and cinnamon; sprinkle over muffins. Bake at 350 degrees for 20 to 25 minutes, until a toothpick inserted in center comes out clean. Makes 12 to 15 large muffins.

*Emily Lynch*
*Iroquois, SD*

## Mocha Muffins

2 c. all-purpose flour
¾ c. plus 1 T. sugar
2½ t. baking powder
1 t. cinnamon
½ t. salt
1 c. milk
2 T. plus ½ t. instant coffee granules, divided
½ c. butter, melted
1 egg, beaten
1½ t. vanilla extract, divided
1 c. mini semi-sweet chocolate chips, divided
½ c. cream cheese, softened

Whisk together flour, sugar, baking powder, cinnamon and salt in a large bowl. Stir together milk and 2 tablespoons coffee granules in a separate bowl until coffee is dissolved. Add butter, egg and one teaspoon vanilla; mix well. Stir into dry ingredients until just moistened. Fold in ¾ cup chocolate chips. Fill greased or paper-lined muffin cups ⅔ full. Bake at 375 degrees for 17 to 20 minutes. Cool for 5 minutes before removing from pans to wire racks. Combine cream cheese and remaining coffee granules, vanilla and chocolate chips in a food processor or blender. Cover and process until well blended. Refrigerate spread until serving time. Serve spread on side. Makes 16 muffins.

*Paige Woodard*
*Loveland, CO*

Mocha Muffins

# Cranberry Upside-Down Muffins

2½ c. all-purpose flour
½ c. sugar
1 T. baking powder
½ t. salt
1¼ c. milk
⅓ c. butter, melted and slightly cooled
1 egg, beaten

Combine flour, sugar, baking powder and salt in a large bowl; blend well. Add milk, butter and egg to flour mixture; stir just until moistened. Spoon Cranberry Topping into 18 greased muffin cups. Spoon batter over topping, filling each cup ⅔ full. Bake at 400 degrees for 16 to 18 minutes, until a toothpick inserted in center comes out clean. Immediately invert onto a wire rack placed on wax paper; serve warm. Makes 1½ dozen.

## Cranberry Topping:

½ c. cranberries, halved
½ c. chopped nuts
⅓ c. brown sugar, packed
¼ c. butter
½ t. cinnamon

Combine all ingredients in a small saucepan. Cook over medium heat until brown sugar dissolves. Cool 10 minutes.

*Barbara Girlardo*
*Pittsburgh, PA*

Cranberry
Upside-Down Muffins

## Butter-Rum Muffins

⅔ c. butter, softened
1⅓ c. sugar
4 eggs
4 c. all-purpose flour
2 T. baking powder
¼ t. salt
2 c. milk
1 t. butter flavoring
1 t. rum extract
11-oz. pkg. butterscotch chips

Combine butter, sugar and eggs in a large bowl; beat with an electric mixer at medium speed until well blended. Stir together flour, baking powder and salt in a separate bowl. Stir together milk, flavoring and extract in another bowl. Add the milk mixture to butter mixture alternately with flour mixture; stir well. Fold in butterscotch chips. Fill lightly greased muffin cups ⅔ full. Bake at 350 degrees for 15 to 20 minutes, until a toothpick inserted in center comes out clean. Makes 3 dozen.

*Diana Krol*
*Nickerson, KS*

Emma's Gingerbread Muffins

## Emma's Gingerbread Muffins

½ c. butter, softened
½ c. shortening
¾ c. sugar
3 eggs
½ c. molasses
¼ c. light corn syrup
3 c. all-purpose flour
2 t. cinnamon
2 t. ground ginger
1 t. nutmeg
1 t. baking soda
1 c. buttermilk

Combine butter and shortening in a large bowl. Beat with an electric mixer at medium speed until creamy. Add sugar; beat just until combined. Add eggs, one at a time, beating after each addition. Add molasses and corn syrup; beat just until blended. Sift together flour and spices. Dissolve baking soda in buttermilk; add the milk mixture to butter mixture alternately with flour mixture, stirring just until combined. Fill greased and floured muffin cups ⅔ full. Bake at 350 degrees for 15 minutes, or until a toothpick inserted in center comes out clean. Makes 2½ dozen.

*Bernadette Dobias*
*Houston, TX*

# Mom's Orange Bow Knots

*I still love going home to find these amazing rolls in Mom's kitchen! The recipe goes back a few generations in my family. Quick breads may be easier, but nothing tastes better than yeast bread.*

1¼ c. milk
½ c. shortening
⅓ c. sugar
¾ t. salt
1 env. active dry yeast
2 eggs, beaten
¼ c. orange juice
2 T. orange zest
5 c. all-purpose flour, divided

Heat milk just to boiling. Combine milk, shortening, sugar and salt in a bowl; let cool to about 110 to 115 degrees. Dissolve yeast in milk mixture. Add eggs, orange juice and orange zest; beat well. Stir in 2 cups flour; let stand 10 minutes. Stir in remaining flour. Cover with a tea towel; let rise until doubled, one to 2 hours. Punch down dough; roll out ½-inch thick on a floured surface. Cut into 10-inch by ½-inch strips. Tie each strip loosely in a bow; arrange on lightly greased baking sheets. Cover and let rise again, 30 minutes to one hour. Bake at 375 degrees for 15 minutes, or until golden. Cool; spread with Orange Frosting. Makes 2 to 3 dozen.

## Orange Frosting:
1 c. powdered sugar
2 T. orange juice
1 t. orange zest

Stir together all ingredients, adding powdered sugar to desired consistency.

*Katie Majeske*
*Denver, PA*

# Auntie Kay Kay's Sticky Buns

2 16-oz. pkgs. frozen bread dough
½ c. cinnamon-sugar
½ c. butter
½ c. sugar
½ c. brown sugar, packed
½ c. vanilla ice cream

Place frozen bread dough in a lightly greased 13"x9" baking pan. Cover pan with plastic wrap sprayed with non-stick vegetable spray; thaw dough in refrigerator overnight. Remove thawed dough from pan and cut into bite-size pieces; roll each piece in cinnamon-sugar to coat. Place coated dough pieces in pan. Melt butter, sugars and ice cream in a saucepan over medium-low heat; stir until smooth. Pour butter mixture over coated dough pieces. Bake at 400 degrees for 20 minutes. Serves 6 to 8.

*Jen Sell*
*Farmington, MN*

*Everyone loves having my Auntie Kay Kay visit! She always starts making these sticky buns the day before so they are ready to bake the next morning. —Jen*

Auntie Kay Kay's
Sticky Buns

Supreme Caramel
Apple Rolls

## Supreme Caramel Apple Rolls

*This is one of my family's most-requested recipes. One time after serving them, one of my seven brothers told me, "These rolls are so bad, I need to take the rest home with me to eat!"*

21-oz. can apple pie filling
½ c. caramel ice cream topping
Optional: ½ c. chopped pecans
8-oz. pkg. cream cheese, softened
⅓ c. powdered sugar
2 8-oz. tubes refrigerated crescent rolls
½ c. sugar
½ c. brown sugar, packed
½ c. butter, melted

Combine pie filling and ice cream topping in a large bowl; pour into a greased 13"x9" baking pan. Sprinkle pecans, if using, over mixture. Combine cream cheese and powdered sugar in a bowl; set aside. Separate crescent roll dough into 2 rectangles; press perforations to seal. Spread half of cream cheese mixture over each rectangle. Starting with long side of each rectangle, roll up and seal edges. Cut each roll into 12 slices with a serrated knife. Stir together sugar and brown sugar in a bowl; dip slices in melted butter and then coat with sugar mixture. Arrange slices in baking pan. Bake at 400 degrees for 25 to 30 minutes, until center rolls are golden. Immediately invert onto a serving plate. Serve warm. Makes 2 dozen rolls.

*Tracey Graham*
*Churubusco, IN*

Creamy Cinnamon Rolls

## Creamy Cinnamon Rolls

*These delectable bites make a great breakfast treat anytime. You can even make the dough ahead of time. Just place rolls in the pan, cover with greased plastic wrap, refrigerate overnight and let them rise the following morning until double in bulk, approximately two hours.*

16-oz. pkg. frozen white bread dough, thawed
2 T. butter, melted
⅔ c. brown sugar, packed
½ c. chopped nuts
1 t. cinnamon
½ c. whipping cream
⅔ c. powdered sugar
1 T. milk

Roll dough into an 18"x6" rectangle on a lightly floured surface. Brush with melted butter. Combine brown sugar, nuts and cinnamon. Sprinkle evenly over dough. Roll up jelly-roll style, starting with a long side. Cut into 20 slices; arrange cut-side down in a greased 13"x9" baking pan. Cover and let rise until almost double in bulk, about 1½ hours. Uncover and pour cream over rolls. Bake at 350 degrees for 25 to 30 minutes. Mix together powdered sugar and milk; drizzle over warm rolls. Makes 20 rolls.

*Sheila Plock*
*Boalsburg, PA*

Overnight Blueberry
French Toast

Make-Ahead Pumpkin
Pie French Toast

## Overnight Blueberry French Toast

*This delicious recipe has become a holiday tradition at our house...my husband and children love it! It's easy to make the night before; then in the morning, just pop it in the oven.*

1 baguette loaf, sliced 1-inch thick
6 eggs
3 c. milk
1 c. brown sugar, packed and divided
vanilla extract to taste
nutmeg to taste
¼ c. chopped pecans
2 c. blueberries
Optional: maple syrup

Arrange baguette slices in a lightly greased 13"x9" baking pan; set aside. Whisk together eggs, milk, ¾ cup brown sugar, vanilla and nutmeg in a large bowl. Pour mixture evenly over baguette slices. Cover and chill overnight. Just before baking, sprinkle remaining brown sugar, pecans and blueberries over top. Bake, uncovered, at 350 degrees for 50 minutes, or until golden and bubbly. Serve with maple syrup, if desired. Serves 6 to 8.

Gloria Bills
Plymouth, MI

## Make-Ahead Pumpkin Pie French Toast

*It's a great Sunday morning breakfast...it can bake while you get ready for church. It's also super-easy for husbands to whip up so Mom can sleep in just a bit on Saturday morning!*

1 loaf French, Italian, challah or Hawaiian bread,
    cut into 1-inch slices
3 eggs, beaten
1½ c. milk
1 c. half-and-half
½ c. egg substitute
1 T. pumpkin pie spice
1 t. vanilla extract
¼ t. salt
½ c. brown sugar, packed
1 to 2 T. butter, sliced

Arrange bread slices in bottom of a greased 13"x9" baking pan. Whisk together eggs, milk, half-and-half, egg substitute, spice, vanilla and salt. Stir in brown sugar; pour mixture over bread slices. Refrigerate, covered, overnight. Dot top with butter and bake, uncovered, at 350 degrees for 40 to 45 minutes. Serves 8.

Jennifer Yandle
Indian Trail, NC

# Cream Cheese Danish

*Did you get out of bed on the wrong side today?
You'll feel so much better after you've tasted this!*

2 8-oz. pkgs. cream cheese, softened
¾ c. sugar
1 egg yolk, beaten
2 t. lemon juice
1 t. vanilla extract
2 8-oz. tubes refrigerated crescent rolls
2 c. powdered sugar
4 to 5 T. milk

Blend together cream cheese and sugar in a large bowl; add egg yolk, lemon juice and vanilla. Set aside. Layer one tube of crescent rolls in bottom of a greased 13"x9" baking pan; press seams together. Spread cream cheese mixture over top; layer remaining tube of rolls on top of cream cheese. Bake at 350 degrees for 15 to 20 minutes, until golden. Let cool. Mix together powdered sugar and milk to a thin consistency; drizzle over top. Cut into slices to serve. Serves 15 to 20.

*Robin Long*
*Newberry, SC*

Cream Cheese Danish

Dutch Puffed Apple
Pancake

## Dutch Puffed Apple Pancake

*An old-fashioned favorite that puffs up high in the oven and then falls when taken out...fun to make, delicious to eat!*

¼ c. butter, melted
1 Granny Smith apple, cored, peeled and
    thinly sliced
½ c. chopped walnuts
4 eggs
1 c. milk
⅔ c. all-purpose flour
2 T. sugar
1 t. vanilla extract
¼ t. cinnamon
⅛ t. salt
½ c. sweetened, dried cranberries
3 T. brown sugar, packed
Optional: maple syrup

Spread butter in a 9" glass pie plate; arrange apple slices and walnuts over butter. Bake at 425 degrees for about 5 minutes, until apples begin to soften and walnuts are lightly toasted. Beat together eggs, milk, flour, sugar, vanilla, cinnamon and salt in a large bowl with an electric mixer at medium speed. Stir in cranberries. Remove pie plate from oven; spray inside edges with non-stick vegetable spray. Pour batter over apples and walnuts; sprinkle with brown sugar. Bake, uncovered, at 425 degrees for about 25 minutes, until center is set and edges are puffed and golden. Cut into wedges and serve immediately with maple syrup, if desired. Serves 4.

*Vickie*
*Gooseberry Patch*

## Finnish Pancakes

*A moist, custard-like treat that can be served with syrup, jelly or honey.*

3 T. butter
4 eggs
2 c. milk
1 c. all-purpose flour
1 T. sugar
1 t. vanilla extract
⅛ t. salt

Melt butter in a 13"x9" baking pan in a 400-degree oven; set aside. Place eggs in a blender; blend well. Add milk, flour, sugar, vanilla and salt; blend thoroughly. Pour into a pan; bake at 400 degrees for 35 minutes. Serves 4.

*Corinne Ficek*
*Normal, IL*

### berry sweet, too!
Top pancakes with something other than syrup...spoonfuls of fruity jam or homemade preserves, fresh berries and a dusting of powdered sugar or a drizzle of honey are all scrumptious.

# Tangy Cranberry Breakfast Cake

*This yummy coffee cake has three fantastic layers!*

2 c. all-purpose flour
1⅓ c. sugar, divided
1½ t. baking powder
½ t. baking soda
¼ t. salt
2 eggs, divided
¾ c. orange juice
¼ c. butter, melted
2 t. vanilla extract, divided
2 c. cranberries, coarsely chopped
Optional: 1 T. orange zest
8-oz. pkg. cream cheese, softened

Combine flour, one cup sugar, baking powder, baking soda and salt in a large bowl; mix well and set aside. Combine one egg, orange juice, butter and one teaspoon vanilla in a small bowl; mix well and stir into flour mixture until well combined. Fold in cranberries and zest, if using. Pour into a greased 9" round springform pan and set aside. Beat together cream cheese and remaining ⅓ cup sugar in a small bowl until smooth. Add remaining egg and one teaspoon vanilla; mix well. Spread over batter; sprinkle with Topping. Place pan on a baking sheet; bake at 350 degrees for one hour, or until toothpick inserted in center comes out clean. Let cool on wire rack for 15 minutes before removing sides of pan. Serves 12.

## Topping:
6 T. all-purpose flour
¼ c. sugar
2 T. butter, diced

Combine flour and sugar in a small bowl. Cut in butter with a pastry blender or fork until crumbly.

Tangy Cranberry
Breakfast Cake

Cherry Streusel Coffee Cake

## Cherry Streusel Coffee Cake

*This easy-to-assemble coffee cake recipe won "Best of Show" several years ago at a county fair, and it's been requested at many social events.*

16½-oz. pkg. yellow cake mix, divided
1 env. active dry yeast
1 c. all-purpose flour
2 eggs, beaten
⅔ c. warm water
5 T. butter, melted
21-oz. can cherry pie filling
2 T. sugar
Optional: chopped nuts

Combine 1½ cups dry cake mix, yeast, flour, eggs and warm water (110 to 115 degrees); stir for 2 minutes. Spread in a lightly greased 13"x9" baking pan. Blend melted butter and remaining cake mix; set aside. Spoon pie filling over batter in pan. Crumble butter mixture over pie filling. Sprinkle sugar over top. Bake at 375 degrees for 30 minutes. Let cool. Drizzle Glaze over cooled cake; sprinkle nuts on top, if desired. Serves 15.

### Glaze:
1 c. powdered sugar
1 T. corn syrup
1 to 2 T. water

Combine powdered sugar and corn syrup. Stir in enough water to form a glaze consistency.

*Joyceann Dreibellis*
*Wooster, OH*

## Orange-Walnut Brunch Cake

*Don't save this yummy cake just for special occasions...enjoy it anytime!*

16.3-oz. tube refrigerated jumbo biscuits
⅓ c. sugar
¼ c. walnuts, finely chopped
1 T. orange zest
2 T. butter, melted
½ c. powdered sugar
3 T. cream cheese, softened
2 T. orange juice

Grease a 9" round cake pan. Separate biscuit dough into 8 biscuits. Place one biscuit in center of pan. Cut remaining biscuits in half, forming 14 half-circles. Arrange pieces around center biscuit with cut sides facing same direction. Combine sugar, walnuts and orange zest in a small bowl; mix well. Brush butter over tops of biscuits and sprinkle with walnut mixture. Bake at 375 degrees for 20 minutes, or until golden. Combine powdered sugar, cream cheese and enough orange juice for desired drizzling consistency in a separate bowl. Blend until smooth; drizzle over warm cake. Cool for 10 minutes. Serves 6 to 8.

*Jackie Smulski*
*Lyons, IL*

# Niles Coffee Cake

*I had a dear elderly friend, Martha, who rented me a room when I was younger. She would make this delicious coffee cake, and we couldn't keep out of it. She always called it "Niles Coffee Cake" after the church she attended in Niles, Michigan. I loved her dearly, and I always think of her when I make this coffee cake.*

16-oz. pkg. frozen white bread dough
1 c. chopped pecans or walnuts
½ c. cook & serve butterscotch pudding mix
½ c. butter
½ c. brown sugar, packed

Let frozen bread dough stand at room temperature for one hour the night before baking. Cut dough into 16 pieces and roll into balls. Spray a Bundt® pan with non-stick vegetable spray; sprinkle nuts into bottom of pan. Arrange dough balls in pan; sprinkle with pudding mix and set aside. Melt butter and brown sugar in a small saucepan over medium-high heat. Pour hot mixture over dough balls. Cover pan; let rise overnight at room temperature, until double in size. Bake at 325 degrees for 25 to 30 minutes, until rolls are light golden. Turn out onto a decorative plate; serve warm. Serves 6 to 8.

*Dawn Wright*
*Marysville, OH*

# Trudy's Cherry Coffee Cake

*This was given to me by my friend Kelley...it's a recipe from her mother, Trudy. I like to make it with different fruit fillings, such as blueberry or apple, and various nuts, such as pecans or almonds. My son requests it often!*

1¾ c. biscuit baking mix, divided
1 egg, beaten
½ c. sugar
¼ c. milk
½ t. vanilla extract
⅛ t. salt
21-oz. can cherry pie filling, partially drained
½ c. brown sugar, packed
⅓ c. chopped walnuts
½ t. cinnamon
3 T. butter, diced

Combine 1½ cups baking mix, egg, sugar, milk, vanilla and salt. Stir until smooth. Pour mixture into a lightly greased 8"x8" baking pan. Spoon pie filling over mixture in pan. Mix together remaining baking mix, brown sugar, nuts, cinnamon and butter using a pastry blender or fork until crumbly. Sprinkle over pie filling. Bake at 375 degrees for 30 minutes. Cut into squares. Serves 6 to 8.

*Dawn Menard*
*Seekonk, MA*

### comforting breakfast
Coffee cakes are usually best served warm and accompanied with a steaming cup of coffee.

Walnut-Maple
Streusel Cake

# Walnut-Maple Streusel Cake

*This cake keeps well, so you can bake it a day before and store it, wrapped in plastic, at room temperature.*

2 c. all-purpose flour
1 t. baking powder
1 t. baking soda
½ t. salt
½ c. butter, room temperature
¾ c. sugar
2 eggs, beaten
1 t. vanilla extract
8-oz. container sour cream
Optional: powdered sugar

Whisk together flour, baking powder, baking soda and salt in a medium bowl; set aside. Beat butter and sugar in a large bowl with an electric mixer at medium-high speed until fluffy. Beat in eggs and vanilla. Beat in flour mixture alternately with sour cream, mixing just until blended. Spoon half of batter into a buttered and floured Bundt®

pan. Spoon two-thirds of Walnut Filling over batter. Spread remaining batter over filling; smooth top. Dot with remaining filling. Bake at 350 degrees for 40 minutes, or until a toothpick inserted in center comes out clean. Cool cake in pan on a wire rack for 15 minutes. Run a knife around pan sides to loosen; turn cake out onto a serving platter and dust with powdered sugar, if desired. Serves 12.

## Walnut Filling:
½ c. all-purpose flour
2 T. butter, softened
1 t. cinnamon
1¼ c. chopped walnuts
½ c. maple syrup

Mix together flour, butter and cinnamon in a small bowl with a pastry blender or fork until crumbly. Stir in nuts and syrup.

*Sarah Oravecz*
*Gooseberry Patch*

Esther's Delicious
Breakfast Treat

## Esther's Delicious Breakfast Treat

*These goodies freeze well. Wrap them in aluminum foil...then just reheat in a warm oven for a quick breakfast.*

1 c. brown sugar, packed
½ to ¾ c. chopped nuts
⅓ c. maple syrup
6 T. butter, softened and divided
8-oz. pkg. cream cheese, softened
¼ c. powdered sugar
2 10.2-oz. tubes refrigerated biscuits

Combine brown sugar, nuts, syrup and 4 tablespoons butter in an ungreased 13"x9" baking pan; set aside. Beat cream cheese, powdered sugar and remaining butter with an electric mixer at medium speed until smooth; set aside. Press biscuits into 4-inch circles; spoon one tablespoon cream cheese mixture onto center of each. Fold dough over cream cheese, forming finger-shaped rolls. Arrange rolls in 2 rows, seam-side down, over brown sugar mixture in pan. Bake at 350 degrees for 20 to 30 minutes, until golden. Let cool for several minutes; turn out onto a serving plate. Serves 8 to 10.

*Esther Goodner*
*Danville, IL*

## Sweet Blintz Soufflé

*Mom always pulled this yummy recipe out for company and holidays. It's light, refreshing and unusual.*

12 frozen blintzes, any variety
4 eggs, beaten
1 t. vanilla extract
¼ c. sugar
⅛ t. salt
1½ c. sour cream
½ c. butter, melted and slightly cooled
Garnish: applesauce or sour cream

Arrange frozen blintzes folded-side down in a 13"x9" glass baking pan coated with non-stick vegetable spray. Beat eggs, vanilla, sugar and salt together in a bowl; stir in sour cream and butter. Spoon over blintzes. Bake, uncovered, at 350 degrees for 40 to 45 minutes, until golden. Garnish with applesauce or sour cream. Serves 6.

*Lori Rosenberg*
*University Heights, OH*

*breakfast in bed*
Surprise your sweetie with a breakfast tray filled with his or her favorite morning meal, a newspaper and a hot cup of coffee.

## Blueberry & Cream Cheese Strata

*This berry-filled strata is just right for a leisurely breakfast with family & friends.*

16-oz. loaf white bread, crusts removed, cubed and divided
2 c. frozen blueberries, divided
3-oz. pkg. cream cheese, cut into ¼-inch cubes
4 eggs
2 c. milk
⅓ c. sugar
1 t. vanilla extract
¼ t. salt
¼ t. nutmeg

Place half of bread in a greased 8"x8" baking pan; top with one cup blueberries. Top with cream cheese, remaining bread and remaining blueberries; set aside. Beat eggs, milk, sugar, vanilla, salt and nutmeg with an electric mixer at medium speed until blended. Pour over bread mixture and refrigerate for 20 minutes to overnight. Bake, uncovered, at 325 degrees for one hour. Serves 4 to 6.

*Kathy Grashoff*
*Fort Wayne, IN*

## Sausage & Cherry Tart with Walnuts

1 c. all-purpose flour
⅔ c. walnuts, ground
6 T. chilled butter, cubed
1 T. sugar
½ t. dry mustard
¼ t. salt
⅛ t. cayenne pepper
1 to 2 T. milk
½ lb. ground pork breakfast sausage
1 onion, finely diced
½ to 1 c. dried tart cherries or cranberries
½ c. chopped walnuts
¼ t. dried thyme
2 eggs, beaten
1 c. whipping cream
3-oz. pkg. crumbled Gorgonzola cheese

Combine flour, ground walnuts, butter, sugar, dry mustard, salt and cayenne pepper in a food processor. Pulse just until mixture resembles bread crumbs. Add one tablespoon milk; pulse until dough comes together. If dough is too crumbly, add more milk until it holds together. Shape dough into a ball and press evenly into a lightly greased 9" round tart pan. Freeze for 30 minutes. Bake crust at 350 degrees for 15 to 20 minutes, until golden. Remove from oven and set aside. Brown sausage and onion in a skillet over medium heat; drain well. Stir in cherries or cranberries, walnuts and thyme. Set aside. Whisk eggs and cream in a bowl until smooth. Spoon sausage mixture into baked crust; sprinkle with cheese. Pour egg mixture over all. Bake at 350 degrees for 15 to 20 minutes, until golden and a toothpick inserted in center comes out clean. Cool 15 minutes before serving. Serves 8.

*Sharon Demers*
*Dolores, CO*

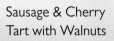

Sausage & Cherry
Tart with Walnuts

# Yummy Brunch Strata

*All you need to accompany this feed-a-crowd dish is a tray of sweet rolls, a big pot of hot coffee and fellowship!*

⅓ c. oil
2 c. cooked ham, diced
3 c. sliced mushrooms
3 c. zucchini, diced
1½ c. onion, diced
1½ c. green, red or yellow pepper, diced
2 cloves garlic, minced
2  8-oz. pkgs. cream cheese, softened
½ c. half-and-half
1 doz. eggs, beaten
4 c. day-old bread, cubed
3 c. shredded Cheddar cheese
salt and pepper to taste

Heat oil in a large skillet over medium-high heat. Add ham, vegetables and garlic. Sauté for 3 to 5 minutes, until tender. Drain; set aside. Beat together cream cheese and half-and-half in a large bowl with an electric mixer at medium speed. Stir in vegetable mixture and remaining ingredients; blend lightly. Pour into 2 greased 11"x7" baking pans. Bake, uncovered, at 350 degrees for 35 to 40 minutes, until a knife inserted near center comes out clean. Let stand 10 minutes; cut into squares. Serves 16.

Lynn Williams
Muncie, IN

Yummy
Brunch Strata

## Creamy Crab Bake

*An elegant breakfast casserole that is ideal for a bridal or Sunday brunch get-together.*

2 eggs, beaten
2 c. milk
2 c. seasoned croutons
8-oz. pkg. shredded Cheddar cheese
1 T. dried, minced onion
1 T. dried parsley
1 lb. crabmeat
salt and pepper to taste
¼ c. grated Parmesan cheese

Combine eggs, milk, croutons, Cheddar cheese, onion and parsley in a large bowl. Stir in crabmeat; sprinkle with salt and pepper. Spoon into a lightly greased 13"x9" baking pan; sprinkle with Parmesan cheese. Bake at 325 degrees for 45 to 55 minutes, until a knife inserted in center comes out clean. Serves 8.

*Diana Chaney*
*Olathe, KS*

## Cozy Breakfast Casserole

*A hearty, savory hot dish that I always made on Christmas Eve to pop in the oven on Christmas morning…now that my boys are older, they still request this every year.*

4 eggs, beaten
2 c. milk
½ t. dry mustard
6 slices bread, cubed
1 lb. breakfast sausage links, browned, drained & sliced
8-oz. pkg. shredded Cheddar cheese

Combine eggs, milk and mustard in a large bowl; mix well and set aside. Layer bread cubes, sausage and cheese in a greased 13"x9" baking pan. Pour egg mixture over top; refrigerate overnight. Bake, covered, at 350 degrees for 45 minutes. Uncover and bake for 10 more minutes. Serves 4 to 6.

*Robin Robertson*
*East Stroudsburg, PA*

## Summer Swiss Quiche

*This is an excellent breakfast or brunch dish to serve when the garden harvest kicks in.*

½ lb. bacon
2 zucchini, thinly sliced
I green pepper, chopped
I onion, chopped
8 eggs, beaten
I c. milk
¼ c. biscuit baking mix
6 slices Swiss cheese

Cook bacon in a skillet over medium heat until crisp; remove from pan and set aside. Sauté zucchini, green pepper and onion in bacon drippings in same skillet over medium heat. Mix eggs, milk and baking mix in a bowl. Pour egg mixture into a lightly greased 13"x9" baking dish. Spoon zucchini mixture over egg mixture. Cover with crumbled bacon; arrange cheese slices on top. Bake, uncovered, at 350 degrees for 30 to 35 minutes, until a toothpick inserted in center comes out clean. Cut into squares. Serves 8 to 10.

*Rebecca Barna*
*Blairsville, PA*

Summer Swiss Quiche

## Classic Quiche Lorraine

*This recipe makes two quiches...just add a fresh fruit salad for an oh-so-easy brunch with friends.*

1 lb. bacon, cut into 1-inch pieces
2 9-inch pie crusts
8-oz. pkg. shredded Swiss cheese
8-oz. pkg. shredded Cheddar cheese
8 eggs, beaten
2 c. whipping cream
1 T. Worcestershire sauce
1 T. pepper
⅛ t. salt

Cook bacon in a skillet over medium-high heat until crisp; drain on paper towels. Arrange pie crusts in two 9-inch pie plates; sprinkle bacon into crusts. Mix together cheeses in a bowl; sprinkle over bacon. Whisk together remaining ingredients in a separate bowl. Divide egg mixture between crusts. Bake at 350 degrees for 45 minutes, or until golden. Let stand about 10 minutes; cut into wedges and serve warm. Makes 2 quiches; each serves 6.

*Francie Stutzman*
*Clinton, OH*

### just for you

Bake a quiche in muffin or custard cups for oh-so-simple individual servings. When making minis, reduce the baking time by about 10 minutes and check for doneness with a toothpick.

## Herbed Sausage Quiche

*For a savory pie crust, spread 2½ tablespoons softened butter in a pie plate and firmly press 2½ cups buttery cracker crumbs or seasoned dry bread crumbs into the butter. Freeze until firm; pour in filling and bake as directed.*

1 c. ground pork breakfast sausage, browned
  and drained
3 eggs, beaten
1 c. whipping cream
1 c. shredded Cheddar cheese
1 sprig fresh rosemary, chopped
1½ t. Italian seasoning
¼ t. salt
¼ t. pepper
9-inch pie crust, baked

Mix together all ingredients except pie crust in a bowl; spread into crust. Bake, uncovered, at 450 degrees for 15 minutes. Reduce heat to 350 degrees, cover with foil and bake for 9 more minutes. Cut into wedges to serve. Serves 8.

*Cherylann Smith*
*Efland, NC*

Herbed Sausage Quiche

Simply Scrumptious Frittata

## Simply Scrumptious Frittata

*A tasty way to use any remaining ham from Sunday dinner...try different cheeses for variety.*

1 T. oil
½ c. onion, chopped
½ c. green pepper, chopped
1 to 2 cloves garlic, minced
4 potatoes, peeled, cubed and cooked
¾ c. cooked ham, cubed
8 eggs, beaten
salt and pepper to taste
¾ c. shredded Cheddar cheese

Heat oil in a heavy oven-proof skillet over medium heat. Add onion and green pepper; cook and stir until tender. Add garlic; cook for one more minute. Stir in potatoes and ham; cook until heated through. Reduce heat to medium-low; add eggs, salt and pepper. Cook until eggs are firm on bottom, about 5 minutes. Top with cheese; bake at 350 degrees for 5 to 10 minutes, until cheese melts. Cut into wedges. Serves 4.

*Jill Valentine*
*Jackson, TN*

## Bacon & Chile Quiche

*This quiche is our favorite for holiday brunches. You can use diced ham instead of bacon. I also like to add fresh asparagus. May be made a day ahead and reheated when needed.*

4 eggs, beaten
1½ c. milk
4-oz. can diced green chiles, drained
½ t. salt
⅛ t. cayenne pepper
8-oz. pkg. shredded Cheddar or Swiss cheese
1 T. all-purpose flour
8 slices bacon, chopped and crisply cooked
9-inch pie crust

Combine eggs, milk, chiles and seasonings in a bowl; mix well. Toss cheese with flour in a separate bowl. Add cheese mixture and bacon to egg mixture; stir. Pour into unbaked pie crust. Bake at 350 degrees for 40 to 45 minutes. Let stand 10 minutes before cutting into wedges. Serves 6.

*Darlene Weathers-Gast*
*Fairfield, CA*

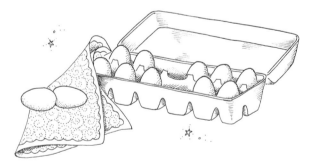

# Crab, Corn & Pepper Frittata

*When it is in season, use fresh corn.*

6 eggs, beaten
⅓ c. corn
⅓ c. mayonnaise
¼ c. milk
2 T. green onions, chopped
2 T. red pepper, chopped
salt and pepper to taste
1 c. crabmeat
1 c. shredded Monterey Jack cheese
Garnish: chopped green onions

Whisk together eggs, corn, mayonnaise, milk, onions, red pepper and salt and pepper to taste. Gently stir in crabmeat. Pour into a greased 10" pie plate. Bake at 350 degrees for 15 to 20 minutes. Sprinkle with cheese and bake for 5 more minutes, or until cheese is melted. Garnish with green onions. Serves 4 to 6.

*Stacie Avner
Delaware, OH*

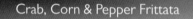

Crab, Corn & Pepper Frittata

# Breakfast Pie

*Nothing says "Rise & shine!" on a lazy weekend morning like the heavenly aroma of this pie in the oven.*

3 eggs, beaten
½ c. milk
½ t. salt
pepper to taste
5 T. butter, melted
3 c. frozen shredded hashbrowns, thawed
1 c. cooked ham, finely chopped
½ c. onion, finely chopped
½ c. green pepper, chopped
¼ c. diced pimento, drained
1 c. shredded sharp Cheddar cheese

Whisk together eggs, milk, salt and pepper in a bowl; set aside. Drizzle butter over a 9" pie plate; pat hashbrowns into bottom and up sides to form a crust. Bake at 425 degrees for 25 minutes, or until golden; cool. Sprinkle crust with ham, onion, green pepper, pimento and cheese; top with egg mixture. Reduce heat to 375 degrees; bake 35 to 40 minutes, until eggs are set. Let stand for 10 minutes before serving. Serves 4 to 6.

*Sharon Tillman*
*Hampton, VA*

# Country-Style Breakfast Pizza

*A surefire breakfast hit...you'll get requests for this recipe!*

13.8-oz. tube refrigerated pizza crust dough
Optional: garlic salt
24-oz. pkg. refrigerated mashed potatoes
10 eggs, beaten
Optional: chopped vegetables, cooked ham or
  sausage
8-oz. pkg. shredded Colby Jack cheese
4-oz. pkg. crumbled bacon pieces
Garnish: tomatoes, sliced; green onions, sliced

Spread pizza dough in a pizza pan sprayed with non-stick vegetable spray; sprinkle with garlic salt, if desired, and set aside. Place mashed potatoes in a microwave-safe bowl; microwave on high setting for about 3 minutes, until heated through. Spread potatoes over dough. Cook eggs as desired, adding vegetables, ham or sausage, if desired. Spread egg mixture evenly over potatoes. Sprinkle with cheese; top with bacon. Bake at 350 degrees for 22 to 25 minutes, until cheese is melted and crust is golden. Garnish with sliced tomatoes and sliced green onions. Serves 8.

*Jackie Balla*
*Walbridge, OH*

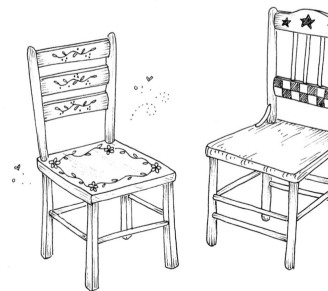

Country-Style Breakfast Pizza

# Haystack Eggs

*This is one of my dad's favorite breakfast treats. Mom has been making it for him for almost as long as I can remember!*

1¾-oz. can shoestring potatoes
4 eggs
1 c. shredded Cheddar cheese
6 slices bacon, crisply cooked and crumbled

Spread potatoes evenly over bottom of a greased 9" pie plate. Make 4 indentations in potatoes almost to bottom of pie plate. Carefully break one egg into each indentation. Bake at 350 degrees for 8 to 10 minutes, until eggs are almost set. Sprinkle with cheese and bacon. Return to oven; bake 2 to 4 more minutes, until eggs are set and cheese melts. Cut into 4 wedges; serve immediately. Serves 4.

*Melissa Cassulis*
*Bridgewater, NY*

Haystack Eggs

# Sweet & Spicy Bacon

*Try this easy-to-fix bacon at your next brunch...guests will love it!*

½ c. brown sugar, packed
2 T. chili powder
1 t. ground cumin
1 t. cumin seed
1 t. ground coriander
¼ t. cayenne pepper
10 thick slices bacon

Line a 15"x10" jelly-roll pan with aluminum foil. Place a wire rack on pan and set aside. Combine all ingredients except bacon. Sprinkle mixture onto a large piece of wax paper. Press bacon slices into mixture, turning to coat well. Arrange in a single layer on wire rack in pan; place pan on center rack of oven. Bake at 400 degrees for 12 minutes; turn bacon over. Bake for 10 more minutes, or until deep brown but not burned. Drain on paper towels; serve warm. Serves 4 to 5.

*Zoe Bennett*
*Columbia, SC*

# Mom's Texas Hash

*Simply said...this is good!*

1 lb. ground beef
2 onions, sliced
1 green pepper, chopped
14½-oz. can stewed tomatoes
½ t. to 1 t. chili powder
1 t. salt

Brown beef, onions and green pepper in a skillet; drain. Stir in remaining ingredients. Cook over medium heat about 8 minutes, until heated through. Spoon into an ungreased one-quart casserole dish. Bake, uncovered, at 350 degrees for 15 to 20 minutes. Serves 4.

*Ginger O'Connell*
*Hazel Park, MI*

# Sausage Balls

*My mom and I have made this tasty recipe for many family gatherings, including the morning after my wedding. It's so simple and uses only three ingredients.*

16-oz. pkg. ground pork breakfast sausage
16-oz. pkg. shredded sharp Cheddar, Pepper Jack or mozzarella cheese
1 c. all-purpose flour

Combine all ingredients in a large bowl. Knead together until completely blended. Form mixture into one to 1½-inch balls. Place balls one inch apart on parchment paper-lined baking sheets. Bake at 350 degrees for 15 to 20 minutes, until golden and and sausage is no longer pink. Cool slightly before serving. May be baked and refrigerated up to one week in a plastic zipping bag and warmed at serving time. Makes 3 to 4 dozen.

*Joanna Watson-Donahue*
*Lubbock, TX*

## Oven-Fried Bacon Potatoes

3 T. butter, melted
1½ lb. red potatoes, cut into ¼-inch slices
¼ t. salt
¼ t. pepper
6 slices bacon
Garnish: thyme leaves

Coat a cast-iron skillet with melted butter. Layer potatoes in skillet; season each layer with salt and pepper. Arrange uncooked bacon slices on top. Bake, uncovered, at 425 degrees for 40 minutes, or until bacon is crisp and potatoes are tender. Garnish with thyme leaves. Serves 6 to 8.

*Patricia Tilley*
*Sabine, WV*

## Brown Sugar Baked Oatmeal

*When I was a little girl, Mom would have freshly baked oatmeal-raisin cookies ready when I came home from school. This recipe reminds me of them… such a warm & cozy memory.*

½ c. butter, softened
½ c. brown sugar, packed, or ½ c. honey
2 eggs, beaten
3 c. long-cooking oats, uncooked
2 t. baking powder
1 t. salt
1 c. milk
Optional: chopped dried fruit or nuts
Optional: applesauce, honey, maple syrup

Blend together butter and brown sugar or honey. Add eggs; mix well. Stir in oats, baking powder, salt, milk and fruit or nuts, if using. Pour into a greased 8"x8" baking pan; bake at 350 degrees for 30 minutes. Serve with applesauce, honey or maple syrup, if desired. Serves 4 to 6.

*Sharon Demers*
*Dolores, CO*

## Glorious Cheese Grits

4 c. water
1 c. long-cooking grits, uncooked
3 c. shredded sharp Cheddar cheese, divided
2 T. butter
1½ t. garlic salt
1 t. Worcestershire sauce
1 egg, beaten
1 lb. pork breakfast sausage, browned and drained

Bring water to a boil in a large saucepan over high heat. Stir in grits; bring to a second boil. Reduce heat; cover and cook for 5 minutes, stirring occasionally. Remove from heat. Add 2 cups cheese, butter, garlic salt and Worcestershire sauce; mix thoroughly until cheese is melted. Stir egg slowly into mixture. Transfer half of mixture to a buttered 2-quart casserole dish. Add cooked sausage; top with remaining grits mixture. Cover and refrigerate at least 8 hours. To serve, let stand at room temperature for 30 minutes. Bake, uncovered, at 350 degrees for 40 minutes. Remove from oven and top with remaining cheese. Return to oven for several minutes, until cheese is melted. Serves 4 to 6.

*Angela Matos*
*Ocoee, FL*

*We southern girls know a thing or two about grits...my recipe really dresses them up. I have taken it to several covered-dish functions, and so many people ask what it is, because they have never had grits this yummy before! You're gonna love every spoonful. –Angela*

Oven-Fried Bacon Potatoes

Pumpkin Biscotti

## Pumpkin Biscotti

*Slices of biscotti are so nice to give to a co-worker along with a teabag...a welcome morning treat. Try a gingerbread muffin or quick bread mix, too... scrumptious!*

4 eggs, beaten
1 c. butter, melted and slightly cooled
1 t. vanilla extract
2 14-oz. pkgs. pumpkin muffin or quick bread mix
12-oz. white or milk chocolate chips, divided
1 to 3 T. all-purpose flour

Combine eggs, butter and vanilla in a large bowl; stir until well blended. Blend in dry muffin or quick bread mix and ½ cup chocolate chips; stir again. Mixture will be sticky. Add enough flour to form a smooth dough; knead on a lightly floured surface for several minutes. Divide dough in half; shape each half into an oval loaf and flatten slightly. Place on a lightly greased baking sheet and bake at 350 degrees for 30 to 40 minutes, until golden. Remove from oven and set aside to cool 15 to 20 minutes. Cut loaves into one-inch thick slices with a serrated knife; arrange on baking sheet. Return to oven and continue to bake 15 more minutes. Remove from oven and set aside to cool. Melt remaining chocolate chips and drizzle over slices; cool. Serves 6 to 8.

*Wendy Lee Paffenroth*
*Pine Island, NY*

# Best-Ever Breakfast Bars

1 c. granola
1 c. quick-cooking oats, uncooked
1 c. nuts, coarsely chopped
½ c. all-purpose flour
¼ c. brown sugar, packed
⅛ t. cinnamon
½ c. dried fruit, chopped into small pieces
2 T. ground whole flaxseed meal
⅓ c. canola oil
⅓ c. honey
½ t. vanilla extract
1 egg, beaten

Combine granola, oats, nuts, flour, sugar, cinnamon, dried fruit and flaxseed meal in a large bowl. Whisk together oil, honey and vanilla; stir into granola mixture. Add egg; stir to blend. Press mixture into a parchment paper-lined 8"x8" baking pan. Bake at 325 degrees for 30 to 35 minutes, until lightly golden around edges. Remove from oven and cool 30 minutes to one hour. Slice into bars. Serves 8 to 12.

*Mary Ann Lewis*
*Olive Branch, MS*

Best-Ever Breakfast Bars

That Yummy Bread
(page 50)

Kathy's Bacon Popovers
(page 52)

Mile-High Buttermilk Biscuits
(page 65)

Butterfly Yeast Rolls
(page 68)

# HEARTWARMING BREADS, ROLLS & BISCUITS

Sweet & savory delights to enjoy with any meal

# No-Knead Oatmeal Bread

*Spread peanut butter or softened butter on this slightly sweet and so-yummy favorite.*

2 envs. active dry yeast
½ c. warm water
1 c. quick-cooking oats, uncooked
½ c. light molasses
⅓ c. shortening
1½ c. boiling water
1 T. salt
6¼ c. all-purpose flour, divided
2 eggs, beaten

Dissolve yeast in warm water (110 to 115 degrees) in a small bowl; let stand about 5 minutes. Combine oats, molasses, shortening, boiling water and salt in a large bowl; stir until shortening is melted. Cool until lukewarm. Stir in 2 cups flour; add eggs and beat well. Stir in yeast mixture. Add remaining flour, 2 cups at a time, mixing well after each addition until a stiff dough forms. Beat vigorously about 10 minutes, until smooth. Place dough in a lightly greased bowl, turning to coat top. Cover tightly; place in refrigerator at least 2 hours to overnight. Turn dough out onto a floured surface. Form into 2 loaves; place seam-side down in greased 8"x4" loaf pans. Cover; let rise in a warm place (85 degrees), free from drafts, 2 hours, until double in bulk. Bake at 375 degrees for about 40 minutes. If top begins to brown too fast, cover with aluminum foil during last half of baking time. Makes 2 loaves.

Hattie Douthit
Crawford, NE

No-Knead Oatmeal Bread

# Honey-Wheat Bread

*Nothing makes your home smell more inviting than homemade bread baking in the oven!*

½ c. honey
2 env. active dry yeast
2 t. salt
2 c. milk
4½ c. all-purpose flour
4 c. whole-wheat flour
2 eggs, beaten
½ c. butter, melted
additional melted butter

Mix together honey, yeast and salt in a large bowl; set aside. Heat milk until warm (110 to 115 degrees). Add milk, flours, eggs and butter to honey mixture. Knead until a smooth, stretchy consistency is reached. Place in a greased bowl; cover dough with a tea towel and set in a warm place. Let rise about 2 to 3 hours, until double in bulk. Punch down; divide dough and form into 5 round loaves. Place loaves on lightly greased baking sheets, 2 to 3 loaves per sheet. Let rise for one more hour. Bake at 350 degrees for 25 to 30 minutes. Remove from oven and brush tops of loaves with butter. Makes 5 loaves.

*Brenda Ervin*
*Festus, MO*

# Italian Bread

*We love this bread with homemade vegetable soup or spaghetti…it disappears very quickly!*

2 envs. active dry yeast
2½ c. warm water
¼ c. olive oil
¼ c. sugar
2 t. salt
7 c. all-purpose flour
¼ c. cornmeal
1 egg white
1 T. cold water

Dissolve yeast in warm water (110 to 115 degrees) in a large bowl. Stir in oil, sugar and salt. Add flour; mix well. Shape into a ball and place in a greased bowl, turning to coat well. Cover and let rise until double in bulk, about one hour. Punch down. Divide into 3 equal parts; shape into loaves. Place loaves crosswise on a greased baking sheet that has been sprinkled with cornmeal. Cover; let rise for 30 minutes. Make 4 diagonal slices in top of each loaf. Bake at 400 degrees for 25 to 30 minutes. Whisk together egg white and cold water; brush onto loaves. Bake for 5 more minutes. Makes 3 loaves.

*Francie Stutzman*
*Dalton, OH*

# Boston Brown Bread

*An old-fashioned, hearty bread that's delicious served warm, spread with butter or cream cheese!*

1 c. raisins
1 c. boiling water
1 c. all-purpose flour
1 c. whole-wheat flour
1 c. cornmeal
¼ c. brown sugar, packed
1½ t. baking soda
1 t. salt
2 c. buttermilk
1 c. molasses

Place raisins in a small bowl; cover with boiling water and let stand 15 minutes. Combine dry ingredients in a large mixing bowl; mix well and set aside. Drain raisins and pat dry; combine with buttermilk and molasses. Add buttermilk mixture to flour mixture; stir just until blended. Pour into a greased 9"x5" loaf pan; bake at 350 degrees for one hour. Makes one loaf.

*Regina Vining*
*Warwick, RI*

# Dilly Bread

*Don't dally, this bread is a must-have!*

1 pkg. active dry yeast
¼ c. warm water
1 c. small-curd cottage cheese
2 T. sugar
1 T. onion, minced
1 T. butter
2 t. dill seed
1 t. salt
¼ t. baking soda
1 egg
2½ c. all-purpose flour
butter, melted
salt to taste

Dissolve yeast in warm water (110 to 115 degrees) in a cup. Combine cottage cheese, sugar, onion, butter, dill seed, salt, baking soda, egg and yeast mixture in a large bowl. Add flour one cup at a time to form a stiff dough, mixing well after each addition. Cover bowl; place in warm place and let rise one hour and 25 minutes to 1½ hours, until double in bulk. Punch down and let rise 50 more minutes to one hour. Place dough in greased 8" round baking pan; let rise another 30 to 40 minutes. Bake at 350 degrees for 40 to 45 minutes. Brush with melted butter and sprinkle with salt while still warm. Makes one loaf.

*Jeanine Boehm*
*Pittsburgh, PA*

# That Yummy Bread

1 c. milk
¼ c. shortening
2 T. sugar
2½ t. salt
2 envs. active dry yeast
1 c. warm water
7 c. all-purpose flour, divided
1 egg, beaten
1 to 2 T. butter, melted

Heat milk just to boiling in a saucepan; stir in shortening, sugar and salt. Cool to lukewarm and set aside. Dissolve yeast in warm water (110 to 115 degrees), and add to milk mixture. Pour into a bowl and add 4 cups flour; stir and beat. Gradually add remaining flour; stir. Let dough rest 10 minutes; turn dough out onto a floured surface and knead until smooth. Place dough in a greased bowl, turning to coat. Cover and let rise in a warm place (85 degrees), free from drafts, until double in bulk. Punch down dough; shape into 2 balls. Roll each ball into a ¼-inch-thick 15-inch by 9-inch rectangle. Brush with egg. Spread Herb Filling to one inch from edges of dough; roll up jelly-roll style, starting at short edge. Pinch edges to seal; place in 2 greased 9"x5" loaf pans, seam-side down. Brush with butter; cover and let rise in a warm place 55 minutes, or until double in bulk. Slash tops of loaves with a knife; bake at 375 degrees for one hour. Let cool on a wire rack before slicing. Makes 2 loaves.

## Herb Filling:
2 c. fresh parsley, chopped
2 c. green onions, chopped
1 clove garlic, minced
2 T. butter
1 egg, beaten
¾ t. salt
pepper and hot pepper sauce to taste

Sauté parsley, onions and garlic in butter; cool slightly. Add egg. Add salt, pepper and hot pepper sauce.

*Francie Stutzman*
*Dalton, OH*

That Yummy Bread

# Rosemary & Onion Bread

16-oz. frozen bread dough, thawed
1 to 2 T. olive oil
¼ c. chopped onion
1 to 2 t. dried rosemary

Coat dough with oil; place on a lightly greased baking sheet. Press onion and rosemary into dough. Bake at 350 degrees for 30 to 40 minutes, until golden. Serves 6.

*Donna Clement*
*Latham, NY*

# Garden Path Herbal Bread

*When we moved out to the country, I began tucking a few herb plants here & there in my flower gardens. I enjoyed cooking with them so much, I planted herbs all along the edge of a path that leads from my back door to the barn!*

1 c. all-purpose flour
1 c. plain yogurt
2 T. Dijon mustard
2 t. baking powder
½ t. salt
3 eggs, beaten
½ c. grated Parmesan cheese
¼ c. fresh oregano, minced
¼ c. fresh chives, minced
¼ c. fresh thyme, minced

Stir together flour, yogurt, mustard, baking powder, salt and eggs in a large bowl; blend well. Add cheese and herbs; mix well. Pour batter into an 8"x4" loaf pan sprayed with non-stick vegetable spray. Bake at 400 degrees for 45 minutes. Remove loaf to wire rack to cool completely. Makes one loaf.

*Brenda Smith*
*Delaware, OH*

# Kathy's Bacon Popovers

*Mmm...bacon! An easy tote-along breakfast to enjoy on the go.*

2 eggs
1 c. milk
1 T. oil
1 c. all-purpose flour
½ t. salt
3 slices bacon, crisply cooked and crumbled

Whisk together eggs, milk and oil. Beat in flour and salt just until smooth. Fill 12 greased and floured muffin cups ⅔ full. Sprinkle bacon evenly over batter. Bake at 400 degrees for 25 to 30 minutes, until puffed and golden. Serve warm. Makes one dozen.

*Kathy Grashoff*
*Fort Wayne, IN*

# Garlic Bubble Bread

16-oz. frozen bread dough, thawed
¼ c. butter, melted
1 T. dried parsley
1 t. garlic powder
½ t. garlic salt
Optional: sesame or poppy seed

Cut dough into one-inch pieces. Combine butter, parsley, garlic power and garlic salt in a small bowl. Dip dough pieces into butter mixture to coat; layer in a buttered 9"x5" loaf pan. Sprinkle sesame or poppy seed over top, if desired. Cover dough with plastic wrap; let rise in a warm place (85 degrees), free from drafts, about one hour, until double in bulk. Bake at 350 degrees for 30 minutes, or until golden. Cool completely in pan on a wire rack. Serves 4 to 6.

*Joanne Grosskopf*
*Lake in the Hills, IL*

Mini Cheddar Loaves

## Mary's Sweet Corn Cake

*Masa harina means "dough flour" in Spanish. It's often used to make tortillas and tamales, although you'll love it in this corn cake. Look for it in the baking or ethnic foods aisle.*

½ c. butter, softened
⅓ c. masa harina
¼ c. water
10-oz. pkg. frozen corn, thawed
⅓ c. sugar
3 T. yellow cornmeal
2 T. whipping cream
¼ t. baking powder
¼ t. salt

Beat butter in a large bowl with an electric mixer at medium speed until creamy. Gradually beat in masa harina; beat in water and set aside. Place corn in a food processor or blender. Pulse to chop corn coarsely; stir chopped corn into butter mixture. Combine sugar and remaining ingredients in a separate bowl; stir until well blended. Stir sugar mixture into butter mixture. Pour into a lightly greased 8"x8" baking pan; cover pan with aluminum foil. Set pan into a 13"x9" baking pan; add water one-third up around smaller pan. Bake at 350 degrees for 50 minutes to one hour, until a toothpick inserted in center comes out clean. Uncover smaller pan; let stand for 15 minutes. Scoop out servings with a small scoop; serve warm. Serves 8.

*Mary Murray*
*Mount Vernon, OH*

## Mini Cheddar Loaves

3½ c. biscuit baking mix
2½ c. shredded Cheddar cheese
2 eggs, beaten
1¼ c. milk

Combine biscuit mix and cheese in a large bowl. Combine eggs and milk in a separate bowl and beat well; stir egg mixture into cheese mixture. Pour into 2 greased 7"x4" loaf pans or 3 greased 6"x3" loaf pans. Bake at 350 degrees for 40 to 55 minutes, until a toothpick inserted in center comes out clean. Cool completely in pans on wire racks. Makes 2 or 3 loaves.

*Mary King*
*Ashville, AL*

Cheesy Batter Bread

## Cheesy Batter Bread

6⅓ c. all-purpose flour, divided
2 T. sugar
1½ t. salt
2 env. active dry yeast
2¼ c. shredded Cheddar cheese, divided
1 c. milk
1 c. water
2 T. butter
1 egg, beaten

Combine 1⅓ cups flour, sugar, salt, yeast and 2 cups cheese in a large bowl; set aside. Combine milk, water and butter in a saucepan over medium-low heat until very warm (110 to 115 degrees) and butter is almost melted. Gradually stir milk mixture into dry ingredients. Beat with an electric mixer at medium speed for 2 minutes.

Add egg and one cup of remaining flour; increase speed to high and beat for 2 minutes. Stir in enough remaining flour with a wooden spoon to make a stiff batter. Cover dough with a tea towel and let rest for 10 minutes. Pour into 2 lightly greased 9"x5" loaf pans. Cover and let rise in a warm draft-free place about one hour, until double in bulk. Sprinkle with ¼ cup cheese; bake at 375 degrees for 25 minutes, or until lightly golden. Remove loaves from pans; cool on wire racks. Makes 2 loaves.

*Wendy Meadows*
*Gratis, OH*

Cheese-Stuffed Biscuits

## Cheese-Stuffed Biscuits

*My kind of recipe...down-home goodness, ready to serve in a jiffy!*

10-oz. tube refrigerated flaky biscuits
8-oz. pkg. Cheddar cheese, sliced into 10 cubes
1 T. milk
1 t. poppy seed

Separate dough into 10 biscuits. Open a small pocket in side of each biscuit; tuck a cheese cube into each pocket. Press dough together to seal well. Place biscuits on an ungreased baking sheet. Cut a deep "X" in top of each biscuit. Brush with milk and sprinkle with poppy seed. Bake at 400 degrees for 10 to 12 minutes, until golden. Serve warm. Makes 10 biscuits.

*Angie Venable*
*Gooseberry Patch*

## Cornbread

*This is a must-have at our house with beef stew.*

1 c. all-purpose flour
1 c. yellow cornmeal
½ c. sugar
4 t. baking powder
¾ t. salt
1 c. plus 2 T. milk
1 egg
¼ c. plus 2 t. oil, divided

Combine flour, cornmeal, sugar, baking powder and salt in a large bowl. Stir in milk and egg; beat for one minute. Add ¼ cup oil and beat for one additional minute. Place remaining oil in an 8"x8" baking pan; tilt pan to coat edges. Spread batter in pan. Bake at 425 degrees for 25 minutes, or until golden. Serves 4 to 6.

*Kendra Walker*
*Hamilton, OH*

## Hazelnut-Raisin Cornbread

*This recipe won a blue ribbon once at the Iowa State Fair!*

1 c. golden raisins
1 c. boiling water
2 c. all-purpose flour
1 t. baking soda
⅛ t. salt
1 c. butter
1 c. sugar
2 eggs
14¾-oz. can cream-style corn
1 c. hazelnuts, finely crushed
Garnish: honey, crushed hazelnuts

Place raisins in a small bowl; cover with boiling water and let stand 20 minutes. Sift together flour, baking soda and salt. Cream together butter and sugar in a separate bowl; stir in eggs and then flour mixture. Drain raisins and pat dry. Stir raisins, corn and nuts into mixture. Mix well and pour into two 8"x4" greased and floured loaf pans. Bake at 350 degrees for 50 minutes to one hour, until a toothpick inserted in center comes out clean. Turn out of pans; garnish with honey and crushed hazelnuts on top. Makes 2 loaves.

*Robin Carmen*
*Des Moines, IA*

---

### kid-friendly project

The kids can make homemade butter in no time...wonderful on warm bread! Just fill a jar with heavy cream, add a tight-fitting lid and roll or shake until the butter forms.

---

## Cheddar Biscuits

2¼ c. biscuit baking mix
½ c. shredded Cheddar cheese
2 T. fresh parsley, chopped
⅓ c. milk
¼ c. sour cream
2 T. Dijon mustard
I egg, beaten

　　Combine baking mix, cheese and parsley in a large bowl; stir just until blended. Combine milk, sour cream and mustard in a small bowl; stir well. Add sour cream mixture to baking mix mixture, stirring just until blended. Place dough on a lightly floured surface; knead 10 times. Pat dough into a ½-inch-thick circle; cut with a 2-inch biscuit cutter. Arrange biscuits on ungreased baking sheets; brush tops lightly with beaten egg. Bake at 425 degrees for 12 to 15 minutes, until golden. Serve warm. Makes 3 dozen.

*Christine Schnaufer*
*Geneseo, IL*

## Angel Biscuits

*My mother would make this up every Sunday afternoon so we could have fresh-baked bread all week. The dough will keep for several weeks in the refrigerator.*

2 envs. active dry yeast
I c. warm water
2 c. buttermilk
¾ c. oil
¼ c. sugar
6 c. all-purpose flour
4 t. baking powder
1½ t. salt
¼ t. baking soda

　　Dissolve yeast in warm water (110 to 115 degrees) in a large bowl; let stand for several minutes. Stir in buttermilk, oil and sugar. Combine remaining ingredients in a large bowl; stir into buttermilk mixture. Cover bowl and place in refrigerator overnight. Remove dough and roll out on a floured board to ½-inch thickness. Cut out biscuits with a round biscuit cutter or the rim of a glass tumbler; place on an ungreased baking sheet. Bake at 400 degrees for 12 to 15 minutes, until golden. Makes 4 dozen.

*Molly Wilson*
*Rapid City, SD*

Cheddar Biscuits

Anytime Cheesy Biscuits

## Anytime Cheesy Biscuits

*So easy...you can whip them up in minutes!*

2 c. biscuit baking mix
⅔ c. milk
½ c. shredded Cheddar cheese
¼ c. butter, melted
¼ t. garlic powder

Mix together baking mix, milk and cheese until a soft dough forms; beat vigorously for 30 seconds. Drop by rounded tablespoonfuls onto an ungreased baking sheet. Bake at 450 degrees for 8 to 10 minutes, until golden. Whisk together butter and garlic powder; spread over warm biscuits. Makes about 1½ dozen.

*Naomi Cooper*
*Delaware, OH*

## Country Biscuits Supreme

*These are terrific with beef stew.*

2 c. all-purpose flour
4 t. baking powder
2 t. sugar
½ t. salt
½ t. cream of tartar
½ c. shortening
⅔ c. milk

Sift together dry ingredients. Cut in shortening with a pastry blender or fork until crumbly. Add milk; stir just until moistened. Turn dough out onto a lightly floured surface; knead gently for about 30 seconds. Roll out to ½-inch thick; cut with a biscuit cutter. Arrange biscuits on an ungreased baking sheet. Bake at 425 degrees for 10 to 12 minutes, until golden. Makes 12 to 15 biscuits.

*Gretchen Hickman*
*Galva, IL*

*easy how-to*
Making biscuits and there's no biscuit cutter handy? Try Mom's little trick...just use the rim of a glass tumbler or the open end of a clean, empty soup can.

## Sweet Potato Biscuits

*Spread with rich apple butter or honey for a touch of sweetness.*

1½ c. all-purpose flour
1½ c. whole-wheat flour
1 T. baking powder
1½ t. salt
½ t. cinnamon
½ t. baking soda
½ c. butter
15-oz. can sweet potatoes, mashed, juice drained
    and reserved

Mix together dry ingredients in a large bowl. Cut in butter, mashed sweet potatoes and ½ cup reserved juice until a soft dough forms. Add more juice as needed. Knead and roll out on a floured surface, about ½-inch thick. Cut with a 2¾-inch biscuit cutter and place on an ungreased baking sheet. Bake at 450 degrees for 10 to 12 minutes. Makes 15 to 16 biscuits.

*Becca Brasfield*
*Burns, TN*

## Peppery Biscuit Sticks

*Biscuits or bread sticks…these tasty tidbits are great for dipping in soups, stews and sauces.*

2 c. all-purpose flour
2 T. sugar
2 t. baking powder
1¼ t. pepper, divided
¼ t. baking soda
¼ t. garlic powder
6 T. butter, chilled
½ c. grated Parmesan cheese
1 egg, beaten
1 c. buttermilk, divided

Combine flour, sugar, baking powder, ¼ teaspoon pepper, baking soda and garlic powder in a large bowl. Cut in butter with a pastry blender or fork until crumbly. Stir in cheese. Make a well in center; set aside. Mix egg and ½ cup buttermilk in a small bowl; stir into flour mixture until just moistened. Turn out dough onto a lightly floured surface; knead just until dough holds together. Pat into a 12"x6" rectangle. Brush lightly with additional buttermilk; sprinkle with remaining pepper and press lightly into dough. Cut into twenty-four 6-inch-long strips. Arrange one inch apart on ungreased baking sheets; bake at 450 degrees for 8 minutes, or until golden. Makes 2 dozen.

*Virginia Watson*
*Scranton, PA*

*make it special*
Cookie cutters make breakfast a treat…
use them to cut out biscuit dough, shape
pancakes or cut shapes from the centers
of French toast. Use mini cutters to make
the sweetest pats of butter!

Peppery Biscuit Sticks

Mile-High
Buttermilk Biscuits

# Cream Biscuits

2 c. all-purpose flour
3 T. sugar
1 T. baking powder
½ t. salt
1¼ c. whipping cream
milk

Combine flour, sugar, baking powder and salt in a large bowl; stir well. Gradually add cream, stirring until mixture forms a soft dough. Shape dough into a ball. Knead dough 6 times on a lightly floured surface; roll out to ⅓-inch thickness. Cut dough into circles with rim of a glass tumbler and place on an ungreased baking sheet. Brush tops of biscuits with milk; bake at 425 degrees for 10 to 15 minutes, until golden. Makes one dozen.

*Jodi Bielawski*
*Manchester, NH*

## make 'em tender
For the flakiest biscuits, stir just until moistened and gently roll or pat the dough...don't overmix it.

# Mile-High Buttermilk Biscuits

*The secret? Use a sharp biscuit cutter and don't twist it when cutting out your biscuits...you'll be amazed how high they rise!*

2 c. all-purpose flour
1 T. baking powder
1 t. salt
½ c. shortening, chilled in freezer
⅔ to ¾ c. buttermilk
¼ c. butter, melted

Mix together flour, baking powder and salt. Cut in shortening with a pastry blender or fork until crumbly. Stir in buttermilk until incorporated and dough leaves sides of bowl. Dough will be sticky. Knead dough 3 to 4 times on a lightly floured surface. Roll out to ½-inch thickness, about 2 to 4 passes with a rolling pin. Cut dough with a biscuit cutter, pressing straight down with cutter. Place biscuits on a parchment paper-lined baking sheet. Bake at 500 degrees for 8 to 10 minutes. Brush tops of warm biscuits with melted butter. Makes about one dozen.

*Staci Meyers*
*Montezuma, GA*

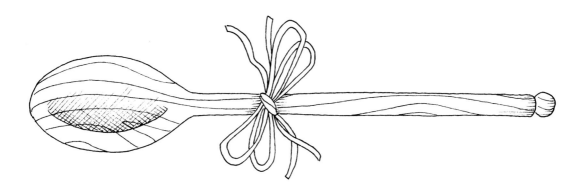

# Grandma Hilda's Sweet Biscuits

*Every summer at the end of July, it was our family's tradition to travel to "Little Grandma's" farm to help with the hay-making. We always looked forward to having these biscuits with every meal.*

6 c. all-purpose flour
1 c. sugar
1 c. shortening
3 T. plus 1 t. baking powder
1 t. salt
3 eggs, beaten
1 c. milk

Mix together flour, sugar, shortening, baking powder and salt in a large bowl; mix well. Beat eggs and milk together in a separate bowl. Add to flour mixture and blend well. Roll out on a floured surface; cut with 3-inch round cookie cutter. Bake at 375 degrees for 15 to 20 minutes, or until golden. Makes 4 dozen.

*Reggie Jarvi*
*Hancock, MI*

# Orange-Glazed Chocolate Rolls

3 c. all-purpose flour, divided
2 env. active dry yeast
1 t. salt
1 t. cinnamon
1¼ c. water
⅓ c. sugar
⅓ c. butter
1 egg
Optional: ½ c. raisins
1 c. semi-sweet chocolate chips

Stir together 1½ cups flour, yeast, salt and cinnamon in a large bowl. Combine water, sugar and butter in a saucepan over medium-low heat, stirring constantly until butter is almost melted (115 to 120 degrees). Add sugar mixture to flour mixture; blend until smooth. Mix in egg; stir in remaining flour. Fold in raisins, if desired; cover dough and let rise in a warm place (85 degrees), free from drafts, for one hour, until double in bulk. Punch down dough; let rest for 10 minutes. Fold in chocolate chips; fill greased muffin cups ⅔ full. Cover; let rise until double in bulk. Bake at 425 degrees for 10 to 15 minutes, until golden. Remove from pan and cool completely. Drizzle with Glaze before serving. Makes about 1½ dozen.

## Glaze:
½ c. powdered sugar
3 t. orange juice

Combine sugar and juice in a small bowl; stir until smooth and creamy.

*Geneva Rogers*
*Gillette, WY*

Orange-Glazed
Chocolate Rolls

# Butterfly Yeast Rolls

*I have been baking these delicious rolls for years, and they are the best! The rolls rise to perfection and are golden and flaky...sure to delight family & friends.*

1 env. active dry yeast
¼ c. warm water
1 c. milk
¼ c. sugar
¼ c. shortening
1 t. salt
3½ c. all-purpose flour, divided
1 egg, beaten

Dissolve yeast in warm water (110 to 115 degrees) in a small bowl; let stand for 5 minutes. Heat milk in a small saucepan over low heat just until boiling; let cool slightly. Combine milk, sugar, shortening and salt in a large bowl. Add 1½ cups flour and beat well. Beat in yeast mixture and egg. Gradually knead in remaining flour to form a soft dough. Place in a greased bowl, turning once. Cover and let rise in a warm place for 2 hours. Punch dough down; turn out on a floured surface. Shape into 36 walnut-size balls; place 3 balls in each cup of a greased muffin tin. Cover and let rise for 45 minutes. Bake at 400 degrees for 12 to 15 minutes, until golden. Makes one dozen.

*Janis Parr*
*Ontario, Canada*

Butterfly Yeast Rolls

# Old-Fashioned Icebox Rolls

*A very old tried & true recipe from my mother and aunt. This is also a good dough to use for making cinnamon rolls.*

1 env. active dry yeast
¼ c. warm water
½ c. boiling water
⅓ c. shortening
⅓ c. sugar
½ c. cold water
½ t. salt
1 egg, beaten
3¾ c. all-purpose flour

Dissolve yeast in warm water (110 to 115 degrees) in a small bowl; let stand for several minutes. Pour boiling water over shortening and sugar in a separate large bowl. Add yeast mixture, cold water, salt, egg and flour. Mix and knead until smooth. Cover and place in refrigerator overnight. Form into golf ball-size pieces and place in a greased 13"x9" baking pan. Cover; let rise until double in bulk. Bake at 400 degrees for 12 to 18 minutes, until golden. Makes 2 dozen.

*Muriel Gundy*
*Morley, MI*

Mother's Rolls

# Mother's Rolls

1 env. active dry yeast
¾ c. warm water
3½ c. biscuit baking mix, divided
1 T. sugar
¼ c. butter, melted
additional melted butter

Dissolve yeast in warm water (110 to 115 degrees); let stand 5 minutes. Place 2½ cups biscuit mix in a large bowl; stir in sugar. Add yeast mixture, stirring vigorously. Sprinkle work surface generously with remaining biscuit mix. Place dough on surface and knead 15 to 20 times. Shape heaping tablespoons of dough into balls; arrange on a lightly greased baking sheet. Cover dough with a damp tea towel; set aside in a warm place to rise, about one hour. Brush rolls with melted butter. Bake at 400 degrees for 12 to 15 minutes, until golden. Remove rolls from oven; brush again with melted butter while hot. Makes 15 rolls.

*Amy Hansen*
*Louisville, KY*

Marie's Yeast Rolls

## Marie's Yeast Rolls

1 env. active dry yeast
2 c. warm water
4 c. self-rising flour
½ c. butter, melted
¼ c. sugar
1 egg, beaten

Dissolve yeast in warm water (110 to 115 degrees) in a large bowl. Add remaining ingredients; stir well. Fill well-greased muffin cups ¾ full. Bake at 425 degrees for 20 minutes, or until golden. Makes 3 dozen.

*Marie Stewart*
*Pensacola, FL*

*microwave magic*
A convenient place to let yeast dough rise is inside your microwave. Heat a mug of water on HIGH for 2 minutes. Then remove the mug, place the covered bowl of dough inside and close the door.

## Stone-Ground Corn Rolls

2 c. milk
¾ c. cornmeal
½ c. sugar
½ c. shortening
1½ t. salt
1 env. active dry yeast
¼ c. warm water
2 eggs, beaten
6 c. all-purpose flour

Combine milk and cornmeal in a large saucepan; cook over medium heat 15 minutes, or until mixture thickens, stirring frequently. Remove from heat; add sugar, shortening and salt and stir until blended. Cool slightly. Dissolve yeast in warm water (110 to 115 degrees) in a small bowl. Add eggs and yeast mixture to milk mixture, stirring to blend; gradually stir in flour. Place dough on a lightly floured surface and knead about 5 minutes, until smooth. Shape dough into 2-inch balls; arrange dough balls 2 inches apart on a greased baking sheet. Cover and let rise in a warm place (85 degrees), free from drafts, for one hour, or until double in bulk. Bake at 375 degrees for 15 minutes, or until golden. Makes one dozen.

*Tina Goodpasture*
*Meadowview, VA*

## Sunday Dinner Potato Rolls

2 env. active dry yeast
2 c. warm water
1 c. warm mashed potatoes
½ c. sugar
½ c. butter, softened
1¼ T. salt
2 eggs, beaten
7½ c. all-purpose flour, divided
3 T. butter, melted

Dissolve yeast in warm water (110 to 115 degrees) in a large bowl. Add potatoes, sugar, butter, salt and eggs; blend well. Gradually add 3½ cups flour, beating with an electric mixer at medium speed; continue beating for 2 minutes. Gradually stir in remaining flour. Turn dough out onto a floured surface and knead until smooth and elastic (about 10 minutes). Brush dough with melted butter; place in a bowl, cover with plastic wrap and chill 2 hours. Punch down dough; cover with plastic wrap and refrigerate overnight. Punch down dough and knead lightly 4 or 5 times. Divide dough in half; shape each half into 24 rolls. Place rolls on lightly greased baking sheets; cover and let rise in a warm place (85 degrees), free from drafts, for one hour, or until double in bulk. Bake at 325 degrees for 40 minutes, or until golden. Makes 4 dozen.

*Mary Murray*
*Mount Vernon, OH*

## Grandma's Irish Soda Bread

*My grandma was 100 percent Irish, and she knew how to make the best Irish soda bread around. Serve it warm from the oven, topped with a pat of butter... there's nothing better!*

3 c. all-purpose flour
⅔ c. sugar
1 t. baking powder
1 t. baking soda
1 t. salt
1½ c. raisins
2 eggs, beaten
1¾ c. buttermilk
2 T. butter, melted and slightly cooled

Sift dry ingredients together into a large bowl; stir in raisins and set aside. Combine eggs, buttermilk and melted butter in a separate bowl, blending well. Add egg mixture to flour mixture; stir until well blended. Pour batter into 2 greased 9"x5" loaf pans. Bake at 350 degrees for one hour. Remove loaves to wire rack to cool completely. Makes 2 loaves.

*Jennifer Savino*
*Joliet, IL*

*flavored butter*
Stir together softened butter and your favorite chopped herbs from the garden or, for a sweet variety, stir in cinnamon-sugar or honey. Everyone will love this extra treat to spread on homemade breads and rolls!

# Golden Raisin Buns

1 c. water
½ c. butter
1 t. sugar
¼ t. salt
1 c. all-purpose flour
4 eggs
½ c. golden raisins

Combine water, butter, sugar and salt in a large saucepan; bring to a boil over high heat. Remove from heat; add flour, stirring until mixture pulls away from sides of pan. Add eggs, one at a time, beating well after each addition. Stir in raisins. Drop by heaping tablespoonfuls onto an ungreased baking sheet; bake at 375 degrees for 30 minutes, or until golden. Makes 2 dozen

*Sharon Hoskins*
*Warrensburg, MO*

Golden Raisin Buns

Mom's Raisin Bread

## Mom's Raisin Bread

*Everyone loved Mom's Raisin Bread. When I got married, Mom gave me the recipe...I finally got her to actually measure ingredients! My children love it too.*

1 c. milk
¼ c. margarine
2 t. salt
½ c. golden raisins
1 env. active dry rapid-rise yeast
2 T. sugar
½ c. warm water
2 eggs, beaten
5 c. all-purpose flour, divided
Optional: beaten egg, milk or softened margarine

Heat milk just to boiling in a small saucepan over low heat; stir in margarine and salt. Add raisins and let cool. Dissolve yeast and sugar in warm water (110 to 115 degrees) in a large saucepan. When milk mixture cools, add it to yeast mixture; stir in eggs. Beat in flour, one cup at a time. When dough gets heavier, start to knead it, adding more flour if too sticky. Knead for about 10 minutes. Place dough in a large greased pan; cover. Set pan in an unheated oven with a pan of hot water placed on rack below it. Let rise for one hour. Punch dough down; let rise for 30 more minutes. Knead dough again; form into 2 loaves and place in 2 greased 8½"x4½" loaf pans. Cover and let rise again for 30 minutes. Brush loaves with egg, milk or margarine, if desired. Bake at 375 degrees for 30 to 45 minutes, until golden. Makes 2 loaves.

*Suzanne Pletsch*
*Chicago, IL*

## Champion Banana Bread

*My grandma taught me most of what I know about baking. This simple recipe was hers...I wish I knew where she got it! I even won the Champion Ribbon at the county fair with this recipe when I was a young girl. My family belongs to a little old country church, and it has been published in their cookbook several times as well.*

2 eggs, beaten
1 c. sugar
½ c. butter, softened
3 bananas, mashed
½ c. evaporated milk
1 t. vanilla extract
2 c. all-purpose flour
1 t. baking powder
1 t. baking soda
½ t. salt

Blend together eggs, sugar and butter; add bananas, milk and vanilla. Stir in dry ingredients; mix well. Pour batter into a 9"x5" loaf pan sprayed with non-stick vegetable spray. Bake at 350 degrees for 40 to 50 minutes. Makes one loaf.

*Michelle Mahler*
*Osceola, WI*

Gran Gran's
Sweet Bread

# Gran-Gran's Sweet Bread

½ c. butter, softened
½ c. shortening
2 c. sugar
3 eggs, beaten
2 t. vanilla extract
2 env. active dry yeast
1 c. warm water
8 c. all-purpose flour
½ t. salt
2 c. warm milk
16-oz. pkg. raisins
½ c. butter, melted
¼ c. sugar

Blend together butter and shortening in a large bowl. Gradually add sugar, eggs and vanilla, beating well after each addition. Dissolve yeast in warm water (110 to 115 degrees) in a cup; let stand 5 minutes. Whisk together flour and salt. Gradually stir flour and salt with a large wooden spoon into butter mixture alternately with yeast mixture and warm milk. Mix well; stir in raisins. Turn dough out onto a floured surface. Knead, adding additional flour until dough is smooth and elastic. Return dough to bowl. Lightly spray dough with non-stick vegetable spray; cover with wax paper and a tea towel. Let rise 6 to 8 hours or overnight, until double in bulk. Punch down; divide into 6 equal portions and place in 6 greased 9"x5" loaf pans. Cover and let rise again 4 to 6 hours, until double in bulk. Drizzle melted butter over loaves; sprinkle each loaf with 2 teaspoons sugar. Bake at 350 degrees for 30 minutes, or until a toothpick inserted in center comes out clean. Cool on wire racks. Makes 6 loaves.

*Susan Rodgers*
*Mohnton, PA*

# Honey Koek Loaf

2 c. all-purpose flour
1 c. sugar
1 t. baking soda
1 t. cinnamon
½ t. ground ginger
½ t. nutmeg
½ t. ground cloves
½ t. baking powder
½ t. salt
½ c. honey
1 c. boiling water

Combine dry ingredients in a large bowl; mix well. Add honey and boiling water; stir together. Pour batter into a greased 9"x5" loaf pan. Bake at 350 degrees for one hour. Cool in pan for 10 minutes; remove loaf to wire rack to cool completely. Makes one loaf.

*Tawnia Hultink*
*Ontario, Canada*

# Holiday Eggnog Bread

2 eggs, beaten
1 c. sugar
1 c. eggnog
½ c. butter, melted and slightly cooled
1 t. vanilla extract
2¼ c. all-purpose flour
2¼ t. nutmeg
2 t. baking powder

Combine eggs, sugar, eggnog, butter and vanilla in a large bowl; blend well. Add remaining ingredients; stir until moistened. Lightly grease bottom of a 9"x5" loaf pan; pour batter into pan. Bake at 350 degrees for 35 to 45 minutes, until a toothpick inserted in center comes out clean. Cool in pan on a wire rack for 10 minutes. Remove from pan. Cool completely on wire rack before slicing. Makes one loaf.

*Summer Staib*
*Broomfield, CO*

## Cranberry-Pecan-Coconut Loaf

2 c. all-purpose flour
2 t. baking powder
1 t. salt
1 c. butter, softened
1 c. sugar
3 eggs
2 t. vanilla extract
⅔ c. milk
1½ c. cranberries
¾ c. pecans, coarsely chopped
½ c. sweetened flaked coconut

Combine flour, baking powder and salt in a large bowl; stir and set aside. Combine butter, sugar, eggs and vanilla in a separate large bowl; mix well with an electric mixer at low speed. Add flour mixture to butter mixture alternately with milk, beginning and ending with flour mixture; mix just until blended. Fold in cranberries, pecans and coconut; spread in 4 greased 8"x4" mini loaf pans. Bake at 350 degrees for one hour and 45 to 50 minutes, until a toothpick inserted in center comes out clean. Cool completely in pans on wire racks. Makes 4 loaves.

*Diana Pindell*
*Wooster, OH*

## Velvet Pumpkin Bread

3 c. all-purpose flour
2 t. baking soda
2 t. baking powder
2 t. cinnamon
1 t. salt
2 c. sugar
1½ c. oil
4 eggs, well beaten
2 c. canned pumpkin

Sift together flour, baking soda, baking powder, cinnamon and salt. Combine sugar and oil in a separate large bowl and mix well; blend flour mixture into sugar mixture. Add eggs and pumpkin; mix well. Pour into 2 greased 9"x5" loaf pans; bake at 350 degrees for one hour, or until a toothpick inserted in center comes out clean. Cool completely in pans on wire racks. Makes 2 loaves.

*Toni LePrevost*
*Parma, OH*

*tasty trivia*
The American tradition of serving coffee and sweet cake along with gossip actually evolved from the tradition of English tea.

Cranberry-Pecan-Coconut Loaf

## Last Hurrah of Summer Peach Bread

*Every late August, I'd take the kids to our family cabin in northern Minnesota for one last week of freedom. On the way home, we'd stop at the small town market and buy Colorado peaches for this recipe. The kids are grown now, but every time I make this bread, I remember all of our joyful trips and how blessed I am. Feel free to use fresh, frozen or canned peaches...all work deliciously.*

3 c. all-purpose flour
2 c. sugar
1½ t. salt
1 t. baking soda
4 eggs, beaten
1 c. oil
2 t. almond extract
1 t. vanilla extract
3 to 4 c. peaches, peeled, pitted and chopped
Optional: 1 c. chopped nuts

Combine flour, sugar, salt and baking soda in a large bowl; mix well. Add eggs and oil; stir just until moistened. Stir in extracts, peaches and nuts, if desired. Spread into 2 greased 9"x5" or four 7"x4" loaf pans. For regular pans, bake at 350 degrees for 50 minutes to one hour. For small pans, bake for 35 minutes, or until a toothpick inserted in center comes out clean. Cool in pans for 10 to 15 minutes; remove from pans. Pour Glaze over warm loaves. Cool completely. Wrap in wax paper and then aluminum foil. Makes 2 regular or 4 small loaves.

### Glaze:

2 c. powdered sugar
2 T. milk
1 T. butter, melted
1 t. almond extract
½ t. vanilla extract

Mix all ingredients in a bowl to make a thin glaze.

*Jackie Flaherty*
*Saint Paul, MN*

## Jane's Sweet Bubble Bread

*This tasty recipe came from an old friend of mine. She was close to retirement age years ago when we taught school together.*

½ c. butter, melted
1½ c. sugar
1½ t. cinnamon
2 16-oz. loaves frozen bread dough, thawed
1 c. chopped nuts, divided
2 T. dark corn syrup, divided

Place melted butter in a small bowl; mix sugar and cinnamon in a separate small bowl. Form dough into walnut-size balls; roll in butter and then in cinnamon-sugar. Place half of dough balls in a greased Bundt® pan. Sprinkle with ¼ cup nuts; drizzle with one tablespoon corn syrup. Pack remaining dough balls on top. Sprinkle with ¼ cup nuts; drizzle with remaining corn syrup. Cover and let rise until double in bulk. Bake at 350 degrees for 25 minutes. Cool for 3 minutes; invert onto a serving plate and top with remaining nuts. Serves 10 to 12.

*JoAnn*
*Gooseberry Patch*

# Mini Butterscotch Drop Scones

2 c. all-purpose flour
½ c. brown sugar, packed
2 t. baking powder
¼ t. salt
⅓ c. butter, softened
1 c. butterscotch chips
½ c. pecans, toasted and chopped
1 egg, beaten
⅔ c. whipping cream
½ t. vanilla extract
Optional: powdered sugar

Combine flour, brown sugar, baking powder and salt in a large bowl, stirring until blended. Cut in butter with a pastry blender or fork until crumbly. Stir in chips and nuts. Combine egg, cream and vanilla in a separate bowl, whisking until well mixed. Add egg mixture to flour mixture, stirring just until moistened. Drop by rounded tablespoonfuls onto parchment paper-lined baking sheets. Bake at 375 degrees for 12 to 15 minutes, until golden. Remove from pans and cool on wire racks. Sprinkle with powdered sugar, if desired. Makes 3 dozen.

*Margaret Welder*
*Madrid, IA*

Chocolate-Cherry
Cream Scones

## Chocolate-Cherry Cream Scones

2 c. all-purpose flour
¼ c. sugar
1 T. baking powder
½ t. salt
½ c. dried cherries, chopped
¼ c. mini semi-sweet chocolate chips
1¼ c. whipping cream
Optional: additional whipping cream, coarse sugar

Combine flour, sugar, baking powder and salt in a bowl; whisk to blend well. Add cherries and chocolate chips. Pour cream into dry ingredients, continuing to stir until a soft, sticky dough is formed. Turn out onto a lightly floured surface and knead 8 to 10 times. Pat dough into a ½-inch to ¾-inch-thick circle; cut into 8 wedges. Place wedges one inch apart on a parchment paper-lined baking sheet. Brush with additional cream and sprinkle generously with coarse sugar, if desired. Bake at 425 degrees for about 15 minutes, or until golden and springy to touch. Makes 8 scones.

*Michelle Stewart*
*West Richland, WA*

## Cranberry-Orange Scones

*I received this recipe from a friend a few years ago. The scones are not only yummy, but quick & easy to make too.*

2 c. biscuit baking mix
½ c. sugar
½ c. butter, softened
1 egg, beaten
½ c. dried cranberries
½ c. chopped pecans
1 T. orange zest
2½ to 3 T. buttermilk or light cream
Optional: beaten egg white, raw or sanding sugar

Combine baking mix, sugar and butter in a bowl until crumbly. Make a well in center and add egg; stir to blend. Stir in cranberries, pecans and zest. Add buttermilk or cream as needed for dough to form a soft ball. Place dough on lightly floured surface and knead 3 or 4 times. Flatten dough and shape into an 8-inch circle. Cut dough into wedges using a serrated knife. Brush with egg white and sprinkle with sugar, if desired. Arrange on a lightly greased baking sheet and bake at 400 degrees for 10 to 15 minutes, until golden. Serves 8 to 10.

*Joyce LaMure*
*Sequim, WA*

Greek Pizza
(page 126)

Tuscan Pork Loin
(page 99)

The Best-Yet Buffalo
Wings (page 118)

Baked Ham in Peach
Sauce (page 94)

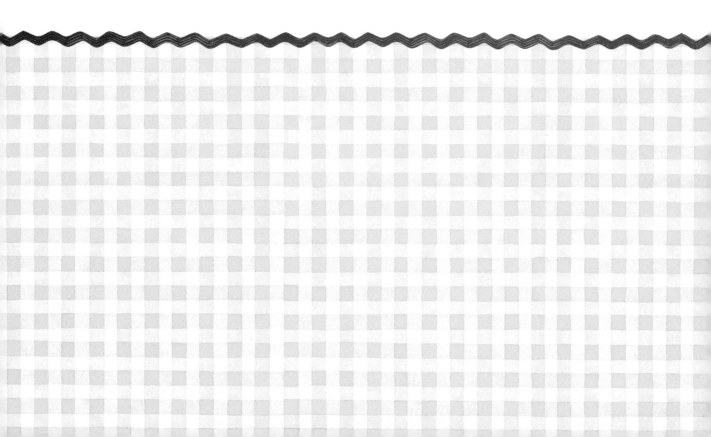

# BEST BAKED ENTRÉES

*Must-have main dishes for every occasion*

# Easy Beef Burgundy

*A simple-to-make version of this classic dish…great for company.*

2 lbs. stew beef cubes
2  10¾ oz. cans cream of mushroom soup
2  4-oz. cans mushrooms, drained
2 c. red wine or beef broth
1½-oz. pkg. onion soup mix
3 to 4 c. egg noodles, cooked

Combine all ingredients except noodles in a 2-quart baking dish. Bake at 350 degrees for 3 hours, stirring occasionally. Serve over prepared noodles. Serves 6 to 8.

*Laurie Aitken*
*Walden, NY*

Easy Beef Burgandy

# Mama's Scrumptious Roast Beef

14-oz. can garlic-seasoned chicken broth
1 c. white wine or chicken broth
3 T. red steak sauce
2 T. brown steak sauce
2 T. balsamic vinegar
2-oz. pkg. onion soup mix
1 T. all-purpose flour
12 to 14 baby carrots
2 red peppers, thinly sliced
2 bunches green onions, chopped
5 to 6 cloves garlic, minced
3 to 4-lb. beef rump roast
salt and pepper to taste

Combine broth, wine or broth, steak sauces, vinegar and soup mix in a large bowl; set aside. Place flour in a large oven bag; shake bag to coat and arrange in a roasting pan. Place vegetables and garlic in bag; place roast in bag on top of vegetables. Drizzle broth mixture over roast; season with salt and pepper. Cut six one-inch holes in top of roasting bag with a knife tip. Close bag with nylon tie provided. Bake at 325 degrees for 3 hours, or until roast is tender. Remove roast to a serving platter; let stand 15 minutes before slicing. Serve vegetables with roast. Serves 6 to 8.

*Debbie Donaldson*
*Andalusia, AL*

# Beef Brisket in a Bag

*Pineapple juice and soy sauce are the secret ingredients that make this brisket taste wonderful.*

3 to 4-lb. beef brisket
pepper and paprika to taste
1 T. all-purpose flour
8-oz. can pineapple juice
3 T. soy sauce
1½ oz. pkg. onion soup mix

Rub brisket with pepper and paprika. Shake flour in a large oven bag and place brisket in bag, fat-side up. Place bag in a 13"x9" baking pan. Combine pineapple juice, soy sauce and soup mix; pour mixture over brisket. Close bag with nylon tie provided; cut six ½-inch slits in top. Bake at 325 degrees for 3 hours. Remove from oven; place brisket on cutting board and pour remaining bag contents into baking pan. Slice brisket against grain; arrange slices over juices in baking pan. Baste with juices; cover pan with aluminum foil and return to oven for one more hour, basting occasionally. Serves 6 to 8.

*Meg Venema*
*Kirkland, WA*

**try this!**
For dark, rich-looking gravy, add a spoonful or 2 of brewed coffee. It will add color to pale gravy but won't affect the flavor.

# Becky's BBQ Beef for a Crowd

*This is a very flexible recipe...just the thing for a take-it-easy cookout. It holds well in a slow cooker, freezes well and reheats well in the microwave.*

5 to 6-lb. beef chuck roast
½ to 1 t. salt
½ to 1 t. pepper
2 14½-oz. cans stewed or crushed tomatoes
2 onions, chopped
3 T. sugar
2 T. smoke-flavored cooking sauce
Optional: vinegar to taste

Place roast in an ungreased large roasting pan; sprinkle with salt and pepper to taste. Mix remaining ingredients except vinegar. If mixture is too sweet, add vinegar, about one teaspoon at a time, if desired. Pour mixture over roast. Cover and bake at 325 degrees for 4 hours, basting occasionally. Serves 10 to 12.

Becky Hall
Belton, MO

*I've used this recipe for large groups, cooking 12 to 15 pounds of meat at a time, doubling the other ingredients and increasing the baking time to 6 hours. The smoke flavoring adds so much, so don't omit it!*
—Becky

# Peppered Beef in Parsley Crust

2 T. whole peppercorns
4 T. butter, softened
1 c. fresh parsley, chopped
2 lb. tenderloin roast

Grind peppercorns until coarse in texture and spread evenly on a large platter. Blend together butter and parsley in a small bowl. Spread butter mixture over roast, covering all sides evenly. Place roast on platter and roll in cracked peppercorns until roast is coated. Bake at 425 degrees for one hour, or until meat thermometer registers 135 degrees; this will produce a rare roast. Let rest before carving. Serves 6.

# Family Swiss Steak

*So quick & easy to make...just stir it up and pop it the oven. Delicious over egg noodles.*

1½ lbs. beef round steak, cut into 6 serving-size
    pieces
2 c. onion, sliced
10½-oz. can beef broth
4½-oz. jar sliced mushrooms, drained
¼ t. salt
¼ t. pepper
¼ c. cold water
2 T. cornstarch

Place steak in a large oven-proof skillet or Dutch oven; set aside. Combine remaining ingredients except water and cornstarch; mix well and pour over steak. Cover and bake at 325 degrees for 2½ to 3 hours, until beef is tender. Combine water and cornstarch in a small bowl; stir into beef mixture. Bake 15 more minutes, or until gravy is thickened. Serves 6.

Sharon Crider
Junction City, KS

Peppered Beef in
Parsley Crust

# Boycott-Your-Grill Beef Kabobs

*Skewers that bake in the oven...perfect for a rained-out cookout!*

1 c. oil
2/3 c. soy sauce
1/2 c. lemon juice
1/4 c. Worcestershire sauce
1/4 c. mustard
2 cloves garlic, minced
1 T. pepper
1/8 t. hot pepper sauce
3 lbs. beef sirloin steak, cut into 2-inch cubes
2 green peppers, cut into 1-inch squares
2 8-oz. pkgs. mushrooms
20-oz. can pineapple chunks, drained

Combine all ingredients except steak, vegetables and pineapple in a bowl. Pour over steak; cover and refrigerate for 24 hours. Thread steak, vegetables and pineapple onto skewers. Arrange on greased baking sheets. Bake at 400 degrees for 8 to 10 minutes. Turn and continue baking until steak is done. Serves 4.

*Kathy Solka*
*Ishpeming, MI*

# Honey & Brown Sugar Meatloaf

*My father-in-law raises honeybees and shares the honey with us. One day I experimented with it, and this has become my husband's favorite meatloaf recipe. It is simply delicious. He also likes to use the leftovers to make hot meatloaf sandwiches the next day...yum!*

2 1/2 lbs. ground beef
1 sleeve saltine crackers, crushed
1 egg, beaten
2 c. catsup, divided
1/2 c. honey
1/2 c. brown sugar, packed

Mix beef, cracker crumbs, egg and 1/2 cup catsup in a large bowl until thoroughly mixed. Shape into a loaf and place in an ungreased 13"x9" baking pan. Spread 1/2 cup catsup on top of loaf. Bake at 350 degrees for one hour and 15 minutes. Mix honey, brown sugar and remaining catsup together with a whisk. Remove meatloaf from oven and pour glaze over the top. Place meatloaf under the broiler until glaze starts to bubble. Let cool slightly before slicing. Serves 6 to 8.

*Lea Ann Burwell*
*Charles Town, WV*

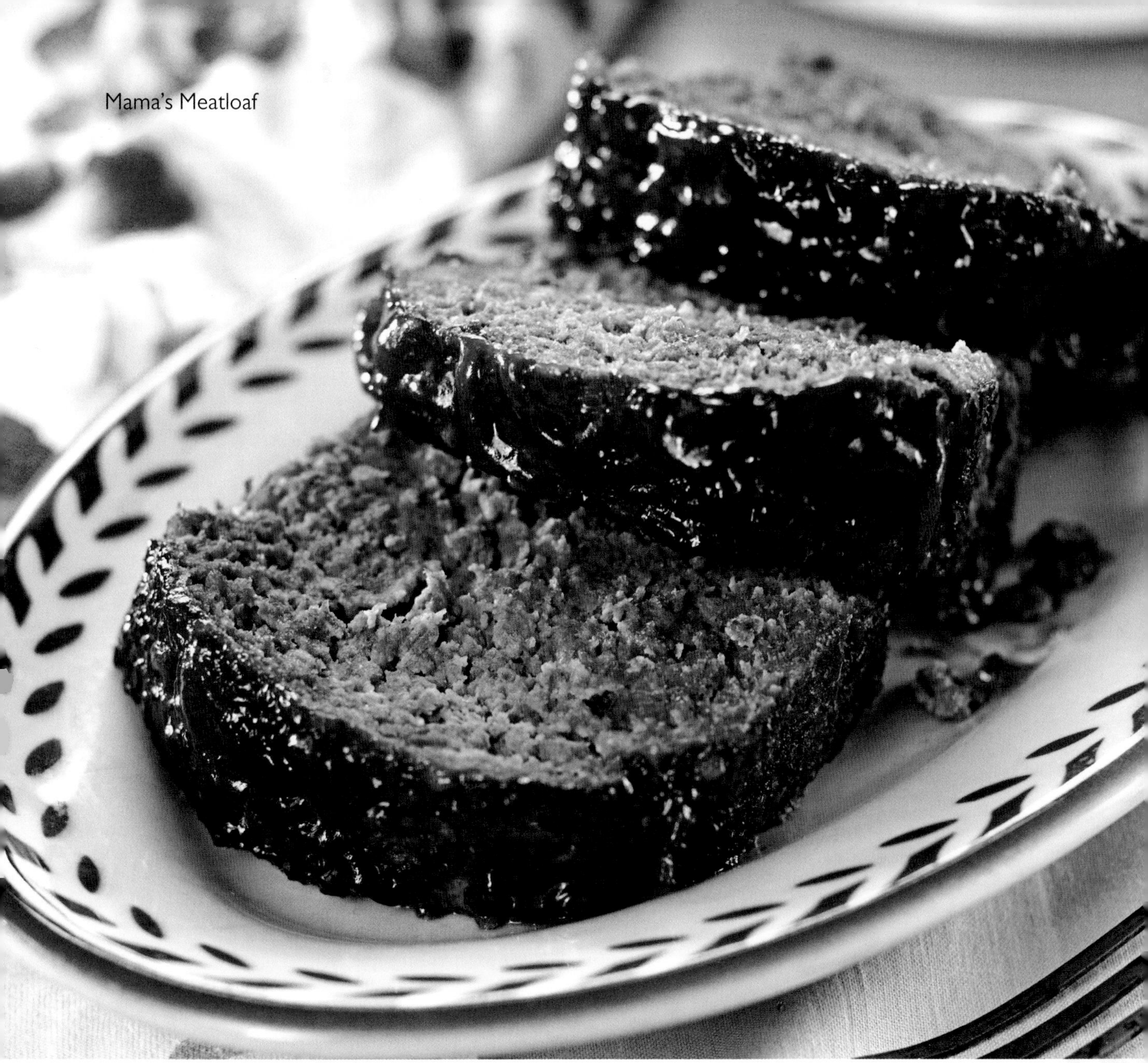

Mama's Meatloaf

## Mama's Meatloaf

1½ lbs. ground beef
2 eggs, beaten
¾ c. milk
⅔ c. saltine cracker crumbs
salt and pepper to taste
Optional: 2 t. onion, chopped
¼ c. catsup
1 T. lemon juice
2 t. brown sugar, packed
1 t. mustard

Mix together beef, eggs, milk, cracker crumbs, salt, pepper and onion, if desired, in a large bowl. Form into a loaf and place in an ungreased 9"x5" loaf pan. Bake, covered, at 350 degrees for 45 minutes. Mix remaining ingredients; spread over meatloaf. Bake, uncovered, 15 more minutes. Serves 6 to 8.

*Maxine Blakely*
*Seneca, SC*

Cheesy Beef & Bacon
Burger Meatloaf

# Cheesy Beef & Bacon Burger Meatloaf

*Minimal prep and maximum flavor make this recipe perfect for busy weeknights or casual get-togethers.*

1 lb. bacon, crisply cooked and crumbled, divided
1½ lbs. ground sirloin
1½ c. shredded Cheddar cheese
2 eggs, beaten
⅓ c. dry bread crumbs
⅓ c. mayonnaise
1 T. Worcestershire sauce
½ t. salt
½ t. pepper
½ c. catsup
¼ t. hot pepper sauce
3 T. Dijon mustard

Set aside ½ cup bacon for topping. Combine remaining bacon, beef, cheese, eggs, bread crumbs, mayonnaise, Worcestershire sauce, salt and pepper in a large bowl; set aside. Mix together catsup, hot pepper sauce and mustard; set aside 3 tablespoons of mixture. Add remaining catsup mixture to beef mixture; blend well. Press into an ungreased 9"x5" loaf pan; spread reserved catsup mixture over top and sprinkle with reserved bacon. Bake, uncovered, at 350 degrees for 50 minutes to one hour, until beef is no longer pink. Remove from oven; let stand 5 to 10 minutes before slicing. Serves 6 to 8.

*Kelly Masten*
*Hudson, NY*

# Savory Salisbury Steak

10¾-oz. can golden mushroom soup, divided
⅓ c. water
1½ lbs. lean ground beef
1 onion, finely chopped
½ c. dry bread crumbs
1 egg, beaten
½ t. salt
⅛ t. pepper

Mix ¾ cup soup and water in a small bowl; set aside. Combine remaining soup and remaining ingredients in a separate bowl. Form into small patties; arrange in a single layer in a lightly greased 13"x9" baking pan. Bake, uncovered, at 350 degrees for 30 minutes. Drain; spoon reserved soup mixture over patties. Bake, uncovered, 10 to 12 more minutes. Serves 4 to 6.

*Dee Dee Plzak*
*Westmont, IL*

# Flat Meatballs & Gravy

*My husband's mother, Arlene Harford, used to make this recipe for her children. David has in turn made it for our three girls, Jennifer, Liz and Stephanie. It continues to be a family favorite.*

2 lbs. ground round
1 egg, beaten
½ c. milk
1 T. all-purpose flour
1 t. salt
½ t. pepper
Optional: 1 onion, diced
2 T. butter
10¾-oz. can cream of mushroom soup
cooked rice

Mix all ingredients except butter, soup and rice together in a large bowl; set aside. Melt butter in a frying pan over medium heat. Scoop beef mixture into frying pan with an ice cream scoop; use spoon to shape into flattened meatballs. Brown over medium heat, turning several times. Remove meatballs to an ungreased 2-quart casserole dish; reserve drippings in pan. Stir soup into drippings; pour over meatballs. Bake, uncovered, at 350 degrees for 30 minutes. Serve over cooked rice. Serves 8.

*Susan Harford*
*Pleasanton, CA*

## Brown Sugar Ham

*For the prettiest presentation, score the ham in a diamond pattern before brushing on the sweet & savory glaze.*

4 to 5-lb. cooked ham
1 c. brown sugar, packed
½ c. spicy mustard
⅓ c. honey
1 T. dried rosemary
1 T. ground cumin

Place ham in an ungreased large roaster pan. Mix together remaining ingredients in a bowl and spread over ham. Bake, covered, at 375 degrees for 35 to 40 minutes. Uncover and bake for 10 to 15 more minutes. Let stand briefly before slicing. Serves 8 to 10.

*Melissa Dawn*
*Kennewick, WA*

## memorable weeknight dinner!
Make meals extra special for your family! Even if no guests are coming for dinner, pull out the good china and light some candles...you'll be making memories together.

## Baked Ham in Peach Sauce

*This ham with its fruity sauce is equally scrumptious served hot at a holiday dinner or cold at a summer picnic.*

7-lb. cooked ham
1 t. whole cloves
2 16-oz. cans sliced peaches, drained
10-oz. jar apricot preserves
1 c. dry sherry or apple juice
1 t. orange zest
½ t. allspice

Place ham in an ungreased 13"x9" baking pan. Score surface of ham in a diamond pattern; insert cloves. Combine remaining ingredients in a blender or food processor. Process until smooth and pour over ham. Cover ham with aluminum foil. Bake at 325 degrees for 30 minutes, basting occasionally with sauce. Uncover and bake for 30 more minutes; continue to baste. Remove ham to a serving platter; slice and serve with sauce from pan. May be served hot or cold. Serves 10.

*JoAnna Nicoline-Haughey*
*Berwyn, PA*

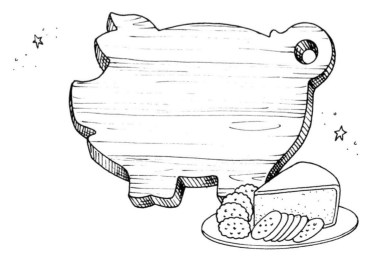

Cheryl's Country-Style Ribs

## Spicy Pork Packets

*Sometimes I replace the plain corn with a can of sweet corn & diced peppers to add a bit of extra color.*

14-oz. can chicken broth
2 c. instant rice, uncooked
1½ T. spicy taco mix, divided
⅛ t. cayenne pepper
⅛ t. salt
⅛ t. pepper
15¼-oz. can corn, drained
⅓ c. green onion, sliced
4 boneless pork chops

Heat broth to boiling in a medium saucepan; remove from heat. Add rice, one teaspoon taco mix, cayenne pepper, salt and pepper. Cover and let stand for about 5 minutes, until liquid is absorbed. Add corn and green onion; set aside. Sprinkle pork chops with remaining taco mix; place each on an 18-inch length of aluminum foil sprayed with non-stick cooking spray. Divide rice mixture evenly over pork chops; fold aluminum foil over to enclose food and seal tightly. Place packets on a baking sheet; cut an "X" to vent foil. Bake at 400 degrees for 45 minutes. Serves 4.

*Virginia Watson*
*Scranton, PA*

## Cheryl's Country-Style Ribs

*Serve these ribs with coleslaw and corn on the cob.*

7 to 8 lbs. country-style pork ribs, sliced into
    serving-size portions
salt to taste
2 onions, sliced
½ c. brown sugar, packed

Place ribs in an ungreased large roasting pan; sprinkle lightly with salt. Top ribs with onion slices, brown sugar and 3⅓ cups Barbecue Sauce. Cover and bake at 350 degrees for 2 hours. Uncover and add remaining sauce. Increase heat to 400 degrees; bake 30 more minutes. Serves 12 to 15.

### Barbecue Sauce:
2 c. catsup
1 c. water
½ c. sugar
½ c. white vinegar
½ c. Worcestershire sauce
2 T. smoke-flavored cooking sauce
1 t. garlic powder
1 t. salt

Combine all ingredients in a bowl and mix well. Keep refrigerated. Makes 4½ cups.

*Cheryl Tesar*
*De Witt, NE*

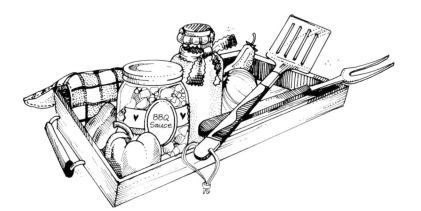

## Western Pork Chops

*For a delicious variation, try substituting peeled, cubed sweet potatoes for the redskins.*

1 T. all-purpose flour
1 c. barbecue sauce
4 pork chops
salt and pepper to taste
4 redskin potatoes, sliced
1 green pepper, cubed
1 c. baby carrots

Shake flour in a large oven bag; place in a 13"x9" baking pan. Add barbecue sauce to bag; squeeze bag to blend in flour. Season pork chops with salt and pepper; add pork chops and vegetables to bag. Turn bag to coat ingredients with sauce; arrange vegetables in an even layer with pork chops on top. Close bag with nylon tie provided; cut six ½-inch slits in top. Bake at 350 degrees for about 40 to 45 minutes, until pork chops and vegetables are tender. Serves 4.

*Kerry Mayer*
*Denham Springs, LA*

## Newlywed Pork Chops

*I first tried this tasty, never-fail recipe years ago when I was newly married. I hope you'll enjoy it too!*

4 boneless pork chops
½ t. garlic salt
⅛ t. pepper
1 onion, sliced
1 lemon, thinly sliced
4 t. dark brown sugar, packed
½ c. catsup

Arrange pork chops in a single layer in a lightly greased 1½-quart casserole dish; sprinkle with garlic salt and pepper. Top each pork chop with a slice each of onion and lemon; sprinkle with one teaspoon brown sugar. Drizzle catsup over pork chops. Cover and bake at 375 degrees for 45 minutes. Uncover; bake for 15 more minutes. Serves 4.

*Stella Hickman*
*Galloway, OH*

---

### perfect pork!

Keep in mind that pork is lean and cooks quickly; overcooking can make it dry and tough. Test thicker cuts of pork for perfect doneness with a meat thermometer.

# Tuscan Pork Loin

4-lb. boneless pork loin roast
8-oz. pkg. cream cheese, softened
1 T. dried pesto seasoning
½ c. baby spinach
6 slices bacon, crisply cooked
12-oz. jar roasted red peppers, drained and divided
1 t. paprika
1 t. salt
½ t. pepper
Optional: baby spinach

Slice pork lengthwise, cutting down center, but not through other side. Open halves and cut down center of each half, cutting to, but not through, other sides. Open pork into a rectangle. Place pork between 2 sheets of heavy-duty plastic wrap and flatten into an even thickness using a rolling pin or flat side of a meat mallet.

Spread cream cheese evenly over pork. Sprinkle with pesto seasoning; arrange spinach over cream cheese. Top with bacon slices and half of red peppers; reserve remaining red peppers for another recipe. Roll up pork lengthwise; tie at 2-inch intervals with kitchen string. Rub pork with paprika, salt and pepper. Place roast seam-side down on a lightly greased rack on an aluminum foil-lined baking sheet. Bake at 425 degrees for 30 minutes, or until a meat thermometer inserted into thickest portion registers 145 degrees. Remove from oven; let stand for 10 minutes. Remove string from pork; slice pork into ½-inch-thick servings. Serve pork slices on a bed of spinach leaves, if desired. Serves 8 to 10.

*Gina McClenning*
*Valrico, FL*

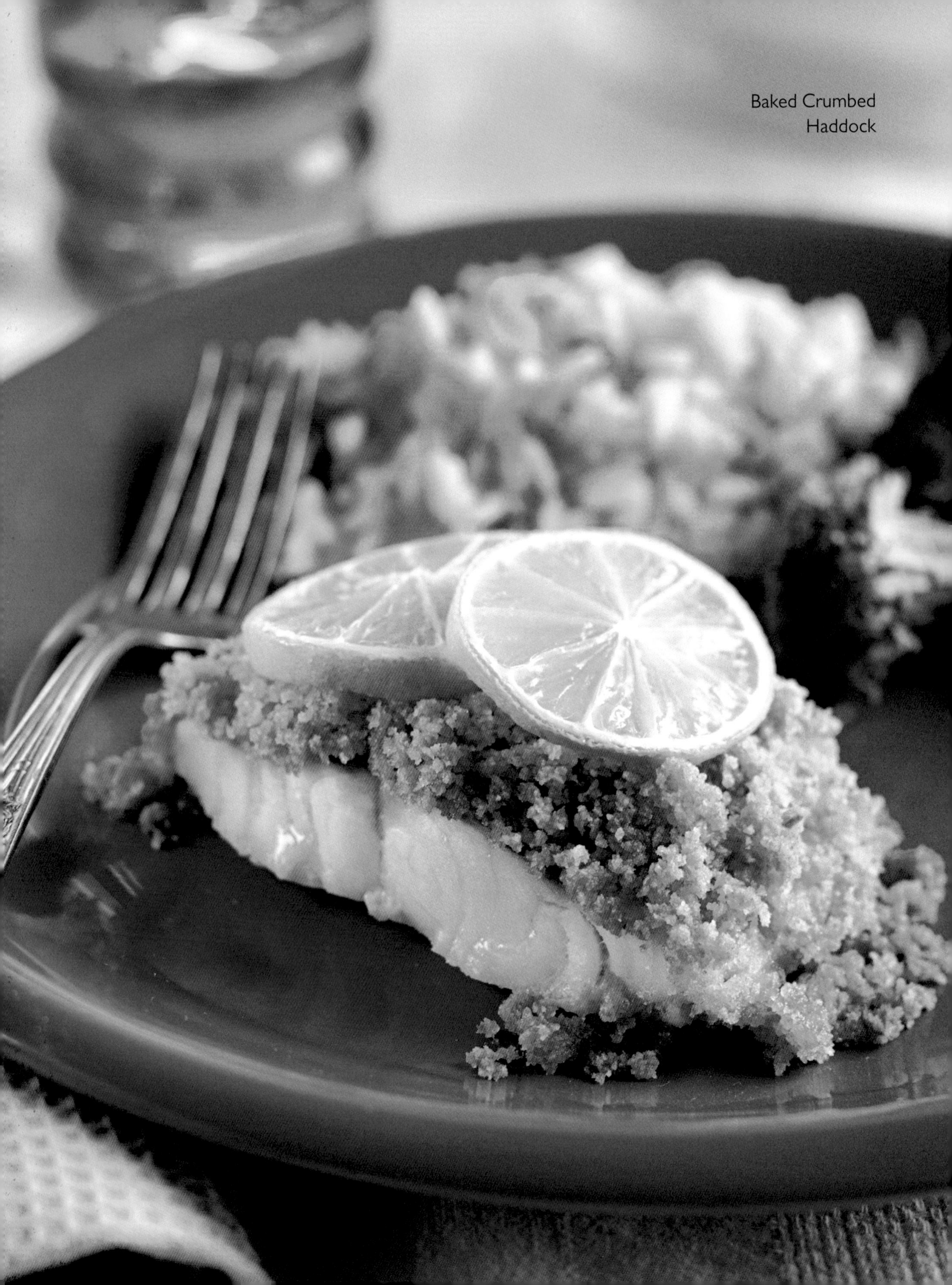

Baked Crumbed Haddock

## Unstuffed Pork Chops

*So tender and good! I like to serve spiced applesauce as a side dish with these pork chops.*

2 T. oil
4 thick pork chops
3 c. dry bread cubes or stuffing mix
¼ c. butter, melted
¼ c. chicken broth
2 T. celery, chopped
2 T. onion, chopped
10¾-oz. can cream of mushroom soup
⅓ c. water

Heat oil in a large skillet over medium heat; add pork chops and brown on both sides. Transfer to a lightly greased 13"x9" baking pan and set aside. Toss together bread cubes or stuffing mix, butter, broth, celery and onion in a large bowl. Spoon heaping mounds of bread crumb mixture over pork chops; set aside. Combine soup and water; pour over pork chops. Bake, covered, at 350 degrees for 30 minutes. Uncover and continue to bake for 10 more minutes, or until juices run clear. Serves 4.

*Elizabeth Blackstone*
*Racine, WI*

### lemon love
Wrap halved lemons in cheesecloth and twine for your dinner guests to squeeze over their fish. The cheesecloth will catch the seeds but allow the juice to run through.

## Baked Crumbed Haddock

*Delicious! Serve with mac & cheese and steamed broccoli for a down-home dinner.*

2 5½-oz. pkgs. onion & garlic croutons
1 c. butter, melted
3 lbs. haddock fillets
Optional: lemon slices

Finely grind croutons in a food processor. Toss together croutons and butter. Place fish in a lightly greased 13"x9" baking pan. Sprinkle crouton mixture over fish. Bake, uncovered, at 350 degrees for 20 to 25 minutes, until fish flakes easily with a fork. Top fish with lemon slices, if desired. Serves 6 to 8.

*Michelle Waddington*
*New Bedford, MA*

## Mediterranean Baked Fish

3½ lbs. whole fish, such as red snapper or
    striped bass, cleaned
juice of 1 lemon
salt and pepper to taste
3 bay leaves
6 T. olive oil
1 medium onion, sliced
2 cloves garlic, chopped
⅔ c. dry white wine or chicken broth
1 T. white wine vinegar
1 c. tomato, chopped
2 T. tomato paste
5 T. Italian parsley, chopped
8 T. dry white bread crumbs
¼ c. feta cheese, crumbled
Garnish: 12 black olives or fresh mint

Wash fish; pat dry. Sprinkle fish cavity with
lemon juice, salt and pepper. Tuck bay leaves
inside. Heat oil in pan over medium heat and cook
onion until transparent. Add garlic and cook for
one minute; add wine, wine vinegar, chopped
tomatoes, tomato paste and parsley. Season with
salt and pepper. Stir well and bring to a boil. Pour
half of sauce into a shallow baking dish or a cast
iron skillet, and place fish on top. Pour on remaining sauce and sprinkle with bread crumbs. Bake,
uncovered, at 375 degrees for 35 to 40 minutes,
until fish is firm. Sprinkle with cheese. Garnish
with olives or fresh mint. Serves 6.

*Theresa M. Nobuyuki*
*Laguna Hills, CA*

## Balsamic Rosemary Chicken

*The zing of balsamic vinegar really adds flavor.*

4 boneless, skinless chicken breasts
2 T. Dijon mustard
salt and pepper to taste
2 T. garlic, minced
¼ c. balsamic vinegar
2 T. water
4 sprigs fresh rosemary

Arrange chicken in an ungreased 11"x7"
baking pan. Spread mustard over chicken; sprinkle
with salt, pepper and garlic. Blend vinegar and
water; sprinkle over chicken. Arrange one sprig
of rosemary on each chicken breast; cover with
aluminum foil and refrigerate for 2 to 3 hours.
Bake, covered, at 350 degrees for 20 minutes;
uncover and bake for 10 more minutes, or until
chicken is golden. Discard rosemary before
serving. Serves 4.

*Bobbi-Jo Thornton*
*Hancock, ME*

### keep it fresh!
Until they're ready for your best recipe,
tuck sprigs of fresh herbs into water-filled
Mason jars or votive holders for a few
days. Not only will they stay fresh longer,
but they'll also look lovely.

Mediterranean
Baked Fish

Sunday Baked Chicken

## Sunday Baked Chicken

3 lbs. chicken
1 T. all-purpose flour
¼ c. water
¼ c. brown sugar, packed
¼ c. catsup
2 T. white vinegar
2 T. lemon juice
2 T. Worcestershire sauce
1 onion, chopped
1 t. mustard
1 t. paprika
1 t. chili powder
salt and pepper to taste
Garnish: lemon wedges

Arrange chicken pieces in a lightly greased 13"x9" baking pan; set aside. Whisk together flour and water in a small saucepan until smooth; add brown sugar, catsup, vinegar, lemon juice and Worcestershire sauce. Cook and stir over medium heat until beginning to boil. Continue cooking and stirring for 2 minutes, or until thick. Add remaining ingredients except lemon wedges; mix well. Pour over chicken; cover and refrigerate for 2 to 4 hours. Remove from refrigerator 30 minutes before baking. Bake, uncovered, at 350 degrees for 35 to 45 minutes, until juices run clear. Garnish with lemon wedges. Serves 4 to 6.

*Linda Behling*
*Cecil, PA*

## Easy Baked Chicken

*This is a yummy quick meal for hurried evenings when I'm running the children back & forth from tennis matches or football practice.*

6 frozen boneless, skinless chicken breasts
10¾-oz. can cream of mushroom soup
10¾-oz. can cream of onion soup
½ c. milk
2 T. margarine, diced
cooked egg noodles

Arrange frozen chicken in a single layer in a lightly greased 13"x9" baking pan. Mix soups and milk together in a bowl; spread mixture over chicken, covering chicken well. Dot chicken with margarine. Cover baking pan with aluminum foil; seal well. Bake at 350 degrees for one to 1½ hours, until cooked through. Serve chicken over egg noodles; spoon sauce from pan over all. Serves 4 to 6.

*Patti Walker*
*Mocksville, NC*

## Buttermilk Baked Chicken

¼ c. butter
¼ c. oil
1 to 1¼ c. all-purpose flour
1 t. paprika
½ t. garlic powder
½ t. Cajun seasoning
½ t. salt
½ t. pepper
4 chicken breasts
1½ c. buttermilk, divided
10¾-oz. can cream of mushroom soup

Melt butter with oil in a 13"x9" baking pan in a 425-degree oven. Combine flour and seasonings. Dip chicken in ½ cup buttermilk; discard buttermilk. Dredge chicken in flour mixture. Arrange chicken skin-side down in baking pan. Bake, uncovered, at 425 degrees for 25 minutes. Turn chicken over and bake for 10 more minutes, or until juices run clear when chicken is pierced with a fork. Stir together soup and remaining one cup buttermilk; spoon over chicken. Cover; bake 10 more minutes. Serve chicken drizzled with sauce in pan. Serves 4.

*Linda Foreman*
*Locust Grove, OK*

## Chicken Mozzarella

*I like portabella mushrooms in this recipe and sometimes I substitute Asiago cheese for a different flavor.*

6 boneless, skinless chicken breasts
¼ to ½ c. all-purpose flour
salt and pepper to taste
4 T. butter, divided
¼ c. white wine or chicken broth
16-oz. pkg. sliced mushrooms
½ c. shredded mozzarella cheese

Flatten chicken breasts to ½-inch thickness using the flat side of a meat mallet or a rolling pin. Dredge in flour, salt and pepper, coating well. Melt 3 tablespoons butter in a skillet over medium heat. Add chicken; cook just until golden on both sides. Remove chicken to an ungreased 13"x9" baking pan. Add wine or broth and remaining butter to skillet; bring to a boil. Add mushrooms; reduce heat and simmer until soft. Top chicken with mushrooms; pour skillet drippings over mushrooms. Bake at 350 degrees for 45 minutes. Sprinkle chicken with cheese; bake for 10 to 15 more minutes, until cheese is melted. Serves 6.

*Mary Gildenpfennig*
*Harsens Island, MI*

**pick a theme**
Weekly theme nights make meal planning simple…have family members choose their favorites! They'll look forward to Spaghetti Monday and Tex-Mex Tuesday… you'll always know the answer to "What's for dinner?"

## South-of-the-Border Chicken

*Scrumptious…makes any meal a fiesta!*

2 T. all-purpose flour
14½-oz. can diced tomatoes with chili seasoning
2 t. diced jalapeños
½ t. salt
15-oz. can black beans, drained and rinsed
6 boneless, skinless chicken breasts
1 yellow pepper, sliced

Shake flour in a large oven bag; place bag in a 13"x9" baking pan. Add tomatoes, jalapeños and salt to bag; squeeze to blend with flour. Add beans and chicken to bag; turn to coat chicken. Top with yellow pepper. Close bag with nylon tie provided; cut six ½-inch slits in top. Bake at 350 degrees for 45 to 50 minutes, until juices run clear when chicken is pierced with a fork. Serves 4.

*Penny Sherman*
*Cumming, GA*

Oven Chicken
Cordon Bleu

## Oven Chicken Cordon Bleu

*Pecans lend a crunchy touch to this favorite.*

4 boneless, skinless chicken breasts
4 t. Dijon mustard, divided
1 t. garlic, minced and divided
4 slices deli ham
4 slices Swiss cheese
olive oil
1 c. chopped pecans

Flatten chicken breasts to ¼-inch thickness using the flat side of a meat mallet or a rolling pin; top each breast with one teaspoon mustard and ¼ teaspoon garlic. Place one slice ham and one slice cheese on each breast; roll up each breast and secure with toothpicks. Brush each roll with oil; dredge in pecans. Place in a greased 13"x9" baking pan; bake at 350 degrees for 35 to 40 minutes. Serves 4.

*Heather Webb*
*Richmond, VA*

Mary's Heavenly
Chicken

## Mary's Heavenly Chicken

1 c. sour cream
1 T. lemon juice
2 t. Worcestershire sauce
2 cloves garlic, finely chopped
2 t. celery salt
1 t. paprika
½ t. pepper
6 boneless, skinless chicken breasts
1½ c. Italian-flavored dry bread crumbs
¼ c. butter, melted and divided
cooked rice or noodles

Combine sour cream, juice, Worcestershire sauce, garlic, celery salt, paprika and pepper in a large bowl. Add chicken and coat well. Cover and refrigerate overnight. Remove chicken from mixture and roll in bread crumbs. Arrange in a single layer in a lightly greased 15"x10" jelly-roll pan. Spoon melted butter over chicken. Bake, uncovered, at 350 degrees for 25 minutes, or until juices run clear when chicken is pierced with a fork. Serve over rice or noodles. Serves 4 to 6.

*Julie Otto*
*Fountainville, PA*

*My stepmom introduced me to this chicken dish when I was about 10 years old. It's a recipe her neighbor, Mary, gave to her, hence the name. It has since become a favorite of my husband and many of our family members. –Julie*

## Grecian Chicken

*I like to put this in the oven before leaving for church.*

8 boneless, skinless chicken breasts
8 to 10 potatoes, peeled and halved
8 to 10 carrots, peeled
2 T. dried rosemary
3 T. olive oil
3 T. lemon juice
salt and pepper to taste
1 t. garlic powder

Place chicken in a greased roasting pan; bake at 450 degrees about 20 minutes, until golden. Add potatoes and carrots to pan; pour in enough water to partially cover vegetables. Sprinkle with rosemary; drizzle with oil and lemon juice. Sprinkle with salt, pepper and garlic powder. Reduce oven to 350 degrees and bake, covered, about 3 hours, until vegetables are tender. Serves 8.

*Lisa Hains*
*Tipp City, OH*

## Chicken à la Kym

*This recipe was my daughter's favorite recipe for company.*

4 boneless, skinless chicken breasts, halved
8 slices Swiss cheese
10¾-oz. can cream of chicken soup
¼ c. white wine or chicken broth
1 c. chicken-flavored stuffing mix
¼ c. butter, melted

Arrange chicken in a lightly greased 13"x9" baking dish; top with cheese slices. Combine soup, wine or broth and stuffing mix; spread over chicken. Drizzle with butter; bake at 350 degrees for 55 minutes. Serves 6 to 8.

*Joann Britton*
*Chesterfield, MO*

# Chicken Kiev

1½ c. dry bread crumbs
½ c. shredded Parmesan cheese
1 t. dried basil
1 t. dried oregano
½ t. garlic salt
½ t. salt
⅔ c. butter, melted and divided
1½ lbs. chicken tenders
¼ c. white wine or chicken broth
¼ c. green onions, chopped
¼ c. dried parsley

Combine bread crumbs, cheese and seasonings in a large bowl. Reserve ¼ cup butter. Dip chicken in remaining melted butter. Dredge chicken in crumb mixture. Arrange chicken in a lightly greased 13"x9" baking pan. Bake, covered, at 375 degrees for 30 to 40 minutes, until chicken is tender. Heat wine or broth, green onions, parsley and reserved butter in a small saucepan over medium heat until heated through. Spoon over chicken and bake, covered, for 5 to 7 more minutes. Serves 6 to 8.

*Grecia Williams*
*Scottsville, KY*

# Glazed Lemon Chicken

*It's so easy to vary the flavor of this glaze! Try rosemary instead of tarragon...use lime juice for the lemon juice.*

1½ lbs. chicken
2 T. butter, melted
2 T. lemon juice
½ t. dried tarragon
salt and pepper to taste

Arrange chicken pieces skin-side down on a broiler pan; set aside. Mix butter, lemon juice and tarragon in a small bowl. Brush half of mixture over chicken; add salt and pepper to taste. Broil for 15 minutes, or until lightly browned. Turn chicken over; brush with remaining mixture and broil 10 to 15 more minutes, until chicken juices run clear when pierced with a fork. Serves 2.

*Kendall Hale*
*Lynn, MA*

Chicken Kiev

Polynesian Chicken

## Polynesian Chicken

*Baked chicken pieces combine with pineapple and orange soy sauce...a delicious taste of the islands!*

2 lbs. chicken, cut up
8¼-oz. can pineapple chunks, drained and
   juice reserved
½ c. orange juice
¼ c. soy sauce
3 T. brown sugar, packed
2 T. dried, minced onion
1 t. ground ginger
¼ t. pepper
¼ c. water
2 t. cornstarch
11-oz. can mandarin oranges, drained
4 c. hot cooked rice

Arrange chicken pieces in a single layer in an ungreased 13"x9" baking pan; set aside. Combine reserved pineapple juice, orange juice, soy sauce, brown sugar, onion, ginger and pepper; pour over chicken. Cover and refrigerate one hour or over-night, turning once. Bake, covered, at 350 degrees for 30 minutes, or until tender. Uncover, and bake 20 to 25 more minutes, until golden and juices run clear when chicken is pierced with a fork. Remove chicken from baking pan; keep warm on a platter. Skim off fat from pan drippings. Combine water and cornstarch with pan juices in a medium saucepan; heat until thickened and bubbly. Stir in pineapple and oranges and warm through; pour over chicken. Serve with cooked rice. Serves 8.

*Norma Burton*
*Meridian, ID*

## Gram Walker's Smothered Chicken

3 to 4 lbs. chicken
1 c. all-purpose flour
salt and pepper to taste
½ c. butter
2.1-oz. env. chicken noodle soup mix
10¾-oz. can cream of mushroom soup
12-oz. can evaporated milk
1 t. poultry seasoning
dried parsley to taste

Dredge chicken pieces in flour; sprinkle with salt and pepper. Melt butter in a large skillet over medium heat. Fry chicken until golden on both sides; transfer to a lightly greased 13"x9" baking pan. Sprinkle with soup mix; pour mushroom soup over top. Combine remaining ingredients in a small saucepan over medium heat; heat through without boiling. Pour over chicken. Bake, uncovered, at 350 degrees for 30 minutes, or until juices run clear when chicken is pierced with a fork. Serves 4.

*Dawn Raskiewicz*
*Alliance, NE*

# Roast Chicken Dijon

*This recipe is so simple and scrumptious...we love it! Sometimes I'll make extra sauce to toss with redskin potatoes and tuck them around the chicken for a meal-in-one.*

3 to 4-lb. roasting chicken
¼ c. Dijon mustard
2 T. lemon juice
1 T. olive oil
salt and pepper to taste

Place chicken on a rack in an ungreased roasting pan. Mix mustard, lemon juice and oil in a small bowl. Brush mixture over chicken; sprinkle with salt and pepper. Bake, uncovered, at 425 degrees for 40 minutes, or until juices run clear when chicken is pierced with a fork. Let stand for several minutes before slicing. Serves 4 to 6.

*Kendall Hale*
*Lynn, MA*

# Roast Chicken & Vegetables

*This is my own creation from about 10 years ago, when I discovered my true love of cooking. Every time I serve this, I get rave reviews from some of the best cooks in my family...it's quite an ego booster!*

3 to 4-lb. roasting chicken
salt and pepper to taste
3 stalks celery, chopped
2 carrots, peeled and chopped
1 onion, chopped
1 tomato, sliced

Place chicken in an ungreased roasting pan. Sprinkle with salt and pepper to taste. Fill chicken cavity loosely with Sage Stuffing, allowing room for stuffing to expand. Place celery, carrots and onion around chicken; add enough water to cover vegetables. Cover; bake at 350 degrees for one hour. Add tomato; cover again and bake for 30 more minutes. Uncover to allow browning; bake for 30 more minutes, or until juices run clear when chicken is pierced with a fork. Place chicken on a platter and carve. Serve stuffing and vegetables separately. Serves 4 to 6.

## Sage Stuffing:
14-oz. pkg. sage-flavored stuffing mix
2 to 2½ c. boiling water
1 egg, beaten
1 onion, chopped
1 stalk celery, chopped
Optional: dried sage to taste

Place stuffing mix in a large bowl. Add water to desired consistency; toss to moisten. Stir in remaining ingredients and sage, if desired, until well blended.

*Beckie Butcher*
*Elgin, IL*

Roast Chicken Dijon

Gran's Rosemary
Roast Chicken

# Gran's Rosemary Roast Chicken

*Tuck some small new potatoes and baby carrots around the chicken for a complete meal...so simple and delicious!*

4-lb. roasting chicken
1 t. salt
¼ t. pepper
1 onion, quartered
8 cloves garlic, pressed
¼ c. fresh rosemary, chopped
¼ c. butter, melted

Place chicken in a large greased roasting pan; sprinkle with salt and pepper. Place onion, garlic and rosemary inside chicken; brush butter over chicken. Bake, uncovered, at 400 degrees for 1½ hours, basting with pan juices, or until golden and juices run clear when chicken is pierced with a fork. Serves 4 to 6.

*Audrey Lett*
*Newark, DE*

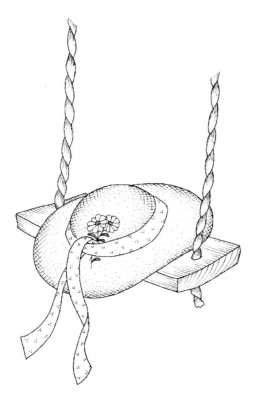

# Delicious Drumsticks

*This is a good recipe that was given to me when I was first married and just learning how to cook. I still enjoy fixing it!*

½ c. all-purpose flour
1 t. salt
½ t. paprika
¼ t. pepper
¼ c. butter, melted and cooled
1½ lbs. chicken drumsticks

Mix flour and seasonings in a shallow bowl; place melted butter in a separate shallow bowl. Dip drumsticks into butter; dredge in flour mixture to coat. Arrange in an ungreased 8"x8" baking pan. Bake, uncovered, at 425 degrees about 50 minutes, until juices run clear when chicken is pierced with a fork. Serves 4 to 6.

*Renae Scheiderer*
*Beallsville, OH*

## buy in bulk

Herbs and spices add lots of flavor to food but can be costly at supermarkets. Instead, purchase them at dollar stores, bulk food stores and even ethnic food stores, where they can be quite a bargain.

## The Best-Yet Buffalo Wings

*These wings are sweet, but the sauce is hot!*

3 lbs. chicken wings
seasoned salt to taste
2-oz. bottle hot pepper sauce
1 c. brown sugar, packed
1 c. water
1 T. mustard seed

Arrange chicken wings on a lightly greased 15"x10" jelly-roll pan. Sprinkle with seasoned salt. Bake at 400 degrees for 20 minutes; turn wings. Bake for 20 to 30 more minutes, until golden and juices run clear when chicken is pierced with a fork; drain. Arrange on serving platter. Combine remaining ingredients in a saucepan; bring to a boil over medium heat. Reduce heat to low; cook until mixture caramelizes and becomes a dark burgundy color, stirring occasionally. Pour sauce over wings before serving or serve on the side for dipping. Makes about 3 dozen.

*Kristen Taylor*
*Fort Smith, AR*

### clean hands

A tray of warm, moistened towels is a must when serving sticky barbecue ribs or chicken wings! Dampen fingertip towels in water and a dash of lemon juice, roll up and microwave on HIGH for 10 to 15 seconds.

## Spicy Sausage & Chicken Creole

*I used this dish to win over my husband and his family while we were dating. He likes his food spicy! Of course, you can use a little less hot pepper sauce, if you prefer.*

14½-oz. can chopped tomatoes
½ c. long-cooking rice, uncooked
½ c. hot water
2 t. hot pepper sauce
¼ t. garlic powder
¼ t. dried oregano
16-oz. pkg. frozen broccoli, corn & red pepper blend, thawed
4 boneless, skinless chicken thighs
½ lb. link Italian sausage, cooked and quartered
8-oz. can tomato sauce

Combine tomatoes, rice, water, hot sauce and seasonings in a 13"x9" baking dish. Cover and bake at 375 degrees for 10 minutes. Stir vegetables into tomato mixture; top with chicken and sausage. Pour tomato sauce over top. Bake, covered, at 375 degrees for 40 minutes, or until juices run clear when chicken is pierced with a fork. Serves 4.

*Carrie Knotts*
*Kalispell, MT*

The Best-Yet Buffalo Wings

Deep South Chicken
& Dumplings

# Deep South Chicken & Dumplings

3 to 4-lb. roasting chicken
salt and pepper to taste
Garnish: fresh parsley

Bake chicken, covered, in an ungreased roasting pan at 350 degrees for 1½ hours. Let chicken cool while preparing Supreme Sauce. Shred chicken; add to simmering sauce in a Dutch oven. Drop Dumplings into sauce by heaping tablespoonfuls. Cover and cook over high heat 10 to 15 minutes, until dumplings are firm and puffy. Discard bay leaves. Add salt and pepper; garnish with fresh parsley. Serves 6.

## Supreme Sauce:

2 T. butter
1 T. oil
½ c. carrot, peeled and diced
½ c. celery, diced
3 cloves garlic, minced
2 bay leaves
5 T. all-purpose flour
6 c. chicken broth
¼ c. whipping cream

Melt butter and oil in a Dutch oven over medium heat. Add vegetables, garlic and bay leaves. Sauté until soft. Stir in flour; add broth, one cup at a time, stirring well after each addition. Simmer until thickened; stir in cream.

## Dumplings:

2 c. all-purpose flour
1 T. baking powder
1 t. salt
2 eggs
¾ to 1 c. buttermilk, divided

Mix flour, baking powder and salt. Whisk together eggs and ¾ cup buttermilk; fold into flour mixture. Stir just until dough forms, adding a little more buttermilk if needed.

# Baked Potatoes & Chicken Sauce

*A few simple ingredients turn baked potatoes into a filling, comforting meal.*

4 baking potatoes
1 to 2 t. oil
2 5-oz. cans chicken, drained and flaked
1 c. sour cream
½ c. mayonnaise
4 t. milk
½ t. seasoned salt
¼ t. pepper
Garnish: chopped fresh parsley

Pierce skins of potatoes several times with a fork; rub oil lightly over potatoes. Bake at 350 degrees for about one hour, until tender. Combine remaining ingredients except parsley in a small saucepan over low heat. Heat through, stirring occasionally, until hot and bubbly. Slice baked potatoes in half lengthwise; place each potato on a plate. Spoon chicken mixture over potatoes. Garnish with fresh parsley. Serves 4.

*Karie Rittenour*
*Delaware, OH*

# Orange-Pecan Cornish Hens

*Great to make during the busy holiday season and perfect served with wild rice.*

½ c. butter, melted and divided
4 1½-lb. Cornish game hens
1 t. salt
1 t. pepper
½ c. orange marmalade
¼ c. orange juice
1 t. cornstarch
½ T. water
½ c. chopped pecans
Garnish: orange slices

Spread one tablespoon butter equally over hens; season with salt and pepper. Tie ends of legs together, if desired, and place on a lightly greased rack in a roasting pan. Bake at 400 degrees for one hour, or until a meat thermometer inserted into thickest part of thigh registers 180 degrees. Blend together remaining butter, marmalade and orange juice in a saucepan; bring to a boil. Blend together a small amount of cornstarch and water in a bowl, slowly adding remaining cornstarch until mixture thickens. Slowly add cornstarch mixture to marmalade mixture, stirring constantly; add pecans. Place hens in a greased 15"x10" jelly-roll pan. Pour glaze over chicken and bake for 10 more minutes, or until glaze begins to turn golden. Garnish with orange slices. Serves 4.

## just-right hens!
Look for the smallest Cornish hens you can find; they'll be the most tender and have the best flavor.

# Turkey-Spinach Quiche

*This recipe is a holiday tradition at our house. I bake it in muffin tins for a nice presentation …my guests love it.*

1 lb. ground turkey sausage, browned and drained
3 c. shredded Cheddar cheese
10-oz. pkg. frozen chopped spinach, cooked and drained
8-oz. can sliced mushrooms, drained
⅔ c. onion, chopped
1 c. mayonnaise
1 c. milk
4 eggs, beaten
1¼ c. biscuit baking mix
2 T. cornstarch

Mix together all ingredients in a large bowl and pour into a greased 9" pie plate. Bake at 350 degrees for 35 to 40 minutes, until golden and set. Serves 4 to 6.

*Jenny Poole*
*Salisbury, NC*

Orange-Pecan Cornish Hens

Stuffed Eggplant Boats

# Stuffed Eggplant Boats

*I just whipped this up one day in my kitchen!*

2 eggplants, halved lengthwise
1 t. salt
2 potatoes, peeled and chopped
4 T. olive oil, divided
1 c. onion, diced
1 red pepper, diced
2 cloves garlic, minced
salt and pepper to taste
8-oz. pkg. shredded mozzarella cheese
1 c. dry bread crumbs
Garnish: fresh parsley

Scoop out the middles of eggplants to form boats, leaving a 2-inch shell. Lightly salt boats; spray with non-stick vegetable spray on all sides. Set aside on a greased baking sheet. Cook potatoes in 3 tablespoons olive oil in a skillet until golden. Remove with a slotted spoon to a separate plate. Add onion, pepper and garlic to skillet. Cook until onion is translucent and pepper is tender. Return potatoes to pan; sprinkle with salt and pepper to taste. Fill eggplant boats with mixture. Top with cheese and bread crumbs; drizzle with remaining oil. Bake at 350 degrees for 30 minutes, or until tender. Garnish with fresh parsley. Serve immediately. Serves 4.

*Michelle Papp*
*Rutherford, NJ*

# Linda's Spring Greens Pizza

*My sister told me she was bringing this pizza to my house for a get-together. A pizza topped with greens? I thought she was crazy! But it was really good… everyone liked it, and it is healthy, too.*

2 c. broccoli flowerets
11 spears asparagus, trimmed
12-inch whole-wheat Italian pizza crust
6-oz. pkg. baby spinach
1 c. grated Parmesan cheese
1 T. garlic, minced
1 t. salt
1 t. pepper
¼ c. chicken broth
1 T. oil
2 c. yellow onion, sliced
3½-oz. pkg. crumbled reduced-fat feta cheese
Garnish: fresh spinach leaves and grape tomato halves

Steam broccoli and asparagus in a steamer basket over boiling water about 5 minutes, until crisp-tender. Drain well; set aside. Place pizza crust on a baking sheet. Bake at 450 degrees for 5 minutes, or until lightly golden; cool. Combine spinach, Parmesan cheese, garlic, salt and pepper in a food processor. Pulse until puréed, adding broth as needed for a smooth consistency; set aside. Heat oil in a large non-stick skillet over medium-high heat. Cook onion, stirring frequently, 4 to 5 minutes, until golden on edges. Spread spinach mixture on pizza crust. Arrange broccoli, asparagus and onion on pizza as desired. Top with feta cheese. Bake at 450 degrees for about 5 minutes, until toppings are hot. Garnish with fresh spinach leaves and grape tomato halves. Cut into wedges. Serves 6 to 8.

*Carolyn Deckard*
*Bedford, IN*

# Greek Pizza

*My husband and I love making this recipe in the summer. Every Saturday morning we go to the farmers' market to buy basil that's been freshly picked that same morning...a tradition we look forward to each summer.*

1 c. basil pesto sauce
12-inch Italian pizza crust
1 c. shredded mozzarella cheese
1½ c. cooked chicken, diced
½ c. red onion, chopped
½ c. green pepper, chopped
¼ c. sliced black olives
Optional: ¼ c. sliced banana peppers
4-oz. container crumbled feta cheese
1 T. fresh oregano
¼ c. tomato, chopped

Spread pesto on pizza crust; sprinkle with mozzarella cheese. Add remaining ingredients in order listed through feta. Bake at 450 degrees for 10 minutes, or until crust is golden and cheese has melted. Sprinkle with oregano and tomato. Serves 6 to 8.

*Dawn Horton*
*Columbus, OH*

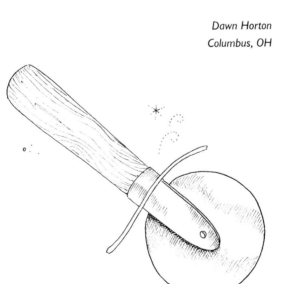

# Homemade Cheese Pizza

*Sure, you could just order your family a pizza, but a homemade pizza has love baked right in!*

1 T. olive oil
1 T. cornmeal
8-oz. can tomato sauce
½ t. sugar
1½ t. dried thyme
1 t. garlic powder
¼ t. pepper
3 T. grated Parmesan cheese
1 onion, finely chopped
28-oz. can diced tomatoes, drained
1 c. shredded white Cheddar cheese
1 c. shredded mozzarella cheese

Prepare Pizza Dough; set aside. Brush oil over a 15"x10" jelly-roll pan; sprinkle with cornmeal. Roll out dough; place on pan. Combine tomato sauce, sugar and seasonings; spread over dough. Top with Parmesan cheese, onion, tomatoes and shredded cheeses. Bake at 400 degrees for 25 to 30 minutes, until edges are golden. Serves 8.

## Pizza Dough:

3 c. all-purpose flour, divided
1 env. rapid-rise yeast
¾ t. salt
2 T. olive oil
1 c. hot water

Mix together 2 cups flour, yeast and salt; set aside. Stir oil into hot water (120 to 130 degrees). Add to flour mixture; mix well. Stir in enough of remaining flour to make a soft dough. Knead on a lightly floured surface until smooth and elastic, about 6 minutes. Cover and let stand for 10 minutes before rolling out.

*Jennifer Niemi*
*Nova Scotia, Canada*

Greek Pizza

Party Ham Casserole (page 142)

Hashbrown-Pork Chop Casserole (page 138)

Oodles of Noodles Casserole (page 148)

Turkey, Almond & Wild Rice Casserole (page 152)

# POTLUCK-PERFECT CASSEROLES

Comforting recipes for easy,
at-home meals or for sharing

Cheeseburger & Fries Casserole

## Cheeseburger & Fries Casserole

*The recipe name says it all...kids will love it!*

2 lbs. ground beef, browned and drained
10¾-oz. can golden mushroom soup
10¾-oz. can Cheddar cheese soup
16-oz. pkg. frozen crinkle-cut French fries
Garnish: chopped tomato, chopped dill pickle

Combine beef and soups; spread mixture in a greased 13"x9" baking pan. Arrange French fries on top. Bake, uncovered, at 350 degrees for 50 to 55 minutes, until fries are golden. Garnish with chopped tomato and dill pickle. Serves 6 to 8.

*Shari Miller*
*Hobart, IN*

### make room

If you're adding more than one baking pan to the oven, remember to stagger them on the racks. Placing one pan directly over another won't allow the food to cook evenly in either.

## Divine Casserole

*I like this with buttery, whipped potatoes...comfort food at its best!*

1 lb. ground beef
6-oz. can tomato paste
1 t. Worcestershire sauce
¼ t. hot pepper sauce
⅛ t. dried oregano
1 onion, chopped
½ c. plus 2 T. butter, melted and divided
8-oz. container small curd cottage cheese
½ c. sour cream
½ c. cream cheese, softened
8-oz. pkg. egg noodles, cooked and divided

Brown beef in a large skillet over medium heat; drain. Add tomato paste, Worcestershire sauce, hot sauce and oregano; heat through and set aside. Sauté onion in 2 tablespoons butter in a separate skillet over medium heat until translucent; place in a medium bowl. Add cottage cheese, sour cream and cream cheese; blend well and set aside. Place half of noodles in an ungreased 2-quart casserole dish. Drizzle with ¼ cup butter; spread with cheese mixture. Toss remaining noodles with remaining butter and spread over cheese mixture. Top with meat mixture. Bake at 350 degrees for 40 minutes, or until bubbly. Serves 4 to 6.

*Tiffany Brinkley*
*Broomfield, CO*

# Beefy Spinach Casserole

*A favorite at any carry-in or potluck.*

1 lb. ground beef
10-oz. pkg. frozen chopped spinach, thawed and
　　drained
1 clove garlic, minced
salt and pepper to taste
16-oz. pkg. wide egg noodles, cooked
2½ c. milk
10¾-oz. can cream of mushroom soup
1 c. American cheese, shredded

Brown beef in a skillet over medium heat; drain. Add spinach, garlic, salt and pepper; cook until heated through. Stir in egg noodles; spoon into a greased 13"x9" baking pan and set aside. Combine milk and soup; mix well to blend and stir gently into beef mixture. Sprinkle with cheese. Cover and bake at 325 degrees for 45 minutes, or until bubbly. Serves 8.

*Bec Royer Williamson*
*Saint Augustine, FL*

# Stuffed Cabbage Casserole

*If you like stuffed cabbage, you'll appreciate this quick & easy variation…no need to roll individual cabbage leaves.*

10 c. cabbage, chopped and divided
2 lbs. ground beef
¾ c. sour cream
1 onion, chopped
½ c. instant rice, uncooked
1 t. salt
1 t. garlic powder
2 10¾-oz. cans tomato soup
½ c. catsup
1 c. shredded Colby cheese

Place 5 cups cabbage in a greased 13"x9" casserole dish; set aside. Combine beef, sour cream, onion, rice, salt and garlic powder; spread over cabbage. Layer remaining cabbage over beef mixture; top with tomato soup and catsup. Sprinkle with cheese. Bake, covered, at 350 degrees for 2 hours. Serves 6 to 8.

*Kelly Schurdell*
*Strongsville, OH*

## save chopping time

Use a garlic press when a recipe calls for minced garlic. Don't bother peeling the clove, just place it in the garlic press and close. The garlic paste is easily removed and ready to add to any recipe. The peel slides off and stays inside the press.

# Pantry Casserole

*Mix a little of this, a little of that and enjoy!*

1 lb. ground beef
2 t. garlic, minced
2 t. poultry seasoning
2 t. dried thyme
1½ t. ground cumin
3 potatoes, thinly sliced
salt and pepper to taste
2 T. butter
1 onion, thinly sliced in rings
2 c. sliced mushrooms
10¾-oz. can cream of chicken soup
¾ c. water
20 saltine crackers, crushed
⅛ t. paprika

Place beef in a large skillet; sprinkle with garlic and seasonings. Heat, stirring frequently, over medium heat until browned. Drain; transfer to an ungreased 13"x9" baking dish. Arrange 2 layers of sliced potatoes over beef mixture, sprinkling each layer with salt and pepper; set aside. Melt butter in the skillet over medium heat; sauté onion and mushrooms until crisp-tender. Spread over potatoes; set aside. Combine soup and water; spread evenly over casserole. Top with cracker crumbs and sprinkle with paprika. Cover and bake at 350 degrees for 1 to 1½ hours, until potatoes are soft. Uncover and bake 10 more minutes, or until golden. Serves 4 to 6.

*Vickie*
*Gooseberry Patch*

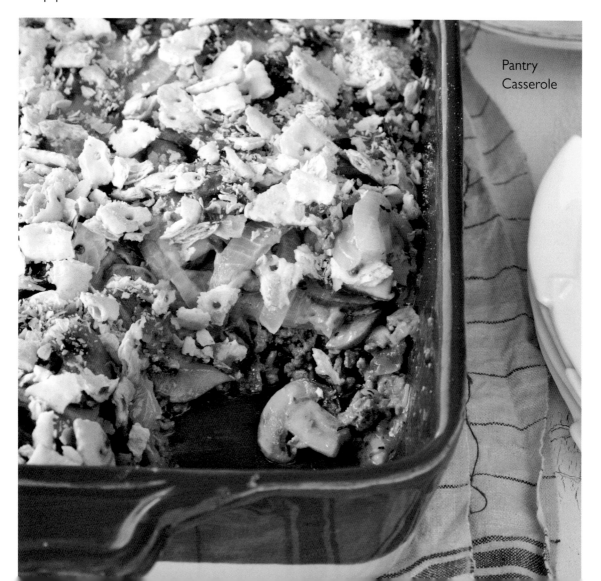

Pantry Casserole

## Mexican Casserole

*I like mild enchilada sauce, but you could choose a hot sauce to spice it up. I think this is the best!*

12 6-inch corn tortillas, quartered
1 lb. ground beef, browned and drained
15-oz. can ranch-style beans
10¾-oz. can cream of chicken soup
10-oz. can enchilada sauce
2 c. shredded Cheddar cheese
14½-oz. can diced tomatoes

Arrange half of tortillas in bottom of a lightly greased 13"x9" baking pan. Place beef on top of tortillas. Mix together beans, soup and enchilada sauce; pour over beef. Sprinkle cheese on top; add remaining tortillas. Pour diced tomatoes on top. Bake, uncovered, at 350 degrees for 45 minutes. Serves 6 to 8.

*Shannon Pettus*
*Rowlett, TX*

## Potato Puff & Ground Beef Casserole

2 lbs. ground beef
10¾-oz. can cream of mushroom soup
10¾-oz. can cream of chicken soup
1⅓ c. milk
6 c. frozen potato puffs
1½ c. shredded Cheddar cheese

Brown beef in a skillet over medium heat; drain. Stir in soups and milk; heat through. Pour into an ungreased 13"x9" baking pan. Layer potato puffs evenly over top. Bake, uncovered, at 375 degrees for 25 minutes, or until puffs are golden. Sprinkle with cheese. Bake 5 more minutes, or until cheese is melted. Serves 8.

*Tina George*
*El Dorado, AR*

## Beefy Chow Mein Noodle Casserole

2 lbs. ground beef
1 onion, chopped
10¾-oz. can cream of celery soup
10¾-oz. can golden mushroom soup
1¼ c. water
1 c. instant rice, uncooked
1 T. Worcestershire sauce
1 t. garlic powder
½ t. salt
5-oz. can chow mein noodles
Garnish: fresh parsley, chopped

Brown beef and onion in a large skillet over medium heat; drain. Stir together soups and remaining ingredients except noodles in a large bowl. Add to beef mixture; mix well. Pour into a lightly greased 13"x9" baking pan. Bake, uncovered, at 375 degrees for 20 minutes, or until bubbly. Sprinkle with chow mein noodles. Bake, uncovered, for 5 to 10 more minutes. Garnish, if desired. Serves 16.

*Vicki Cox*
*Bland, MO*

*plan ahead*
When chopping onions or celery, it takes only a moment to chop a little extra. Place the diced veggies in a plastic zipping bag and tuck them away in the freezer for a quick start to dinner another day.

Beefy Chow Mein Noodle Casserole

Hearty Pierogi Casserole

# Hearty Pierogi Casserole

2 to 3 16.9-oz. pkgs. frozen favorite-flavor
   pierogies
1½ to 2 lbs. smoked pork sausage, sliced into
   bite-size pieces
26-oz. can cream of mushroom soup
3¼ c. milk
2 to 3 c. shredded Cheddar cheese

Bring a large saucepan of water to a boil; add
pierogies and sausage. Cook for 5 to 7 minutes,
until pierogies float; drain. Arrange pierogies
and sausage in a lightly greased 13"x9" glass
baking pan. Combine soup and milk; pour over
top of pierogi mixture. Top with cheese. Bake,
uncovered, at 350 degrees for 30 to 35 minutes,
until bubbly and cheese is lightly golden. Let
stand for 5 minutes before serving. Serves 8.

*Sheryl Maksymoski*
*Grand Rapids, MI*

# Cheesy Sausage-Potato Casserole

*Add some fresh green beans, too, if you like.*

3 to 4 potatoes, sliced
2 8-oz. links sausage, sliced into 2-inch lengths
1 onion, chopped
½ c. butter, sliced
1 c. shredded Cheddar cheese

Layer potatoes, sausage and onion in a 13"x9"
baking pan sprayed with non-stick vegetable
spray. Dot with butter; sprinkle with cheese. Bake
at 350 degrees for 1½ hours. Serves 6 to 8.

*J.J. Presley*
*Portland, TX*

## wrap it up

If you're taking a casserole along to a
potluck or carry-in, secure the lid
with a brightly colored tea towel
wrapped around the baking dish
and knotted at the top. Keep
the serving spoon handy by
tucking it through the knot.

## Hashbrown-Pork Chop Casserole

*Serve a quick vegetable, such as green bean bundles, along with these chops for a flavorful weeknight meal.*

5 bone-in pork chops
1 T. oil
10¾-oz. can cream of celery soup
1 c. sour cream
½ c. milk
32-oz. pkg. frozen shredded hashbrowns, thawed
1 c. onion, chopped
1 c. shredded Cheddar cheese

Brown pork chops on both sides in hot oil in a large skillet over medium heat. Set aside. Combine soup, sour cream and milk in a large bowl; stir in hashbrowns and onion. Spread sour cream mixture in an ungreased 13"x9" baking pan and sprinkle with cheese. Top with pork chops. Bake, uncovered, at 375 degrees for 45 to 50 minutes, until heated through and pork chops are fully cooked. Serves 5.

*Shirley Flanagan*
*Wooster, OH*

### go green
A crisp green salad goes well with almost any comforting main dish. For a zippy lemon dressing, combine ½ cup olive oil, ⅓ cup fresh lemon juice and a tablespoon of Dijon mustard in a small jar and chill; shake jar to blend before serving.

## Grandma Knorberg's Pork Chop Casserole

6 bone-in pork chops
salt and pepper to taste
⅛ t. dried sage
10¾-oz. can cream of mushroom soup
1 c. carrot, peeled and sliced
½ c. water
½ c. celery, sliced

Arrange pork chops in an ungreased 13"x9" baking pan; sprinkle with salt, pepper and sage. Combine remaining ingredients; spoon soup mixture over chops. Bake, covered, at 350 degrees for 45 minutes. Serves 6.

*Shirl Parsons*
*Cape Carteret, NC*

Hashbrown-Pork
Chop Casserole

Mile-High Pork
Chop Casserole

# Mile-High Pork Chop Casserole

*Use red or yellow peppers for color and variety.*

4 boneless pork chops
salt and pepper to taste
2 T. oil
1 c. long-cooking rice, uncooked
1 tomato, sliced
1 yellow pepper, sliced
1 onion, sliced
10-oz. can beef consommé
Garnish: fresh parsley, chopped

Sprinkle pork chops on both sides with salt and pepper. Heat oil in a skillet; cook chops on both sides until golden. Set aside. Sprinkle rice in a lightly greased 11"x7" baking pan. Arrange pork chops on top of rice. Place tomato, yellow pepper and onion slices on top of each pork chop. Pour consommé over all; cover. Bake at 350 degrees for 1½ hours, or until pork chops are tender and rice has absorbed liquid. Garnish with parsley. Serves 4.

*Karen Shepherd*
*Elko, NV*

# Ham-It-Up Casserole

*Use thickly sliced steak fries and smoked ham to give this dish a brand-new flavor.*

16-oz. pkg. frozen French fries
16-oz. pkg. frozen chopped broccoli, cooked
1½ c. cooked ham, cubed
10¾-oz. can cream of mushroom soup
1¼ c. milk
¼ c. mayonnaise
1 c. grated Parmesan cheese

Arrange fries in a greased 13"x9" baking pan. Top with broccoli; sprinkle with ham and set aside. Combine soup, milk and mayonnaise in a small bowl; mix well and pour evenly over ham. Sprinkle with cheese. Bake, uncovered, at 375 degrees for 40 minutes. Serves 4 to 6.

*Lisa Bownas*
*Columbus, OH*

# 3-Bean & Ham Casserole

*Hearty & filling...feeds a crowd!*

3 16-oz. cans baked beans, drained and rinsed
2 16-oz. cans kidney beans, drained and rinsed
1 lb. pork sausage links, sliced into 2-inch pieces
10-oz. pkg. frozen lima beans, cooked
8-oz. can tomato sauce
½ lb. smoked ham, cubed
1 onion, chopped
½ c. catsup
¼ c. brown sugar, packed
1 T. salt
1½ t. pepper
½ t. mustard

Combine all ingredients in an ungreased 3½-quart baking dish; mix well. Bake, uncovered, at 400 degrees for one hour. Serves 16 to 20.

*Melanie Lowe*
*Dover, DE*

# Party Ham Casserole

8-oz. pkg. medium egg noodles, uncooked
   and divided
10¾-oz. can cream of mushroom soup
½ c. milk
1 c. sour cream
2 t. mustard
1 t. dried, minced onion
2 c. cooked ham, cubed
¼ c. dry bread crumbs
1½ T. butter, melted
1 T. grated Parmesan cheese

Measure out half of noodles, reserving rest for another recipe. Cook noodles according to package directions; drain. Combine soup and milk in a small saucepan, stirring over low heat until smooth. Add sour cream, mustard and onion, stirring to combine well. Layer half each of cooked noodles, ham and soup mixture in a lightly greased 1½-quart casserole dish; repeat layers. Toss bread crumbs with melted butter; sprinkle over casserole. Top with cheese. Bake, uncovered, at 350 degrees for 25 to 30 minutes, until golden. Serves 6.

*Barbara Reese*
*Catawissa, PA*

Party Ham Casserole

# Ham & Cauliflower Casserole

*Try substituting broccoli for cauliflower…just as delicious.*

3 c. cooked ham, cubed
3 c. cauliflower flowerets, cooked
1½ c. sliced mushrooms
salt and pepper to taste
2 T. butter
1 c. milk
2 T. all-purpose flour
1 c. shredded Cheddar cheese
½ c. sour cream
1 T. dry bread crumbs

Combine ham, cauliflower and mushrooms in an ungreased 3-quart casserole dish. Sprinkle with salt and pepper and set aside. Melt butter in a saucepan; stir in milk and flour. Cook over medium heat, stirring frequently, until thickened. Stir in cheese and sour cream; continue cooking until cheese has melted and sauce is smooth. Set aside; pour sauce over top of ham mixture. Sprinkle with bread crumbs. Bake, uncovered, at 350 degrees for 30 to 40 minutes, until heated through. Serves 6.

*Darrell Lawry*
*Kissimmee, FL*

# Hearty Ham & Potato Casserole

*This is a good brunch or supper dish. It can be assembled a day ahead and refrigerated. Bring to room temperature before baking.*

26-oz. pkg. frozen shredded hashbrowns, thawed
1 lb. cooked ham, cubed
10¾-oz. can cream of potato soup
½ t. pepper
¼ c. grated Parmesan cheese
1 c. shredded Cheddar cheese
paprika to taste

Combine hashbrowns, ham, soup and pepper in a lightly greased 13"x9" baking dish. Bake, uncovered, at 400 degrees for 25 minutes. Sprinkle with cheeses and paprika; bake 5 more minutes, or until golden. Serves 6 to 8.

*Barbara Czahowski*
*Sugar Land, TX*

# He-Man Casserole

*This recipe was first published in my church cookbook in 1983. So hearty, filled with ham and mashed potatoes…that must be how it got its name!*

6 T. butter
½ c. onion, chopped
½ c. green pepper, chopped
6 T. all-purpose flour
⅛ t. pepper
1½ c. milk
1 c. chicken broth
4 c. cooked ham, cubed
10-oz. pkg. frozen peas, thawed and drained
4 c. mashed potatoes
1 egg, beaten
1 c. shredded Cheddar cheese

Melt butter in a large skillet over medium heat. Add onion and green pepper; cook until tender. Add flour and pepper; stir until smooth. Gradually stir in milk and broth. Cook, stirring until thickened. Stir in ham and peas; pour ham mixture into a lightly greased 3-quart casserole dish. Combine mashed potatoes, egg and cheese in a large bowl. Drop potato mixture by tablespoonfuls onto ham mixture. Bake, uncovered, at 375 degrees for 45 minutes, or until hot and bubbly. Serves 8.

*Linda Barner*
*Fresno, CA*

## Grandma Great's Chicken Casserole

*This hearty casserole was my mother-in-law's special dish. Whether it's a family gathering or church social, everyone loves it!*

4 to 5 boneless, skinless chicken breasts
2 onions, chopped
1 green pepper, chopped
½ c. oil
4-oz. can sliced mushrooms, drained
Optional: 2-oz. jar sliced pimentos, drained
8-oz. pkg. pasteurized process cheese spread, shredded
16-oz. pkg. thin spaghetti, cooked

Place chicken in a large saucepan; add water to cover. Simmer over medium heat about 30 minutes, until tender. Remove chicken and cool. Drain saucepan, reserving 2 cups broth. Cook onions and pepper in oil in the same pan; drain. Stir in reserved broth, mushrooms and pimentos, if desired; bring to a simmer. Chop chicken and add along with cheese and spaghetti. Transfer to a lightly greased 2-quart casserole dish. Bake, covered, at 350 degrees for 30 minutes. Uncover; bake 20 to 30 more minutes, until golden on top and liquid is absorbed. Serves 6 to 8.

*Judy Taylor*
*Butler, MO*

## Chicken Parmigiana Casserole

1 c. Italian-flavored dry bread crumbs
⅓ c. grated Parmesan cheese
1 lb. boneless, skinless chicken breasts, cut into bite-size pieces
2 T. olive oil
16-oz. pkg. penne pasta, cooked
26-oz. jar marinara sauce, divided
1 c. shredded mozzarella cheese, divided

Combine bread crumbs and Parmesan cheese in a large heavy-duty plastic zipping bag. Place chicken in bag and shake to coat. Remove chicken from bag; cook in oil in a medium skillet over medium heat, until browned on all sides. Layer pasta, half of sauce, half of cheese and chicken in an ungreased 13"x9" baking pan. Top with remaining sauce and cheese. Bake, covered, at 350 degrees for 30 minutes, or until heated through and cheese is melted. Serves 6.

# Top-Prize Chicken Casserole

*This crowd-pleasing dish has graced my family's table for decades. Originally prepared by my mother-in-law, it's been taken to many potlucks and church suppers. With its creamy sauce and crunchy topping, it's always a hit.*

2 to 3 c. cooked chicken, cubed
2 10¾-oz. cans cream of mushroom soup
4 eggs, hard-boiled, peeled and chopped
1 onion, chopped
2 c. cooked rice
1½ c. celery, chopped
1 c. mayonnaise
2 T. lemon juice
3-oz. pkg. slivered almonds
5-oz. can chow mein noodles

Combine all ingredients except almonds and noodles in a large bowl; mix well. Place chicken mixture in a lightly greased 3-quart casserole dish. Cover and refrigerate 8 hours to overnight. Stir in almonds. Bake, uncovered, at 350 degrees for 40 to 45 minutes, until heated through. Top with noodles; bake 5 more minutes. Serves 6 to 8.

Betty Lou Wright
Hendersonville, TN

## soak up the flavor
Casseroles really taste better if they're made in advance to allow the flavors to blend. Assemble one the night before, store in the fridge overnight, then pop in the oven to bake the next day for dinner.

Top-Prize Chicken
Casserole

Chicken-Cashew
Casserole

## Chicken-Cashew Casserole

2 10¾-oz. cans cream of mushroom soup
2 c. cooked chicken, diced
1 c. celery, diced
⅔ c. water
½ c. onion, grated
8½-oz. container cashews
8-oz. can sliced water chestnuts, drained and
    coarsely chopped
8-oz. pkg. sliced fresh mushrooms
1 c. buttery round crackers, crushed
2 T. butter, melted
Garnish: green onions, sliced

Combine all ingredients in a bowl, except crackers and butter. Spread in a lightly greased 13"x9" baking pan. Bake, uncovered, at 350 degrees for 30 minutes. Mix together crackers and butter in a bowl; sprinkle over top of casserole. Bake for 10 more minutes. Garnish with green onions. Serves 6.

*Doris Wilson*
*Denver, IA*

## Texas Two-Step Casserole

*I created this recipe after experimenting with a variety of peppers, salsas and rubs.*

1 lb. ground turkey
1 T. olive oil
1 onion, chopped
3 cloves garlic, minced
1 red chile pepper, finely chopped
1 red pepper, chopped
8-oz. pkg. rotini pasta, cooked
¼ c. sour cream
1 c. shredded Cheddar cheese, divided
2¼-oz. can sliced black olives, drained
1 T. butter, softened
½ t. dried parsley
½ t. ground cumin
salt and pepper to taste
Optional: 2 T. salsa

Brown turkey in oil in a skillet over medium heat; drain. Add onion, garlic and peppers to skillet; sauté until soft. Combine turkey mixture, rotini, sour cream, ½ cup cheese, olives, butter, herbs, salt, pepper and salsa, if desired, in a greased 13"x9" baking pan. Top with remaining cheese. Bake, covered, at 350 degrees for one hour. Serves 6 to 8.

*Sybil Boyter*
*Duncanville, TX*

## Zippy Chili Casserole

*Just 20 minutes to bake...how speedy!*

2 T. butter
2 T. all-purpose flour
2 c. milk
1 T. grated Parmesan cheese
4½ c. wide egg noodles, cooked
2 c. turkey, cooked and cubed
1 c. onion, chopped
1½ c. green pepper, chopped
1 T. mustard
1 t. chili powder
2 T. bread crumbs

Melt butter over medium-high heat in a saucepan; sprinkle with flour. Cook, whisking constantly, for 2 minutes. Whisk in milk and cheese. Cook, stirring constantly for 2 minutes, until thickened. Remove from heat. Add noodles, turkey, onion, pepper, mustard and chili powder to saucepan; toss to mix well. Spoon mixture into a greased 2-quart casserole dish and sprinkle with bread crumbs. Bake, uncovered, at 375 degrees for 20 minutes, or until golden and bubbly. Serves 6.

*Kelly Alderson*
*Erie, PA*

## Use Your Noodle Casserole

*Feeling creative in the kitchen, I pulled out all my tasty leftovers, tossed them together and invented this super casserole!*

2 T. butter
2 T. all-purpose flour
1 c. milk
½ c. cooked ham, cubed
½ c. cooked chicken, cubed
1 c. wide egg noodles, cooked
¼ c. celery, chopped
¼ t. salt
¼ t. pepper
¼ c. shredded Cheddar cheese
Optional: paprika to taste

Melt butter in a large saucepan over low heat; stir in flour and heat until bubbly. Slowly add milk, stirring constantly, until mixture is thick and smooth. Remove from heat; stir in ham, chicken, noodles, celery, salt and pepper. Transfer to an ungreased 1½-quart casserole dish. Bake, uncovered, at 400 degrees for 15 minutes. Sprinkle with cheese and paprika, if desired. Bake 5 to 10 more minutes, until cheese is bubbly. Serves 4.

*Jason Keller*
*Carrollton, GA*

## Chicken Noodle Casserole

*My mom created this recipe, and it is a favorite of mine. Nothing turns a day around quicker than coming home to this dish!*

2 T. margarine
2 T. all-purpose flour
1 t. chicken bouillon granules
1 c. boiling water
10¾-oz. can cream of chicken soup
1½ c. cooked chicken, diced
8-oz. pkg. wide egg noodles, cooked
1 c. potato chips, crushed

Melt margarine in a large saucepan over medium heat; stir in flour. Dissolve bouillon in boiling water; add to pan. Stir in soup and chicken; heat through. Add noodles; pour into a greased 2-quart casserole dish. Sprinkle with crushed chips. Bake, uncovered, at 325 degrees for 15 minutes. Serves 4.

*Mary Beth Updike*
*Ottawa, IL*

## Oodles of Noodles Casserole

*To toast the almonds, just spread them on a baking dish and bake at 350 degrees for 10 to 15 minutes, stirring occasionally.*

8-oz. pkg. medium egg noodles, uncooked and divided
2 T. butter
2 T. all-purpose flour
1 t. salt
¼ t. pepper
2 c. milk
1 c. shredded Cheddar cheese
10-oz. pkg. frozen broccoli spears, cooked
2 c. cooked turkey, diced
⅓ c. slivered almonds, toasted

Cook half of noodles according to package directions, reserving rest for another recipe; drain and set aside. Melt butter in a saucepan over low heat; blend in flour, salt and pepper. Stir until smooth and bubbly. Gradually add milk, stirring until thickened. Remove from heat and add cheese; stir until melted. Dice broccoli stems, leaving flowerets intact. Arrange noodles, broccoli stems and turkey in a lightly greased 8"x8" baking pan or individual baking dishes; pour cheese sauce over top. Lightly press broccoli flowerets into cheese layer; sprinkle with almonds. Bake, uncovered, at 350 degrees for 15 minutes. Serves 4.

*Beth Kramer*
*Port Saint Lucie, FL*

Oodles of Noodles Casserole

Southwestern Turkey Casserole

## Southwestern Turkey Casserole

*I like to arrange bowls filled with different toppings so that everyone can garnish with their favorites...sour cream, chopped cilantro, salsa, chopped green onions and extra shredded cheese.*

10¾-oz. can cream of chicken soup
10¾-oz. can cream of mushroom soup
7-oz. can diced green chiles, drained
1 c. sour cream
16 6-inch corn tortillas, cut into strips
2 c. cooked turkey, diced and divided
8-oz. pkg. shredded Cheddar cheese, divided
Garnish: cilantro leaves and chopped green onions

Combine soups, chiles and sour cream in a mixing bowl; set aside. Line bottom of a 13"x9" baking dish with half of tortilla strips. Top with half of turkey. Spread half of soup mixture over turkey; sprinkle with half of cheese. Repeat layers. Bake, uncovered, at 350 degrees for 30 to 45 minutes. Garnish with cilantro and green onions. Serves 6 to 8.

*Amy Butcher*
*Columbus, GA*

## heat it up

Need to thaw a frozen casserole? Up to 2 days before serving, set the frozen casserole in the refrigerator to slightly thaw. When ready to bake, cover loosely with aluminum foil and continue baking 20 to 30 minutes longer, until heated through.

## Garlicky Chicken Casserole

*I created this low-carb variation of chicken enchilada casserole...minus the tortillas!*

½ c. onion, chopped
2 cloves garlic, pressed
2 T. olive oil
2 12-oz. cans chicken, drained
10¾-oz. can cream of mushroom soup
10-oz. can diced tomatoes with green chiles, drained
½ c. shredded Cheddar cheese
4 to 6 T. whipping cream
salt and pepper to taste
Optional: shredded Cheddar cheese and sour cream

Sauté onion and garlic in oil in a skillet over medium heat until onion is translucent. Combine onion mixture and remaining ingredients except toppings in a large mixing bowl; stir well. Pour mixture into a lightly greased 13"x9" baking pan. Bake, uncovered, at 350 degrees for 20 to 25 minutes. Top with cheese and sour cream, if desired. Serves 4 to 6.

*Shellye McDaniel*
*Texarkana, TX*

## Turkey, Almond & Wild Rice Casserole

*The crunch of almonds and the tang of pimentos make this casserole oh-so delicious.*

1 onion, chopped
2 T. butter
½ c. all-purpose flour
2 4½-oz. jars sliced mushrooms, drained and liquid reserved
3 c. half-and-half
½ to 1 c. chicken broth
6 c. cooked turkey, cubed
2 c. prepared long-grain and wild rice
1 c. slivered almonds, toasted
½ c. pimentos, diced
4 T. fresh parsley, chopped
salt and pepper to taste
1 c. dry bread crumbs
¼ c. butter, melted
Garnish: fresh parsley sprig

Sauté onion in butter in a saucepan over medium heat; remove from heat and stir in flour. Set aside. Combine reserved mushroom liquid with half-and-half and enough broth to make 4 cups. Gradually stir into flour mixture; cook and stir until thickened. Add turkey, rice, mushrooms, toasted almonds, pimentos, parsley, salt and pepper. Place in a lightly greased 11"x17" baking pan; set aside. Combine bread crumbs and butter; sprinkle over top of casserole. Bake, uncovered, at 350 degrees for 40 minutes. Garnish, if desired. Serves 6 to 8.

*Shelley Turner*
*Boise, ID*

## Hot Tamale Casserole

*Once you taste this, you'll make it all the time.*

2 lbs. ground turkey
2 1¼-oz. pkgs. taco seasoning mix
2 8½-oz. pkgs. corn muffin mix
2 eggs
1 c. milk
2 c. shredded Monterey Jack cheese, divided
1 c. salsa

Brown turkey in a skillet over medium heat; drain and add taco seasoning. Set aside. Prepare corn muffin mixes with eggs and milk; mix well. Pour half of batter into a greased 13"x9" baking pan. Top with turkey; layer with one cup cheese. Pour remaining batter over cheese and spread evenly. Bake, uncovered, at 350 degrees for 30 minutes. Spread with salsa and sprinkle with remaining cheese. Bake for 10 more minutes. Cool for 15 minutes before serving. Serves 4 to 6.

*Marlene Darnell*
*Newport Beach, CA*

*make your own*
Homemade chicken broth is simple to make. Whenever you boil chicken for a recipe, save the broth and freeze it. When it's time to make broth, thaw and combine with desired amount of chopped onion, chopped carrots, and sliced celery. Simmer, uncovered, for one hour and strain, if desired.

Turkey, Almond & Wild Rice
Casserole

Seafood Bisque Casserole

## Seafood Bisque Casserole

*Oodles of seafood in a velvety cream sauce.*

7 T. butter, divided
½ lb. small shrimp, peeled and cleaned
½ lb. crabmeat, chopped
½ lb. scallops
1 T. shallots, chopped
10 T. sherry or chicken broth, divided
½ t. salt
¼ t. pepper
3 T. all-purpose flour
1½ c. milk
dry bread crumbs
grated Parmesan cheese
Garnish: fresh parsley, chopped

Melt 4 tablespoons butter in a large skillet over medium heat. Add seafood and shallots; sauté for 5 minutes. Sprinkle with 6 tablespoons sherry or broth, salt and pepper; set aside. Melt remaining butter in a small saucepan; add flour, stirring to thicken. Add milk and remaining sherry; stir until smooth. Combine sauce and seafood mixture and place in a lightly greased 8"x8" baking pan. Sprinkle with bread crumbs and Parmesan; bake, uncovered, at 400 degrees for 30 minutes. Garnish, if desired. Serves 6 to 8.

*Linda Stone*
*Cookeville, TN*

## Herbed Seafood Casserole

*This rich seafood dish is tasty with garlic bread and spinach salad.*

1 lb. cooked medium shrimp, chopped
½ lb. lobster, chopped
¼ lb. crabmeat, chopped
4-oz. can sliced mushrooms, drained
¼ c. butter
¼ c. all-purpose flour
2 c. milk
salt and pepper to taste
¼ t. paprika
2 t. fresh chives, finely chopped
2 t. fresh parsley, finely chopped
2 T. white wine or chicken broth
4 T. grated Parmesan cheese

Combine shrimp, lobster, crabmeat and mushrooms in a greased 1½-quart casserole dish; set aside. Melt butter in a medium saucepan over medium-low heat; stir in flour until smooth and bubbly. Gradually add milk, stirring constantly. Continue to cook over low heat, stirring constantly, until thickened and bubbly. Stir in seasonings and wine or broth. Gently stir sauce into seafood mixture; sprinkle with Parmesan cheese. Bake, uncovered, at 350 degrees for 20 minutes; place under a broiler for one minute, or until golden on top. Serves 4.

*Rita Morgan*
*Pueblo, CO*

### add citrus
Serve lemon and lime wedges with seafood casseroles...their citrus taste is a perfect pairing with seafood. Guests can squeeze on as much or as little as they'd like.

# Mock Oyster Casserole

*One of our tastiest recipes...no one will miss the oysters!*

1 eggplant, peeled and sliced into 1-inch cubes
½ c. butter, melted
1½ c. buttery round cracker crumbs
1 egg, beaten
6½-oz. can minced clams, drained and
   liquid reserved
salt, pepper and hot pepper sauce to taste

Drop eggplant into boiling water for 3 minutes. Drain well; set aside. Add butter to cracker crumbs; mix well. Reserve ⅓ cup crumb mixture for topping. Gently mix egg, clams and eggplant. Add crumb mixture, salt, pepper and hot pepper sauce. Add just enough reserved clam liquid to make moist, but not soupy. Pour into a greased 11"x7" baking pan. Top with reserved crumbs and bake, uncovered, at 350 degrees for 45 minutes. Serves 4 to 6.

Dale Duncan
Waterloo, LA

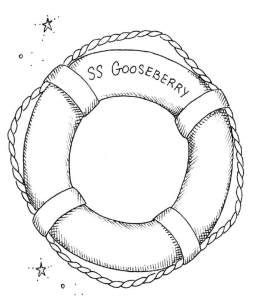

# Party Paella Casserole

*Here's a great use for rotisserie chicken, shrimp and yellow rice.*

2  8-oz. pkgs. yellow rice
1 lb. medium shrimp, peeled and cleaned
1 T. fresh lemon juice
½ t. salt
¼ t. pepper
2 cloves garlic, minced
1½ T. olive oil
2½-lb. lemon-and-garlic deli roast chicken,
   boned and coarsely shredded
5 green onions, chopped
8-oz. container sour cream
1 c. frozen English peas, thawed
1 c. green olives with pimentos, coarsely chopped
1½ c. shredded Monterey Jack cheese
½ t. smoked Spanish paprika

Prepare rice according to package directions. Remove from heat and let cool 30 minutes; fluff with a fork. Meanwhile, toss shrimp with lemon juice, salt and pepper in a bowl. Sauté shrimp and garlic in hot oil in a large non-stick skillet 2 minutes, or just until done. Remove from heat. Combine shredded chicken, cooked rice, onions, sour cream and peas in a large bowl; toss well. Add shrimp and olives, tossing gently. Spoon rice mixture into a greased 13"x9" baking pan. Combine cheese and paprika, tossing well; sprinkle over casserole. Bake, uncovered, at 400 degrees for 15 minutes, or just until cheese is melted and casserole is thoroughly heated. Serves 8.

Party Paella Casserole

# Cajun Crab Casserole

*So easy to prepare…this is one of my weeknight favorites.*

8-oz. can crabmeat, drained
10¾-oz. can cream of mushroom soup
½ c. prepared herb-flavored stuffing mix
½ c. green or red pepper, chopped
½ c. celery, chopped
½ c. mayonnaise
hot pepper sauce and Cajun seasoning to taste

Combine all ingredients in a bowl. Pour into a greased 1½-quart casserole dish or 4 individual baking dishes. Bake, uncovered, at 350 degrees for 45 minutes to one hour, until hot and bubbly. Serves 4.

*Elizabeth Blackstone*
*Racine, WI*

Cajun Crab Casserole

## Shrimply Divine Casserole

*The combination of spinach and shrimp is a perfect pairing!*

8-oz. pkg. spinach egg noodles, cooked
3-oz. pkg. cream cheese, cubed
1½ lbs. medium shrimp, peeled and cleaned
½ c. butter
10¾-oz. can cream of mushroom soup
1 c. sour cream
½ c. milk
½ c. mayonnaise
1 T. fresh chives, chopped
½ t. mustard
Optional: ¾ c. shredded cheese, any flavor

Place noodles in a lightly greased 13"x9" baking pan. Place cream cheese cubes on hot noodles; set aside. Sauté shrimp in butter and pour over noodles and cheese. Mix together remaining ingredients except cheese and pour over shrimp. Sprinkle cheese on top, if desired. Bake, uncovered, at 325 degrees for 20 to 30 minutes, until bubbly and cheese melts. Serves 6.

*Karen Puchnick*
*Butler, PA*

## Rotini-Tuna Casserole

*You can use almost any canned "cream of" soup in this versatile casserole recipe.*

10¾-oz. can cream of chicken soup
1¼ c. milk
16-oz. pkg. rainbow rotini pasta, cooked
14½-oz. can mixed vegetables, drained
6-oz. can tuna, drained
8-oz. can sliced mushrooms, drained
2-oz. jar pimentos, drained
salt and pepper to taste
1 t. dried parsley
½ c. shredded Cheddar cheese
½ c. potato chips, crushed

Mix together soup and milk in a large bowl. Add pasta, vegetables, tuna, mushrooms, pimentos and seasonings; mix well. Pour into an ungreased 2-quart casserole dish; top with cheese and potato chips. Bake, uncovered, at 350 degrees for 30 minutes, or until heated through. Serves 6 to 8.

*Tammy Rowe*
*Bellevue, OH*

# Black Bean Casserole

*A no-fuss casserole...watch it disappear!*

⅓ c. long-cooking brown rice, uncooked
1 c. vegetable broth
1 T. olive oil
⅓ c. onion, diced
1 zucchini, thinly sliced
½ c. sliced mushrooms
½ t. ground cumin
salt to taste
cayenne pepper to taste
15-oz. can black beans, drained and rinsed
4-oz. can diced green chiles, drained
⅓ c. carrots, peeled and shredded
2 c. shredded Swiss cheese, divided

Combine rice and vegetable broth in a saucepan and bring to a boil. Reduce heat to low; cover and simmer for 45 minutes. Set aside. Heat oil in a skillet over medium heat; sauté onion until tender. Stir in zucchini, mushrooms, cumin, salt and cayenne pepper. Cook and stir until zucchini is lightly golden. Mix rice, zucchini mixture, beans, chiles, carrots and one cup cheese in a large bowl. Pour into a greased 13"x9" baking pan; sprinkle with remaining cheese. Cover casserole loosely with aluminum foil. Bake at 350 degrees for 30 minutes. Uncover and bake 10 more minutes, or until bubbly and lightly golden. Serves 6 to 8.

*Tami Bowman*
*Marysville, OH*

# Texas Corn & Green Chile Casserole

8-oz. pkg. cream cheese
¼ c. butter
¼ c. sugar
16-oz. pkg. frozen corn, thawed
7-oz. can diced green chiles
salt and pepper to taste

Combine cream cheese, butter and sugar in a medium saucepan over medium heat; cook until melted. Add corn and chiles; stir until well blended. Sprinkle with salt and pepper. Pour into a greased 1½-quart casserole dish. Bake, uncovered, at 350 degrees for 30 to 40 minutes, until golden around edges. Serves 10.

*Terri King*
*Granger, TX*

# Farmers' Market Casserole

*Any veggies will work well...you just can't go wrong.*

15-oz. can French-style green beans, drained
15-oz. can green peas, drained
15-oz. can whole kernel corn, drained
10-oz. jar pearl onions, cooked
¼ c. butter
3 T. all-purpose flour
1 c. whipping cream
½ c. shredded Cheddar cheese
salt and pepper to taste
1 t. dry mustard
¼ t. Worcestershire sauce
grated Parmesan cheese to taste

Combine vegetables in a lightly greased 13"x9" baking pan. Melt butter in a saucepan over medium heat; stir in flour. Cook until well blended. Gradually stir in cream and continue stirring until sauce is thickened. Add cheese, salt, pepper, mustard and Worcestershire sauce. Stir until cheese is melted; pour over vegetables. Sprinkle with Parmesan cheese. Cover and bake at 350 degrees for 20 to 30 minutes. Serves 6 to 8.

*Brad Warner*
*Marengo, OH*

# Italian Zucchini Casserole

3 zucchini, sliced
3 T. olive oil, divided
1 onion, sliced
1 clove garlic, minced
28-oz. can diced tomatoes
1 T. fresh basil, minced
1½ t. fresh oregano, minced
½ t. garlic salt
¼ t. pepper
1½ c. favorite-flavor stuffing mix
½ c. grated Parmesan cheese
¾ c. shredded mozzarella cheese

Cook zucchini in one tablespoon oil in a skillet over medium heat for 5 to 6 minutes, until tender. Drain and remove from skillet. Sauté onion and garlic in remaining oil for one minute. Add tomatoes, basil, oregano, salt and pepper; simmer, uncovered, for 10 minutes. Remove from heat; gently stir in zucchini. Place in an ungreased 13"x9" baking dish. Top with stuffing mix; sprinkle with Parmesan cheese. Cover and bake at 350 degrees for 20 minutes. Uncover and sprinkle with mozzarella cheese. Bake for 10 more minutes, or until cheese is bubbly and golden. Serves 6 to 8.

Italian Zucchini Casserole

One-Dish Reuben Dinner
(page 166)

Renae's Taco Bake
(page 173)

Cajun Seafood Fettuccine
(page 183)

Chilly-Day Chicken Pot Pie
(page 189)

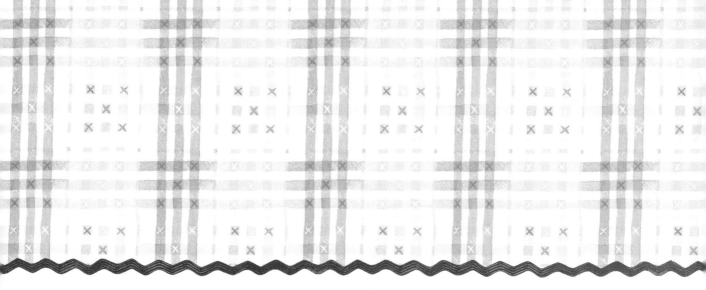

# FAMILY-STYLE ONE-DISH DINNERS

Simple suppers for any night of the week

# Tamale Pot Pie

*Not your "usual" pot pie filling...this will be a hit!*

1 lb. ground beef
2 c. frozen corn, thawed
14½-oz. can diced tomatoes, undrained
2¼-oz. can sliced ripe olives, drained
1 c. plus 2 T. biscuit baking mix, divided
1 T. chili powder
2 t. ground cumin
½ t. salt
½ c. cornmeal
½ c. milk
2 T. chopped green chiles
1 egg, beaten

Brown beef in a large skillet over medium heat; drain. Stir in corn, tomatoes with juice, olives, 2 tablespoons baking mix, chili powder, cumin and salt. Bring to a boil; boil, stirring frequently, one minute. Keep warm over low heat. Stir together remaining baking mix and remaining ingredients until blended. Pour beef mixture into an ungreased 9"x9" baking dish. Spread cornmeal mixture over beef mixture. Bake, uncovered, at 400 degrees for 20 to 30 minutes, until golden. Serves 6.

*Marian Buckley*
*Fontana, CA*

# Hobo Dinner

*My mom and I have made this recipe for years. It's quick, delicious and so easy that the kids can help assemble it.*

1½ lbs. ground beef
1 t. Worcestershire sauce
½ t. seasoned pepper
⅛ t. garlic powder
3 redskin potatoes, sliced
1 onion, sliced
3 carrots, peeled and halved
olive oil and dried parsley to taste

Combine beef, Worcestershire sauce, pepper and garlic powder; form into 4 to 6 patties. Place each patty on an 18-inch length of aluminum foil. Divide slices of potato, onion and carrots evenly and place on each patty. Sprinkle with olive oil and parsley to taste. Wrap tightly in aluminum foil; place on a baking sheet. Bake at 375 degrees for one hour. Serves 4 to 6.

*Denise Mainville*
*Elk Rapids, MI*

## Cornbread-Topped Barbecue Beef

2 lbs. ground beef
1 onion, diced
1 green pepper, diced
14½-oz. can diced tomatoes, drained
11-oz. can corn, drained
½ c. barbecue sauce
3 8½-oz. pkgs. cornbread mix

Brown beef and onion in a skillet over medium heat; drain. Add green pepper, tomatoes and corn; cook, stirring occasionally, until vegetables are tender. Stir in sauce; spread mixture in an ungreased 13"x9" baking pan. Prepare cornbread according to package directions; spread batter over beef mixture. Bake, uncovered, at 400 degrees for 20 to 25 minutes, until golden and a knife tip inserted in center comes out clean. Serves 8 to 10.

*Megan Brooks*
*Antioch, TN*

## One-Dish Reuben Dinner

*An easy version of everyone's favorite hot deli sandwich that's always a hit...yummy and filling!*

16-oz. can sauerkraut, undrained
1 lb. deli corned beef, chopped
2 c. shredded Swiss cheese
½ c. mayonnaise
¼ c. Thousand Island salad dressing
2 c. tomatoes, sliced
¼ to ½ c. pumpernickel or rye soft bread crumbs
2 T. butter, melted

Place undrained sauerkraut in a lightly greased 1½-quart casserole dish. Top with corned beef and cheese. Combine mayonnaise and salad dressing; spread over cheese. Arrange tomatoes on top. Toss together bread crumbs and melted butter; sprinkle over top of casserole. Bake, uncovered, at 350 degrees for 25 to 30 minutes. Let stand 5 minutes before serving. Serves 4 to 6.

*Suzanne Ruminski*
*Johnson City, NY*

### the more the merrier
Mom's best recipes usually make lots of servings, perfect for sharing. Invite to dinner a neighbor or a co-worker you'd like to get to know better...encourage your kids to invite a friend. You're sure to have a great time together!

One-Dish
Reuben Dinner

Cream Cheese Enchiladas

# Beefy Cheddar Bake

1 lb. ground beef
1 onion, chopped
1 green pepper, chopped
2 c. rotini pasta, cooked
14½-oz. can diced tomatoes, drained
10¾-oz. can cream of mushroom soup
8-oz. pkg. shredded sharp Cheddar cheese
6-oz. can French fried onions

Brown beef, onion and pepper in a skillet over medium-high heat; drain. Combine beef mixture and remaining ingredients except French fried onions in a large bowl; mix well. Spread into a lightly greased 13"x9" baking pan; cover with aluminum foil. Bake at 350 degrees for 30 minutes. Remove foil; sprinkle with onions. Bake, uncovered, for 5 to 10 more minutes. Serves 8 to 12.

*Kimberly Keafer*
*Saint Johnsbury, VT*

# Cream Cheese Enchiladas

*This creamy variation on Mexican enchiladas is yummy! It won me 1st place in a local newspaper's holiday cooking contest.*

2 8-oz. pkgs. cream cheese, softened
1 c. sour cream
2 10-oz. cans mild green chile enchilada sauce
¼ c. jalapeños, chopped
1 lb. ground beef, browned and drained
½ c. shredded sharp Cheddar cheese
8 to 12 flour tortillas
1 sweet onion, chopped
½ c. sliced black olives
Garnish: sliced black olives, chopped tomato, shredded lettuce, chopped green onion

Blend together cream cheese, sour cream, enchilada sauce and jalapeños in a large bowl; set aside. Combine ground beef and shredded cheese in another bowl; set aside. Fill each tortilla with one to 2 tablespoons cream cheese mixture and one to 2 tablespoons beef mixture. Sprinkle each with onion and olives; roll up tortillas. Place in a 13"x9" baking dish; cover with remaining cream cheese mixture. Bake, uncovered, at 400 degrees for 30 to 40 minutes; cover if top begins to brown. Garnish with olives, tomatoes, lettuce and green onions. Serves 8.

*Mary Kathryn Carter*
*Platte City, MO*

# Wild Rice Hot Dish

2 lbs. ground beef
½ c. butter
1 lb. sliced mushrooms
1 c. onion, chopped
½ c. celery, chopped
2 c. sour cream
¼ c. soy sauce
2 t. salt
¼ t. pepper
2 c. long-grain and wild rice, cooked
½ c. slivered almonds

Brown beef in a skillet over medium heat. Remove beef from skillet; drain. Melt butter in skillet; sauté mushrooms, onion and celery for 5 to 10 minutes, until tender. Combine sour cream, soy sauce, salt and pepper in a large bowl. Stir in beef, mushroom mixture, cooked rice and almonds. Toss lightly. Place mixture in a greased 3-quart casserole dish. Bake, uncovered, at 350 degrees for one hour, or until heated through. Stir occasionally, adding a little water if needed. Serves 12 to 16.

*June Sabatinos*
*Billings, MT*

## kitchen secret: chopping an onion

Trim the stem and root ends; discard. Remove the papery outer skins. Then stand the onion upright on a cutting board and cut a thin slice off one side. Make vertical slices through the onion to within ¼ inch of the bottom. Rotate the onion 90 degrees and repeat. Finally, turn the onion so that the cut side is flat on the board. Cut vertically through the onion.

# Spaghetti Pie

*A recipe kids big and little will love!*

12-oz. pkg. spaghetti, uncooked
2 T. butter, softened
½ c. grated Parmesan cheese
2 eggs, beaten
1 c. cottage cheese
1 lb. ground beef
½ onion, chopped
¼ c. green pepper, chopped
16-oz. can whole tomatoes, chopped
3 6-oz. cans tomato paste
1 t. sugar
1 t. dried oregano
½ t. garlic salt
½ c. shredded mozzarella cheese

Prepare half of spaghetti according to package directions, reserve remaining noodles for another recipe. Stir in butter; add Parmesan cheese and eggs. Spoon into a greased 10-inch pie plate; spread cottage cheese over top. Set aside. Brown beef, onion and pepper in a skillet; drain. Add remaining ingredients except mozzarella cheese. Stir well; pour over cottage cheese layer. Bake, uncovered, at 350 degrees for 20 minutes; sprinkle with mozzarella cheese. Bake for 5 more minutes, or until cheese melts. Cut into wedges to serve. Serves 6 to 8.

*Tina Stidam*
*Delaware, OH*

Wild Rice Hot Dish

Florence's Meatball
Surprise

## Florence's Meatball Surprise

1 lb. lean ground beef
1 egg, beaten
1 onion, diced
½ green pepper, diced
salt and pepper to taste
2 10¾-oz. cans cream of mushroom soup
16-oz. container sour cream
1¼ c. water
7-oz. pkg. elbow macaroni, cooked
15¼-oz. can peas, drained

Mix beef, egg, onion and green pepper in a medium bowl. Add salt and pepper. Shape mixture into small meatballs. Place meatballs in a skillet over medium heat; brown on all sides. Remove from skillet; drain. Blend together soup, sour cream, water and macaroni in a large bowl. Gently stir in meatballs and peas. Pour meatball mixture into a lightly greased 2-quart casserole dish. Bake, covered, at 350 degrees for 30 to 40 minutes. Serves 6 to 8.

*Kim Watkins*
*Wagoner, OK*

# Renae's Taco Bake

1 lb. ground beef
15-oz. can tomato sauce
1¼-oz. pkg. taco seasoning mix
3 c. elbow macaroni, cooked
8-oz. container sour cream
1 c. shredded Cheddar cheese, divided
¼ c. grated Parmesan cheese
Garnish: green onions, chopped

Brown beef in a skillet over medium heat; drain. Stir in tomato sauce and seasoning mix. Bring to a boil and remove from heat. Combine cooked macaroni, sour cream and ½ cup Cheddar cheese in a bowl. Spoon macaroni mixture into a lightly greased 13"x9" baking pan. Top with beef mixture and remaining cheeses. Bake, uncovered, at 350 degrees for 30 minutes, or until hot and bubbly. Garnish with green onions. Serves 6.

*Renae Scheiderer*
*Beallsville, OH*

Renae's Taco Bake

Company Baked Ziti

## Company Baked Ziti

*Layers of sour cream and two types of cheese…this pasta classic is extra rich and cheesy.*

1 lb. ground beef
1 lb. sweet Italian ground pork sausage
1 onion, chopped
2  26-oz. jars spaghetti sauce
16-oz. pkg. ziti pasta, cooked
6-oz. pkg. sliced provolone cheese
1 c. sour cream
1½ c. shredded mozzarella cheese
½ c. grated Parmesan cheese

Brown beef, sausage and onion in a skillet over medium heat; drain. Stir in sauce; reduce heat to low and simmer 15 minutes. Layer in a greased 13"x9" baking pan as follows: half of pasta, provolone cheese, sour cream, half of sauce mixture, remaining pasta, mozzarella cheese and remaining sauce. Top with Parmesan cheese. Cover and bake at 350 degrees for 30 minutes, or until hot, bubbly and cheeses are melted. Serves 6 to 8.

*Colleen Leid*
*Narvon, PA*

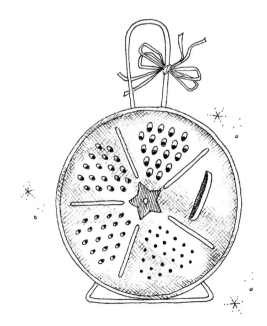

Ravioli Taco Bake

## Ravioli Taco Bake

*I was looking for something easy and different to take to our church potluck supper, so I came up with this recipe. Not only was it a hit…I came home with an empty dish and more than 50 people wanting the recipe!*

1½ lbs. ground beef
1-oz. pkg. taco seasoning mix
¾ c. water
25-oz. pkg. frozen meat-filled ravioli
8-oz. pkg. shredded Cheddar cheese
Optional: sliced black olives

Brown beef in a large skillet over medium heat; drain. Stir in seasoning mix and water. Reduce heat; simmer for 8 to 10 minutes. Place ravioli in a lightly greased 13"x9" baking pan; spoon beef mixture over top. Sprinkle with cheese. Bake, uncovered, at 350 degrees for 25 to 30 minutes, until cheese is melted and bubbly. Sprinkle with olives before serving, if desired. Serves 6 to 8.

*Margie Kirkman*
*High Point, NC*

## Make-Ahead Faux Lasagna

16-oz. pkg. wide egg noodles, uncooked
1 T. butter, melted
8-oz. pkg. cream cheese, softened
1 c. cottage cheese with chives
½ c. sour cream
1 lb. ground beef
⅓ c. dried, minced onion
8-oz. can tomato sauce
salt and pepper to taste

Boil half of noodles for 5 minutes; drain. Reserve remaining uncooked noodles for another recipe. Arrange half of cooked noodles in a lightly greased 2-quart casserole dish. Drizzle evenly with melted butter. Combine cheeses and sour cream in a medium bowl. Spoon cream cheese mixture over noodles. Arrange remaining noodles on top; set aside. Brown beef and onion in a skillet over medium heat; drain well. Combine with tomato sauce, salt and pepper; spoon over noodles. Cover and refrigerate for one to 8 hours. Uncover and bake at 350 degrees for 30 minutes. Cover with aluminum foil and bake for 15 more minutes. Serves 10 to 12.

*Juanita Lint*
*Forest Grove, OR*

"This recipe came from a 1980 North Dakota church cookbook. It is a big hit... as tasty as lasagna but without the effort. That's how the name came about!" —Juanita

## Oven-Baked Ragout

*Shared with me by a friend who can always "whip up" a wonderful meal.*

2 to 2½ lbs. boneless pork, cubed
2 T. oil
¼ c. all-purpose flour
14-oz. can chicken broth
1¼ c. white wine or chicken broth, divided
3 T. dried, minced onion
½ t. seasoned salt
½ t. dried, minced garlic
½ t. dried rosemary
¼ t. pepper
¼ t. dried thyme
¼ t. dried marjoram
2 c. carrots, peeled and sliced
10-oz. pkg. frozen peas, thawed
6 slices bacon
2 c. sliced mushrooms
Garnish: crumbled bacon, dried parsley

Brown pork on all sides, one-third at a time, in hot oil in a Dutch oven; remove and set aside. Add flour to Dutch oven; cook over medium heat for 2 minutes, stirring and scraping bottom of pan. Stir in chicken broth, one cup wine or broth and seasonings. Cook, stirring constantly, until mixture boils and thickens. Remove from heat; stir in browned pork. Cover Dutch oven and bake at 325 degrees for 1½ hours. Stir in carrots and peas; bake, covered, 30 more minutes, or until carrots are tender. Fry bacon in large skillet until crisp; remove, crumble and set aside. Drain, leaving 3 tablespoons drippings in skillet; sauté mushrooms about 3 minutes. Add remaining wine or broth; simmer 3 to 5 minutes. Stir mushroom mixture into Dutch oven. Garnish with reserved bacon and parsley. Serves 6 to 8.

*Nancy Wise*
*Little Rock, AR*

Make-Ahead Faux Lasagna

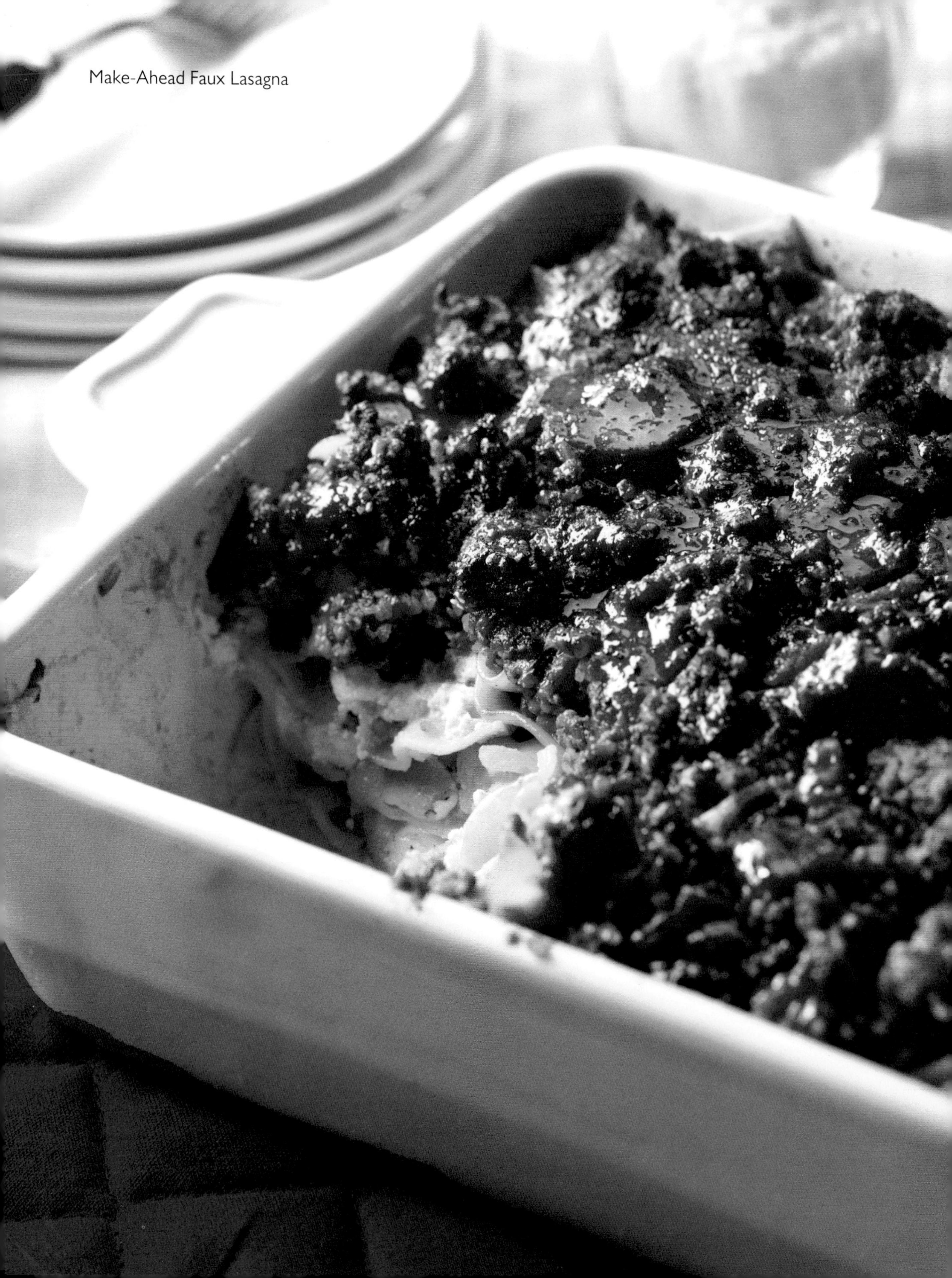

# Penne with Sausage & Cheese

1 lb. hot or mild ground Italian pork sausage
3 cloves garlic, chopped
24-oz. jar marinara sauce with cabernet and herbs
½ t. red pepper flakes
½ t. salt
½ t. pepper
12-oz. pkg. penne pasta, cooked
1 c. shredded mozzarella cheese
Garnish: grated Parmesan cheese, chopped fresh
    parsley

Cook sausage in a skillet over medium heat until browned; drain. Return sausage to pan. Add garlic and cook until tender, about 2 minutes. Stir in sauce and seasonings. Stir sauce mixture into cooked pasta; pour mixture into a greased 12"x8" baking pan. Top with mozzarella cheese. Bake, covered, at 375 degrees for 25 to 30 minutes, until bubbly and cheese has melted. Garnish with Parmesan cheese and parsley. Serves 6.

*Bev Bornheimer*
*Lyons, NY*

Penne with Sausage
& Cheese

## Saucy Pork Chop Scallop

*This recipe was handed down from my grandmother to my mother and then to me. It is very simple, yet oh-so creamy and good.*

4 pork chops
1 T. oil
salt and pepper to taste
10¾-oz. can cream of mushroom soup
½ c. sour cream
¼ c. water
2 T. dried, minced onion
4 c. potatoes, peeled and thinly sliced

Brown pork chops in oil in a skillet over medium heat. Drain; sprinkle with salt and pepper. Blend together soup, sour cream, water, onion, potatoes and additional salt and pepper. Spread into a lightly greased 13"x9" baking pan. Top with browned pork chops. Cover; bake at 375 degrees for one hour and 15 minutes. Serves 4.

*Hope Yates*
*Wesley, AR*

## Pizzeria Sausage Supper

1 lb. ground pork sausage
½ c. onion, chopped
¼ c. green pepper, chopped
2 T. all-purpose flour
14½-oz. can diced tomatoes
4-oz. can mushroom stems & pieces, drained
1 t. fresh oregano, chopped
½ t. fresh basil, chopped
¼ t. garlic powder
⅛ t. pepper
Optional: 4-oz. pkg. sliced pepperoni
10-oz. tube refrigerated biscuits, quartered
2 c. shredded mozzarella cheese
Optional: grated Parmesan cheese

Brown sausage, onion and green pepper in a large ovenproof skillet over medium heat. Drain; sprinkle with flour. Add tomatoes with juice, mushrooms, herbs and seasonings; mix well. Simmer until hot and bubbly, stirring until slightly thickened. Add pepperoni, if desired. Arrange biscuit quarters over mixture in skillet. Sprinkle biscuit layer with mozzarella cheese. Bake, uncovered, at 400 degrees for 12 to 16 minutes, until biscuits are golden. Sprinkle with Parmesan cheese, if desired. Serves 10.

*Kay Jones*
*Cleburne, TX*

## Cheesy Chicken & Mac

*Having company? This make-ahead dish can be popped in the oven right before guests arrive.*

2 c. cooked chicken, diced
2 c. elbow macaroni, uncooked
2 c. milk
2 10¾-oz. cans cream of mushroom soup
2 onions, diced
8-oz. pkg. pasteurized processed cheese spread, diced

Mix all ingredients together in a large bowl; spoon into an ungreased 13"x9" baking pan. Cover with aluminum foil and refrigerate over-night; bake at 350 degrees for one hour. Serves 6 to 8.

*Myra Barker*
*Gap, PA*

## Broccoli-Chicken Lasagna

*A tasty twist on a familiar dish…the kids will love it!*

¼ c. butter
¼ c. all-purpose flour
1 T. chicken bouillon granules
pepper to taste
½ t. Italian seasoning
2 c. milk
2 c. shredded Italian-blend cheese
2 c. broccoli flowerets, cooked
1 c. cooked chicken, diced
4 strips prepared lasagna, divided

Melt butter in a saucepan over medium-low heat; stir in flour, bouillon, pepper and Italian seasoning. Gradually stir in milk; cook and stir until thickened. Add cheese; stir until melted. Mix in broccoli and chicken. Spread ½ cup mixture in the bottom of an 8"x8" baking pan sprayed with non-stick vegetable spray. Top with half of lasagna. Top with half of remaining sauce; repeat layers. Bake, uncovered, at 350 degrees for 30 to 40 minutes. Serves 4 to 6.

*Monica Wilkinson*
*Burton, SC*

*There's nothing like a hot pan of lasagna on a cold winter's night!* –Jo Ann

Chicken Lasagna with
Roasted Red Pepper Sauce

# Chicken Lasagna with Roasted Red Pepper Sauce

4 c. cooked chicken, finely chopped
2 8-oz. containers chive-and-onion cream cheese
10-oz. pkg. frozen chopped spinach, thawed and
   well drained
1 t. seasoned pepper
¾ t. garlic salt
9 no-boil lasagna noodles, uncooked
2 c. shredded Italian 3-cheese blend

Stir together chicken, cream cheese, spinach, pepper and salt. Layer a lightly greased 11"x7" baking pan with a third of Roasted Red Pepper Sauce, 3 noodles, a third of chicken mixture and a third of cheese. Repeat layers twice. Place baking pan on a baking sheet. Bake, covered, at 350 degrees for 50 to 55 minutes, until hot and bubbly. Uncover and bake 15 more minutes. Serves 6 to 8.

# Roasted Red Pepper Sauce:

16-oz. jar creamy Alfredo sauce
12-oz. jar roasted red peppers, drained
¾ c. grated Parmesan cheese
½ t. red pepper flakes

Process all ingredients in a food processor until smooth, stopping to scrape down sides. Makes 3½ cups.

*Jo Ann*
*Gooseberry Patch*

Chicken Spaghetti Deluxe

## Aunt B's Chicken Tetrazzini

*This makes two large trays of cheesy, chickeny pasta...perfect for any church gathering when a covered dish is requested.*

8 c. chicken broth
2 yellow onions, chopped
2 green peppers, chopped
16-oz. pkg. angel hair pasta, uncooked
2 lbs. boneless, skinless chicken breasts, cooked
2 4-oz. cans sliced mushrooms, drained
2 c. butter
1½ c. all-purpose flour
4 c. milk
6 c. pasteurized process cheese spread, cubed
bread crumbs

Simmer broth, onions and peppers in a large stockpot over medium heat until boiling. Add pasta and cook as directed; do not drain. Add chicken and mushrooms; set aside. Combine butter, flour, milk and cheese in a medium saucepan over medium-low heat. Cook and stir until thickened; add to broth mixture and combine well. Pour into two lightly greased deep 13"x9" baking pans; top with bread crumbs. Bake, uncovered, at 350 degrees for 30 minutes, or until hot and bubbly. Serves about 12.

*Bryna Dunlap*
*Muskogee, OK*

## Chicken Spaghetti Deluxe

*This recipe is reminiscent of cold winter days and the inviting smells of Mom's warm kitchen. Best of all, the pasta doesn't need to be cooked ahead of time.*

2 c. cooked chicken, chopped
8-oz. pkg. spaghetti, uncooked and broken into
    2-inch pieces
1 c. celery, chopped
1 c. onion, chopped
1 c. yellow pepper, chopped
1 c. red pepper, chopped
2 10¾-oz. cans cream of mushroom soup
1 c. chicken broth
¼ t. Cajun seasoning or pepper
1 c. shredded Cheddar cheese

Mix chicken, spaghetti, celery, onion, yellow pepper and red pepper in a bowl. Whisk together soup, broth and seasoning in a separate bowl. Add chicken mixture to soup mixture. Spread chicken mixture in a lightly greased 13"x9" baking pan; sprinkle cheese over top. Cover with aluminum foil coated with non-stick vegetable spray. Bake at 350 degrees for 45 minutes. Uncover and bake for 10 more minutes. Serves 8.

*Dorothy Benson*
*Baton Rouge, LA*

*cook & share*
Potluck dinners are a wonderful way to share fellowship with family and friends. Why not make a standing date once a month to try new recipes as well as tried & true favorites?

## Chicken Tex-Mex Bake

2 12½-oz. cans chicken, drained and shredded
2 10-oz. cans mild red enchilada sauce
10¾-oz. can cream of chicken soup
14½-oz. can diced tomatoes
4½-oz. can diced green chiles
2½ c. shredded Mexican-blend cheese, divided
1 c. sour cream
½ c. onion, diced
½ t. pepper
10 flour tortillas, cut into one-inch squares and
 divided
½ c. sliced black olives

Combine chicken, enchilada sauce, soup, tomatoes, chiles and half of cheese; mix well. Blend in sour cream, onion and pepper; set aside. Arrange half of tortillas over bottom of a greased 13"x9" baking pan. Spoon half of chicken mixture over tortillas. Repeat layers, ending with chicken mixture on top. Sprinkle with remaining cheese; top with olives. Cover loosely with aluminum foil; bake at 350 degrees for 40 minutes, or until hot and bubbly. Serves 8.

*Jenny Flake*
*Gilbert, AZ*

## One-Dish Chicken & Gravy

*My grandma used to make this chicken for us…now whenever I make it, I think of her.*

¼ c. butter, melted
3 lbs. chicken
¼ c. all-purpose flour
8 pearl onions
4-oz. jar mushroom stems and pieces, drained
10¾ oz. can cream of mushroom soup
1 c. pasteurized processed cheese spread, cubed
⅔ c. evaporated milk
¾ t. salt
⅛ t. pepper
paprika to taste

Spread butter in a 12"x8" baking pan; set aside. Coat chicken pieces with flour; arrange in baking dish skin-side down in a single layer. Bake, uncovered, at 425 degrees for 30 minutes. Turn chicken over; bake 15 to 20 more minutes, until golden. Top with onions and mushrooms; set aside. Combine soup, cheese, evaporated milk, salt and pepper; pour over chicken. Sprinkle with paprika; cover with aluminum foil. Reduce oven to 325 degrees and bake 15 to 20 more minutes. Serves 4 to 5.

*Jennifer Burkum*
*Maple Grove, MN*

Chicken Tex-Mex Bake

## Chicken-Zucchini Bake

*This recipe proves there's no such thing as too many zucchini!*

1 T. margarine, melted
12-oz. pkg. chicken-flavored stuffing mix
6 c. zucchini, sliced and steamed
1 c. carrots, peeled and grated
3 to 4 lbs. cooked chicken, diced
10¾-oz. can cream of chicken soup
1 c. sour cream
¼ c. onion, chopped

Combine margarine and stuffing mix; spoon half of mixture in bottom of a 13"x9" baking pan. Layer zucchini, carrots and chicken over top; set aside. Mix soup, sour cream and onion together; spoon over chicken. Top with remaining stuffing mixture; bake, uncovered, at 350 degrees for 45 minutes. Serves 6 to 8.

*Julie Brown*
*Provo, UT*

Veggie-Chicken Bake

## Veggie-Chicken Bake

*A quick-to-fix dish that's rich & creamy.*

4 boneless, skinless chicken breasts, cooked
    and diced
1 c. mayonnaise
1 c. shredded Cheddar cheese
2 10¾-oz. cans cream of chicken soup
16-oz. pkg. frozen broccoli and cauliflower, thawed
    and drained
12-oz. pkg. egg noodles, cooked

Combine chicken, mayonnaise, cheese, soup and vegetables. Spoon into an ungreased 13"x9" baking pan; bake, uncovered, at 350 degrees for about 45 minutes, until heated through. Serve over noodles. Serves 6 to 8.

*Theresa Currie*
*Chatham, NJ*

# Brunswick Chicken Bake

*My husband loves a big kettle of down-home Brunswick stew, so when I found this casserole-style recipe, I knew he'd like it too. For a really traditional dish, sometimes I'll substitute a package of frozen sliced okra for one of the packages of succotash.*

2 T. oil
2½ lbs. chicken
1 onion, chopped
2 T. all-purpose flour
1-oz. pkg. Italian salad dressing mix
14½-oz. can diced tomatoes with green peppers
   and onions
1 bay leaf
2 10-oz. pkgs. frozen succotash, thawed

Heat oil in a large skillet over medium-high heat. Brown chicken on all sides about 15 minutes. Drain, reserving 2 tablespoons drippings in skillet. Arrange chicken in an ungreased 13"x9" baking pan and set aside. Add onion to skillet; sauté until tender. Stir in flour and salad dressing mix. Add tomatoes and bay leaf; cook and stir until bubbly. Stir in succotash and heat through. Pour skillet mixture over chicken; cover with aluminum foil. Bake at 350 degrees for one hour, or until juices run clear when chicken is pierced with a fork. Discard bay leaf before serving. Serves 4.

*Jill Valentine*
*Jackson, TN*

## display the love

Family recipes make a memory-filled kitchen wall display. Arrange old recipe cards or clippings in a shadowbox purchased at a crafts store, adding cookie cutters and even mini kitchen utensils. To make it all the more special, place a snapshot of Mom or Grandma preparing her favorite recipe.

# Rooster Pie

*The aroma of country goodness fills the house as it's baking...we can hardly wait to break the golden crust!*

2 c. cooked chicken, cubed
½ c. frozen carrots
½ c. frozen peas
1 onion, diced
3 T. pimentos, chopped
1 T. fresh parsley, chopped
salt and pepper to taste
10¾-oz. can cream of chicken soup
1 c. sour cream
1 c. chicken broth
12 oz. tube refrigerated biscuits

Combine chicken, carrots, peas, onion, pimentos, parsley, salt and pepper; set aside. Combine soup, sour cream and broth; stir into chicken mixture. Spread in a greased 13"x9" casserole dish. Arrange biscuits over top. Bake, uncovered, at 350 degrees for 30 minutes, or until biscuits are golden. Serves 4 to 6.

*Tammy Rowe*
*Bellevue, OH*

Chilly-Day Chicken
Pot Pie

## Chilly-Day Chicken Pot Pie

*This is my family's favorite chicken pot pie recipe... everyone who tries it asks me for the recipe.*

2  9-inch pie crusts
¼ c. margarine
¼ c. all-purpose flour
¼ t. poultry seasoning
⅛ t. pepper
1 c. chicken broth
⅔ c. milk
2 c. cooked chicken, cubed
2 c. frozen mixed vegetables, thawed

Place one crust in an ungreased 9" pie plate; set aside. Melt margarine in a saucepan over medium heat; stir in flour, seasoning and pepper. Cook until mixture is smooth and bubbly. Gradually add broth and milk; bring to a boil. Reduce heat and simmer, stirring constantly until mixture thickens. Stir in chicken and vegetables; cook until heated through. Pour into pie plate. Place second crust over filling; crimp edges and cut vents in top. Bake at 400 degrees for 20 to 30 minutes, until golden. Serves 4.

*Jessica McAlister*
*Fort Worth, TX*

## Cheesy Chicken Enchiladas

2 10¾-oz. cans cream of chicken soup
16-oz. container sour cream
4-oz. can diced green chiles
2¼-oz. can chopped black olives, drained
3 green onions, chopped
1 onion, chopped
3 c. shredded Cheddar cheese
4 to 5 chicken breasts, cooked and diced
10 to 12  10-inch flour tortillas
2 c. shredded Monterey Jack cheese

Mix together soup, sour cream, chiles, olives, onions and Cheese in a large bowl. Set aside 1½ cups of soup mixture for topping; add chicken to remaining mixture. Spoon chicken mixture into tortillas; roll up and place in a lightly greased 13"x9" baking pan. Spoon reserved soup mixture over tortillas; sprinkle with Monterey Jack cheese. Bake, covered, at 350 degrees for one hour. Serves 10 to 12.

*Carrie Kiiskila*
*Racine, WI*

## Overnight Scalloped Turkey

2 10¾-oz. cans cream of mushroom soup
2½ c. milk
8-oz. pkg. pasteurized process cheese spread,
    cubed
4 c. cooked turkey, chopped
7-oz. pkg. elbow macaroni, uncooked
3 eggs, hard-boiled, peeled and chopped
½ c. butter, melted and divided
1½ c. soft bread crumbs

Combine soup, milk and cheese in a large bowl;
add turkey, macaroni and eggs. Stir in ¼ cup
melted butter; transfer to a lightly greased 13"x9"
baking pan. Cover and refrigerate for 8 hours or
overnight. Toss bread crumbs with remaining
butter; sprinkle over top. Bake, uncovered, at
350 degrees for 45 to 50 minutes. Serves 8 to 10.

### mix it up
Jazz up an ordinary casserole with
something new...chile peppers, salsa,
water chestnuts or baby corn.

## Sour Cream Noodle Bake

*To roast garlic, slice off the top of the bulb, making
sure to cut the tips of the cloves. Place in a square of
aluminum foil, drizzle with olive oil, wrap up and
bake at 450 degrees for 25 to 30 minutes. Let cool
enough to handle and then squeeze the cloves out of
the skin.*

1 lb. ground turkey
1 t. salt
¼ t. pepper
1 bulb garlic, roasted
8-oz. can tomato sauce
1 c. cottage cheese
1 c. sour cream
1 c. fontina cheese, shredded
1 bunch green onions, chopped
8-oz. pkg. medium egg noodles, cooked
1 c. shredded Cheddar cheese

Brown turkey in a large skillet sprayed with
non-stick vegetable spray; drain. Sprinkle with salt
and pepper. Stir in garlic and tomato sauce; reduce
heat and simmer for 5 minutes and set aside.
Combine cottage cheese, sour cream, fontina
cheese and green onions in a medium bowl; set
aside. Spread half of turkey mixture in a lightly
greased 2-quart casserole dish; top with half of
noodles and then half of cheese mixture. Repeat
layers. Sprinkle with Cheddar cheese and bake,
uncovered, at 350 degrees for 20 minutes, or until
cheese is bubbly. Serves 4 to 6.

*Tami Bowman*
*Marysville, OH*

# Homemade Turkey Pot Pie

*This recipe has been in our family for years...
a real treat.*

⅓ c. butter
⅓ c. onion, chopped
⅓ c. all-purpose flour
½ t. salt
¼ t. pepper
1¾ c. turkey broth
⅔ c. milk
2½ to 3 c. cooked turkey, chopped
10-oz. pkg. frozen peas and carrots, thawed
2  9-inch pie crusts

Melt butter in a large saucepan over low heat. Stir in onion, flour, salt and pepper. Cook, stirring constantly, until mixture is bubbly; remove from heat. Stir in broth and milk. Heat to boiling, stirring constantly. Boil and stir for one minute. Mix in turkey, peas and carrots; set aside. Roll out one pie crust and place in a 9"x9" baking pan. Pour turkey mixture into pan. Roll remaining crust into an 11-inch square; cut out vents with a small cookie cutter. Place crust over filling; turn edges under and crimp. Bake at 425 degrees for 35 minutes, or until golden. Serves 4 to 6.

*Sarah Sullivan*
*Andrews, NC*

Homemade Turkey
Pot Pie

Cajun Seafood Fettuccine

# Crab-Stuffed Eggplant

*Serving this for dinner is a treat for the whole family...we love it.*

1½ lb. eggplant
5½ T. butter, divided
½ c. dry bread crumbs
¼ c. grated Parmesan cheese
6 to 8 green onions, chopped
2 T. fresh parsley, chopped
1 lb. jumbo lump crabmeat
½ c. mayonnaise
½ c. whipping cream
1 T. all-purpose flour
1 T. Worcestershire sauce
¼ t. salt
¼ t. pepper

Cover eggplant with water in a stockpot; boil for 15 minutes. Drain. When cool enough to handle, cut in half lengthwise and remove pulp, leaving a shell ¼-inch thick. Chop pulp and reserve. Arrange shells in a lightly greased 13"x9" baking pan; set aside. Melt one tablespoon butter in a large skillet; add bread crumbs and sauté until golden. Add cheese and stir to coat; set aside. Melt 4 tablespoons butter in a separate skillet. Add green onions and parsley; sauté for 2 minutes. Add eggplant pulp and remaining ingredients, except remaining butter. Sauté eggplant mixture, stirring constantly, for 3 minutes. Spoon filling into each eggplant shell. Sprinkle with bread crumb mixture; dot with remaining butter. Bake, uncovered, at 400 degrees for 20 minutes. Serves 2 to 4.

*Karen Pilcher*
*Burleson, TX*

# Cajun Seafood Fettuccine

*Sometimes this only serves 4!*

½ c. butter, divided
2 8-oz. pkgs. frozen seasoned vegetable blend
garlic powder and Cajun seasoning to taste
¼ c. all-purpose flour
1 pt. half-and-half
16-oz. pkg. pasteurized processed cheese spread, cubed
1½ lbs. medium shrimp, peeled and cleaned
1½ lbs. crabmeat
12-oz. pkg. egg noodles, cooked
12-oz. pkg. shredded Colby Jack cheese
Garnish: fresh parsley, chopped

Melt ¼ cup butter in a large saucepan; add vegetables and sauté until tender. Sprinkle with garlic powder and Cajun seasoning; set aside. Add ¼ cup water to flour to make a thick paste that is still able to be poured; add to skillet. Stir in half-and-half and cheese spread; continue stirring until cheese is melted. Set aside. Sauté shrimp in remaining butter in a separate skillet until no longer pink. Add shrimp and crabmeat to vegetable mixture and let simmer on medium-low heat for 20 minutes. Stir in egg noodles; pour into an ungreased 13"x9" baking pan. Sprinkle with Colby Jack cheese. Bake, uncovered, at 350 degrees for 20 minutes. Garnish with parsley. Serves 8.

*Sheila Collier*
*Kingwood, TX*

## Swiss Seafood Lasagna

*An elegant twist on the traditional lasagna recipe.*

2 14½ oz. cans stewed tomatoes, chopped
½ c. sliced mushrooms
½ t. dried oregano
½ t. onion powder
⅛ t. salt
⅛ t. pepper
½ c. frozen cooked small shrimp, thawed and
    cleaned
3 T. margarine
3 T. all-purpose flour
1¾ c. milk
1 c. shredded Swiss cheese
8-oz. pkg. crabmeat, chopped
¼ c. white wine or chicken broth
8 strips prepared lasagna
¼ c. grated Parmesan cheese
Garnish: fresh parsley, chopped

Combine undrained tomatoes, mushrooms, oregano, onion powder, salt and pepper in a medium saucepan; bring to a boil. Reduce heat and simmer, uncovered, about 20 minutes, until thickened. Stir in shrimp; set aside. Melt margarine in a second medium saucepan; stir in flour. Add milk; cook and stir over medium heat until thickened and bubbly. Cook and stir one more minute. Stir in Swiss cheese until melted; stir in crabmeat and wine or broth. Layer half of shrimp sauce, half of lasagna strips and half of cheese sauce in an ungreased 2-quart rectangular casserole dish. Repeat layers. Top with Parmesan cheese. Bake, uncovered, at 350 degrees for about 25 minutes, until heated through. Let stand 15 minutes before serving. Garnish with parsley. Serves 6 to 8.

*Kendall Hale*
*Lynn, MA*

## Tuna Noodle Supreme

3 T. butter
¼ c. all-purpose flour
2 c. milk
8-oz. pkg. pasteurized process cheese spread,
    cubed
3 eggs, hard-boiled, peeled and diced
8-oz. pkg. wide egg noodles, cooked
6.4-oz. pkg. tuna, drained and flaked
½ c. sliced mushrooms
salt and pepper to taste
1 c. potato chips, crushed

Melt butter in a large saucepan over medium heat. Stir in flour; cook one minute. Gradually add milk; cook and stir until slightly thickened. Add cheese; stir until melted. Stir in remaining ingredients except chips; mix well. Spoon tuna mixture into a lightly greased 3-quart casserole dish; top with chips. Bake, uncovered, at 350 degrees for 30 minutes, or until hot and bubbly. Serves 6.

Swiss Seafood
Lasagna

Southern-Style
Shrimp & Rice

# Southern-Style Shrimp & Rice

*An updated version of an old-fashioned favorite.*

¾ c. butter, divided
1 onion, sliced
8-oz. pkg. sliced mushrooms
¼ c. green pepper, diced
2 c. long-grain and wild rice, cooked
1½ lbs. medium shrimp, peeled and cleaned
1 T. Worcestershire sauce
hot pepper sauce to taste
salt and pepper to taste
½ c. all-purpose flour
1½ c. chicken broth
½ c. white wine or chicken broth
Garnish: ¼ c. green onion, chopped

Melt ¼ cup butter in a large, heavy skillet over medium heat. Add onion, mushrooms and green pepper; sauté for 8 minutes. Add rice; toss until well blended; spread across bottom of a greased 2-quart casserole dish. Set aside. Combine shrimp, sauces, salt and pepper in a medium mixing bowl. Arrange evenly over vegetable mixture; set aside. Melt remaining butter over medium heat in a saucepan; add flour and whisk for one minute. Add broth and wine or additional broth. Whisk until well blended and slightly thickened; pour evenly over shrimp. Bake, uncovered, at 350 degrees for 25 minutes, or until bubbly. Garnish with green onions. Serves 6.

*Claire Bertram*
*Lexington, KY*

# Zesty Creole Bake

*This recipe is good when you're in the mood for something a little tangy!*

3 c. water
1½ c. instant rice, uncooked
¼ c. butter
1 onion, chopped
1 clove garlic, minced
2 stalks celery, chopped
1 green pepper, chopped
¼ c. all-purpose flour
2 c. milk
½ c. chili sauce
½ t. hot pepper sauce
1 t. salt
¼ t. pepper
1 lb. cod fillets
2 tomatoes, sliced

Bring water to a boil in a saucepan; add rice and stir. Reduce heat; cover and simmer for 20 minutes. Set aside. Melt butter in a skillet over medium heat. Add onion and garlic; cook until tender, about 4 minutes. Add celery and green pepper; cook for about 3 minutes, until tender but not browned. Add flour and stir well; cook for 3 more minutes. Stir in milk and bring just to a boil. Stir in chili sauce, hot sauce, salt and pepper. Place rice in a greased 13"x9" baking pan. Arrange fish fillets over rice in a single layer. Place sliced tomatoes over fish; pour sauce over top. Bake, uncovered, at 400 degrees for 20 minutes, or until fish flakes easily with fork. Serves 4.

*Zoe Bennett*
*Columbia, SC*

Dijon Salmon Bake

# Easy Mexican Bake

*Add a pound of browned ground beef to the beans for a heartier meal...toss a salad, and dinner is ready!*

16-oz. can refried beans
½ c. sour cream
3 c. tortilla chips, broken
10-oz. can diced tomatoes with chiles, drained
1 c. shredded Mexican blend cheese
Garnish: sour cream, lettuce, chopped tomatoes,
    chopped onions

Combine beans and sour cream in a saucepan over medium heat; heat through. Arrange chips evenly in an ungreased 13"x9" baking pan. Spread bean mixture lightly over chips; top with tomatoes and sprinkle with cheese. Bake, uncovered, at 350 degrees for 30 minutes, or until cheese is bubbly. Garnish with sour cream, lettuce, chopped tomatoes, and onions. Serves 3 to 4.

*Christi Sidney*
*Panama City, FL*

# Dijon Salmon Bake

*This is so easy and quick, yet everyone thinks that I made a gourmet dinner!*

6-oz. pkg. baby spinach, cooked, well-drained and
    shredded
1¾ c. prepared rice
½ t. salt, divided
¾ c. sour cream
1 egg
3 T. grated Parmesan & Romano cheese, divided
1 T. Dijon mustard
¼ t. pepper
1 lb. boneless, skinless salmon fillet, sliced ½-inch
    thick on the diagonal
½ t. water

Combine spinach, rice and ¼ teaspoon salt in a large bowl; set aside. Whisk together sour cream, egg, 2 tablespoons cheese, mustard, remaining salt and pepper in a small bowl. Add all sour cream mixture except 4 tablespoons to rice mixture and stir to coat. Place in a greased 1½-quart baking dish; top with salmon. Set aside. Add water to remaining sour cream mixture; mix well and drizzle over salmon. Top with remaining cheese. Bake, uncovered, at 350 degrees for 30 minutes. Let stand 5 minutes before serving. Serves 4.

*Jaunae Phoenix-Bacon*
*Macomb, IL*

Eggplant Parmesan

# Eggplant Parmesan

*This is a down-home dish that's great to enjoy with family & friends no matter what the occasion. Serve it atop spaghetti noodles.*

2 eggs, beaten
1 T. water
2 eggplants, peeled and sliced ¼-inch thick
2 c. Italian-flavored dry bread crumbs
1½ c. grated Parmesan cheese, divided
27¾-oz. jar garden-style pasta sauce, divided
1½ c. shredded mozzarella cheese

Combine eggs and water in a shallow bowl. Dip eggplant slices into egg mixture. Arrange slices in a single layer on a greased baking sheet; bake at 350 degrees for 25 minutes, or until golden. Set aside. Mix bread crumbs and ½ cup Parmesan cheese; set aside. Spread a small amount of pasta sauce in an ungreased 13"x9" baking pan. Layer half of eggplant, one cup sauce, ½ cup remaining Parmesan cheese and one cup crumb mixture. Repeat to make a second layer. Cover and bake for 45 minutes. Uncover; sprinkle with mozzarella cheese and remaining Parmesan cheese. Bake, uncovered, 10 more minutes. Cut into squares. Serves 6 to 8.

*Tammy Dillow*
*Raceland, KY*

## 3-Cheese Spinach Rigatoni

*The best part about this dish is that it is on the
table in fewer than 30 minutes.*

16-oz. pkg. rigatoni pasta, uncooked
3 T. olive oil, divided
10-oz. pkg. frozen chopped spinach, thawed and
   drained
2 c. ricotta cheese
5 T. grated Parmesan cheese, divided
¾ t. salt
¼ t. pepper
Optional: ¼ t. nutmeg
1½ c. shredded fontina cheese, divided
Garnish: additional grated Parmesan cheese

   Cook rigatoni according to package directions.
Drain; toss with one tablespoon oil and place in
a lightly greased 13"x9" baking pan. Combine
spinach, ricotta and 3 tablespoons Parmesan in
a food processor or blender; purée until smooth.
Add salt, pepper and nutmeg, if desired, to spinach
mixture. Stir half of fontina into spinach mixture.
Pour spinach mixture over rigatoni; top with
remaining fontina and Parmesan cheese. Drizzle
with remaining oil. Bake, covered with aluminum
foil, at 450 degrees for 15 to 20 minutes, until
golden and heated through. Garnish with additional Parmesan cheese. Serves 4.

*Audrey Lett*
*Newark, DE*

## Tomato-Basil Pasta Bake

*Your family will love the fresh taste of the
homemade pasta sauce...it's simple to make
using canned tomatoes.*

⅔ c. onion, chopped
2 cloves garlic, minced
2 T. butter
28-oz. can diced tomatoes with Italian herbs,
   undrained
2 T. fresh basil, snipped
¼ t. pepper
½ t. sugar
Optional: 1 T. capers, drained
8-oz. pkg. thin spaghetti, uncooked and divided
½ c. shredded mozzarella cheese

   Sauté onion and garlic in butter in a large
skillet over low heat until onion is tender. Stir in
tomatoes with juice, seasonings and sugar. Bring
to a boil; reduce heat. Simmer, uncovered, for
about 20 minutes. Stir in capers, if desired;
remove from heat. Meanwhile, measure out half
of spaghetti, reserving rest for another recipe.
Cook according to package directions. Drain
spaghetti and add to skillet; toss to coat with
sauce. Spoon into a lightly greased 9"x9" baking
pan. Sprinkle with cheese. Bake at 400 degrees for
5 to 8 minutes, until bubbly and cheese is melted.
Serves 4.

*Lori Van Antwerp*
*Ashley, OH*

*no spills*
When cooking pasta, remember that
rubbing a bit of vegetable oil around the
top of the pot will prevent boilovers!

3-Cheese Spinach
Rigatoni

Green Beans Supreme
(page 210)

Paula's Twice-Baked Potatoes
(page 235)

Aunt Annie's Macaroni
& Cheese (page 236)

Tried & True Apple
Casserole (page 228)

# HOT & BUBBLY SIDES

*Delicious baked side dishes to complete your meal*

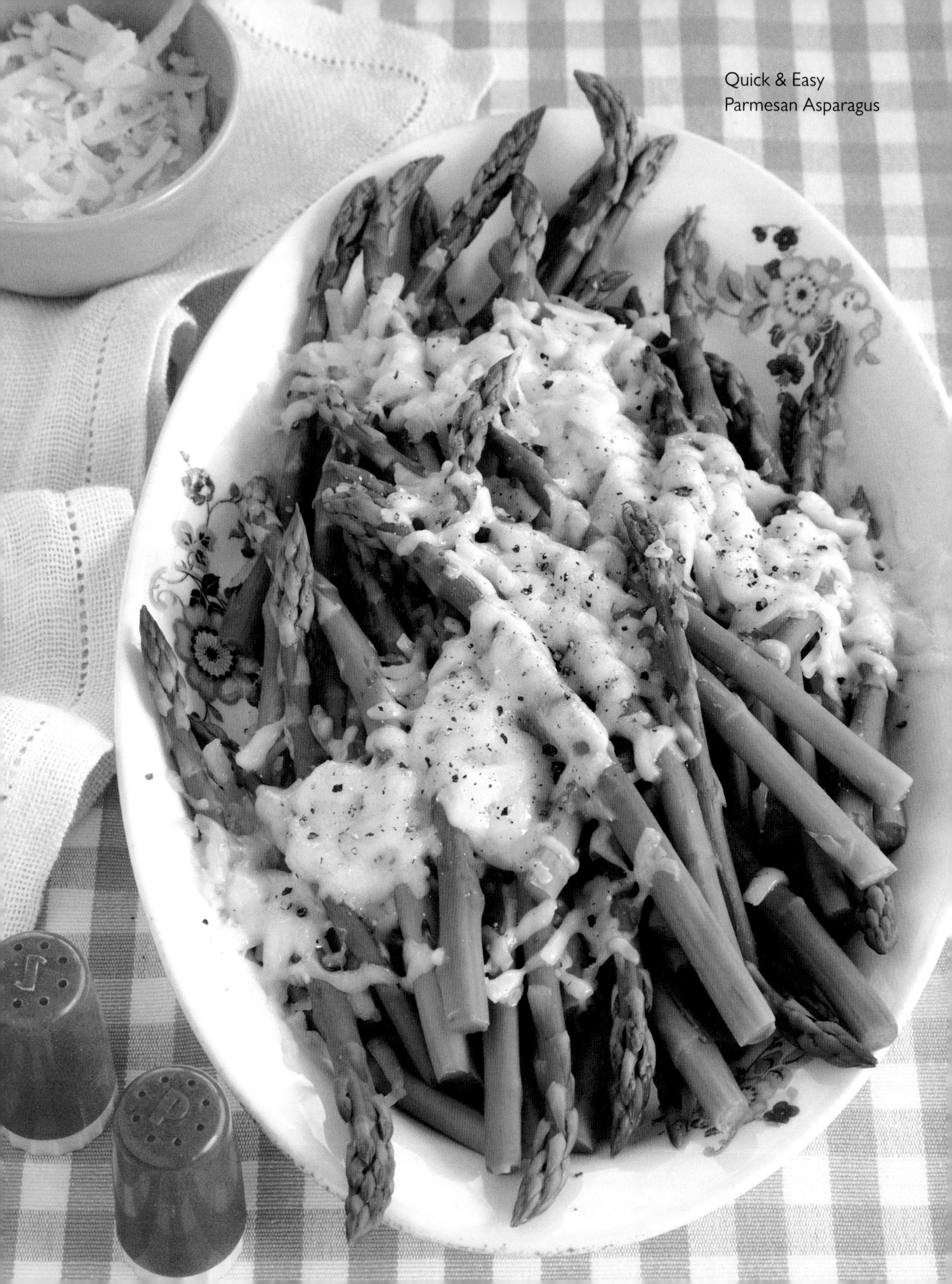

Quick & Easy
Parmesan Asparagus

## Quick & Easy Parmesan Asparagus

*From oven to table in only 15 minutes!*

4 lbs. asparagus, trimmed
¼ c. butter, melted
2 c. shredded Parmesan cheese
1 t. salt
½ t. pepper

Add asparagus and one inch of water in a large skillet. Bring to a boil. Reduce heat; cover and simmer for 5 to 7 minutes, until crisp-tender. Drain and arrange asparagus in a greased 13"x9" baking pan. Drizzle with butter; sprinkle with Parmesan cheese, salt and pepper. Bake, uncovered, at 350 degrees for 10 to 15 minutes, until cheese melts. Serves 8 to 10.

*Paula Smith*
*Ottawa, IL*

---

*a fresh & healthy alternative!*

Cutting back on salt? Drizzle steamed vegetables with freshly squeezed lemon juice…you'll never miss the salt.

---

## Asparagus Casserole

*A creamy, cheesy veggie dish that's especially good with baked ham.*

2 10-oz. cans asparagus spears, drained and ¼ c. liquid reserved
2 eggs, hard-boiled, peeled and sliced
10¾-oz. can cream of mushroom soup
8-oz. pkg. shredded Cheddar cheese, divided
1 c. buttery round crackers, crushed and divided

Spray a 2-quart casserole dish with non-stick vegetable spray. Line bottom of dish with one can of asparagus spears; arrange one sliced egg over top and set aside. Heat soup in a saucepan; stir in reserved asparagus liquid. Spoon half of soup mixture over eggs; sprinkle with one cup cheese and ½ cup cracker crumbs. Repeat layers, ending with crumbs. Bake, uncovered, at 350 degrees for 20 to 30 minutes, until cheese melts. Serves 6 to 8.

*Janet Konrade*
*Spearville, KS*

## Oh-So-Hot Banana Peppers

*My friend, Sherry, brought this to our summer pool party, and it has been my family's favorite ever since. For a milder version, use mild banana peppers and sweet sausage...it's still wonderful!*

18 hot banana peppers
2 lbs. ground hot pork sausage, browned and
    drained
2 6-oz. pkgs. pork-flavored stuffing mix, cooked
1 onion, chopped
1 zucchini, chopped
2 eggs, beaten
½ c. brown sugar, packed
16-oz. pkg. shredded Cheddar cheese

Slice peppers down center of one side lengthwise to open up; run under water, removing seeds. Combine sausage and prepared stuffing in a large bowl; add onion and zucchini. Stir in eggs and brown sugar; mix well. Spoon into peppers; arrange peppers in a lightly greased 13"x9" baking pan. Bake, uncovered, at 350 degrees for 1½ hours. Sprinkle with cheese; bake for 10 more minutes, or until cheese is melted. Serves 12.

*Jean Cerutti*
*Kittanning, PA*

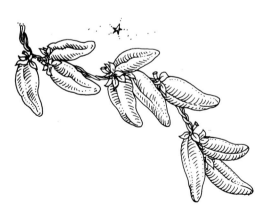

## Aunt Karen's Baked Beans

*These beans have just the right amount of spice. My husband's aunt makes them for all of our family gatherings. I'll pass up dessert to have a second helping of her baked beans!*

½ lb. ground beef
½ c. onion, chopped
2 16-oz. cans baked beans
½ to 1 t. garlic, minced
½ c. catsup
¼ c. barbecue sauce
¼ c. brown sugar, packed
¼ c. sugar
3 T. vinegar
1 T. dry mustard
3 to 5 slices bacon, partially cooked

Brown beef and onion in a skillet over medium heat; drain. Combine beef mixture with beans in a large bowl; stir in remaining ingredients except bacon. Pour into a lightly greased 13"x9" baking dish; lay bacon slices on top. Bake, uncovered, at 350 degrees for 55 to 60 minutes, until bubbly. Serves 8 to 10.

*Melissa Ward*
*Ila, GA*

### freshest veggies

Keep vegetables fresh longer by wrapping them in paper towels and storing in open plastic zipping bags in the refrigerator.

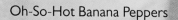
Oh-So-Hot Banana Peppers

Kielbasa Bean Pot

## Kielbasa Bean Pot

*So easy to prepare...so flavorful and filling.*

2 16-oz. cans pork & beans
1 lb. Kielbasa sausage, sliced
1½-oz. pkg. onion soup mix
⅓ c. catsup
¼ c. water
2 t. brown sugar, packed
1 T. mustard
Garnish: sliced green onions

Combine all ingredients except garnish in a 2-quart baking dish. Bake, uncovered, at 350 degrees for one hour. Sprinkle servings with sliced green onions. Serves 6 to 8.

*Sharon Crider*
*Lebanon, MO*

**campfire fun!**
A fun idea for a family get-together...serve up baked beans Western style. Enjoy them with a dinner 'round a campfire. Roast hot dogs, grill corn on the cob, roast potatoes in the coals and finish off the meal with warm biscuits and honey.

## Baked Hominy & Cheese

3 T. butter
¼ c. onion, finely chopped
3 T. all-purpose flour
¾ t. chili powder
salt and pepper to taste
1½ c. milk
2 15-oz. cans white hominy, drained and rinsed
1 c. shredded Cheddar cheese

Melt butter in a large saucepan over medium heat; add onion and cook until tender. Add flour and seasonings; cook and stir until bubbly. Slowly add milk; cook and stir until thickened. Stir in hominy; pour mixture into a lightly greased 1½-quart casserole dish. Top with cheese. Bake, uncovered, at 350 degrees for 35 to 40 minutes. Serves 6.

## Green Beans Supreme

*This isn't your usual green bean casserole.*
*Loaded with cheese and sour cream, it will be*
*your new favorite!*

1 onion, sliced
1 T. fresh parsley, snipped
3 T. butter, divided
2 T. all-purpose flour
½ t. lemon zest
½ t. salt
⅛ t. pepper
½ c. milk
16-oz. pkg. frozen French-style green beans,
   thawed
8-oz. container sour cream
½ c. shredded Cheddar cheese
¼ c. soft bread crumbs

Cook onion slices and parsley in 2 tablespoons
butter in a saucepan over medium heat about
5 minutes, until onion is tender. Blend in flour,
lemon zest, salt and pepper. Stir in milk; heat until
thick and bubbly. Add beans and sour cream; heat
through. Spoon into an ungreased 2-quart baking
dish; sprinkle with cheese. Melt remaining butter
and toss with bread crumbs; sprinkle over beans.
Broil 3 to 4 inches from heat for 3 minutes, or until
golden. Serves 4 to 6.

## Cabbage Pudding

*This is my Grandmother Ellen's recipe from*
*Kentucky. It is always a favorite at carry-ins,*
*and everyone wants the recipe.*

1 head cabbage, cut into 1-inch-thick wedges
1 sleeve saltine crackers, crushed
½ c. butter, diced
salt and pepper to taste
1 to 2 c. milk

Layer half each of cabbage wedges, crushed
crackers, butter, salt and pepper. Repeat layering,
ending with salt and pepper. Pour enough milk
over top to just barely cover cabbage mixture.
Cover and bake at 350 degrees for 45 minutes;
uncover and bake 15 more minutes. Serves 8 to 10.

*Teri Johnson*
*Marion, IN*

### fantastic frozen veggies

Don't hesitate to stock up on frozen
vegetables when they go on sale.
Flash-frozen soon after harvesting, they
actually retain more nutrients than fresh
produce that has traveled for several days
before arriving in the grocery store's
produce section.

Green Beans Supreme

Green Bean Bundles

# Green Bean Bundles

*Easy and delicious! The most obvious time-saver in this recipe is not to make the bundles, but it's definitely worth the effort.*

3 14½-oz. cans whole green beans, drained
8 slices bacon, cut in half crosswise
6 T. butter, melted
½ c. brown sugar, packed
2 to 3 cloves garlic, minced

Gather beans in bundles of 10; wrap each bundle with a half-slice of bacon. Arrange bundles in a lightly greased 13"x9" baking pan. Mix melted butter, sugar and garlic in a small bowl; spoon over bundles. Cover and bake at 375 degrees for 30 minutes. Uncover and bake 15 more minutes. Serves 8.

*Wendy Sensing*
*Brentwood, TN*

# Creamy Cabbage Bake

*This recipe is a favorite at our family cookouts...real comfort food.*

1 head cabbage, coarsely chopped
1 c. carrots, peeled and chopped
1 c. onion, chopped
10¾-oz. can cream of mushroom soup
½ c. plus 2 T. milk
1 t. dried parsley
½ t. seasoned salt
8-oz. pkg. shredded Swiss cheese
8-oz. pkg. shredded Parmesan cheese

Boil cabbage, carrots and onion in water until tender; drain. Combine with remaining ingredients. Transfer cabbage mixture to a greased 13"x9" baking pan. Bake, uncovered, at 350 degrees for 45 minutes. Serves 12.

*Kimberly Burditt*
*Summerville, SC*

# Spicy Carrot French Fries

*The sweet flavor that comes from roasting root vegetables mixed with the spicy seasonings is delicious.*

2 lbs. carrots, peeled and cut into matchsticks
4 T. olive oil, divided
1 T. seasoned salt
2 t. ground cumin
1 t. chili powder
1 t. pepper
ranch salad dressing

Place carrots in a large plastic zipping bag. Sprinkle with 3 tablespoons oil and seasonings; toss to coat. Drizzle remaining oil over a baking sheet; place carrots in a single layer on sheet. Bake, uncovered, at 425 degrees for 25 to 35 minutes, until carrots are golden. Serve with salad dressing for dipping. Serves 4 to 6.

*Kelly Gray*
*Weston, WV*

*"My children didn't know until they were almost grown that this dish was healthy for you, or even that it was a vegetable!"*

*—Kelly*

# Zesty Horseradish Carrots

*This is such an easy make-ahead dish. Assemble it the night before and refrigerate; sprinkle on the topping and then pop it in the oven just before mealtime.*

6 to 8 carrots, peeled and cut into matchsticks
½ c. mayonnaise
2 T. onion, grated
2 T. horseradish sauce
½ t. salt
¼ t. pepper

Cover carrots with water in a saucepan; cook for 6 to 8 minutes over medium heat. Drain, reserving ¼ cup cooking liquid. Combine carrots, reserved cooking liquid and remaining ingredients. Spoon mixture into a lightly greased 9"x9" baking pan; sprinkle with Topping. Bake, uncovered, at 375 degrees for 15 to 20 minutes. Serves 6.

## Topping:
¼ c. dry bread crumbs
1 T. butter, softened
⅛ t. paprika

Combine all ingredients; mix until crumbly.

*Joan White*
*Malvern, PA*

Spicy Carrot French Fries

Patty's Broccoli &
Swiss Casserole

## Patty's Broccoli & Swiss Casserole

*This dish is a family favorite that was passed down to me by my late sister Patricia..."Perfect Patty" we liked to call her. Everything she did or made always came out superbly, including this wonderful casserole. It is quick, easy and delicious, and it is always expected at our family gatherings. No leftovers here!*

1 egg
½ c. mayonnaise
10¾-oz. can cream of mushroom soup
3  10-oz. pkgs. frozen chopped broccoli, thawed
    and drained
1 onion, finely chopped
1 c. shredded Swiss cheese
½ c. bread crumbs
2 T. butter, melted
paprika to taste

Lightly whisk egg in a large bowl; blend in mayonnaise and soup. Stir in broccoli, onion and cheese. Spoon into a lightly greased 1½-quart casserole dish. Toss together crumbs and butter; top casserole with crumb mixture and sprinkle with paprika. Bake, uncovered, at 350 degrees for about 35 minutes, until bubbly. Serves 8.

*Donna Esposito*
*Glenville, NY*

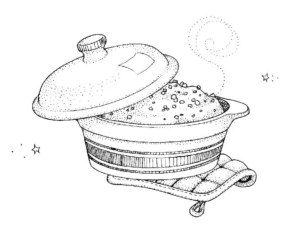

## Roasted Cauliflower

*A tasty substitute for deep-fried cauliflower!*

2 heads cauliflower, cut into flowerets
2 red onions, quartered
¼ c. olive oil
¼ t. garlic powder
½ t. salt
¼ t. pepper

Toss cauliflower with remaining ingredients in a large bowl; spread evenly in a large roasting pan. Cover and bake at 425 degrees, stirring occasionally, for 30 to 35 minutes, until golden. Serves 8 to 10.

*Karen Puchnick*
*Butler, PA*

## Herbed Veggie-Cheese Casserole

*Lots of veggies combine for a delectable cheesy dish.*

10-oz. pkg. frozen green beans
10-oz. pkg. frozen broccoli
10-oz. pkg. frozen cauliflower
10-oz. jar pearl onions, drained
1 c. shredded Cheddar cheese
2 10¾-oz. cans cream of mushroom soup
6-oz. pkg. herb stuffing mix

Cook frozen vegetables separately, until just crisp-tender; drain. Arrange vegetables in layers in a greased 13"x9" baking pan. Arrange onions around outer edge. Sprinkle with cheese; pour soup over all. Bake, uncovered, at 350 degrees for 30 minutes. Remove from oven; sprinkle half of stuffing over top, reserving the rest for another recipe. Bake for 15 more minutes. Serves 8.

*Jo Ann*
*Gooseberry Patch*

Tangy Corn Casserole

# Tangy Corn Casserole

*Great for brunch and casual celebrations, this side dish gets a little kick from a dab of hot sauce.*

10-oz. pkg. frozen corn, thawed and drained
½ c. onion, chopped
½ c. green pepper, sliced into strips
½ c. water
1 c. yellow squash, chopped
1 tomato, chopped
1 c. shredded Cheddar cheese, divided
⅔ c. cornmeal
½ c. milk
2 eggs, beaten
¾ t. salt
¼ t. pepper
¼ t. hot pepper sauce

Combine corn, onion, green pepper and water in a medium saucepan. Bring to a boil; reduce heat to medium-low. Cover and simmer 5 minutes, or until vegetables are crisp-tender. Do not drain. Combine squash, tomato, ¾ cup cheese, cornmeal, milk, eggs, salt, pepper and hot pepper sauce in a large mixing bowl. Add corn mixture to cornmeal mixture; stir to blend. Pour into a greased 1½-quart casserole dish. Bake, uncovered, at 350 degrees for 45 to 50 minutes, until heated through. Top with remaining cheese. Serves 8.

*Dave Slyh*
*Galloway, OH*

# Corn & Onion Casserole

*A "must-have" at Thanksgiving.*

½ c. butter
2 sweet onions, thickly sliced and separated
   into rings
8-oz. container sour cream
1 c. shredded Cheddar cheese, divided
7-oz. pkg. corn muffin mix
1 egg, beaten
½ c. milk
4 drops hot pepper sauce
14¾-oz. can creamed corn

Melt butter in a skillet over low heat; add onions and sauté until golden. Remove from heat; stir in sour cream and ½ cup cheese. Set aside. Combine muffin mix, egg, milk, sauce and corn in a medium bowl; mix well. Spoon muffin mixture into a greased 9"x9" baking pan. Top with onion mixture; sprinkle with remaining cheese. Bake, uncovered, at 350 degrees for one hour. Serves 6.

*Tammy Wright*
*Decatur, TX*

# Kansas Scalloped Corn

*Swiss cheese makes this scalloped corn just a bit yummier!*

2 eggs, slightly beaten
11-oz. can corn, drained, liquid reserved
14¾-oz. can cream-style corn
5-oz. can evaporated milk
4 T. butter, melted
2 T. dried, minced onion
⅛ t. salt
⅛ t. pepper
2 c. saltine crackers, coarsely crushed
8-oz. pkg. Swiss cheese, diced

Combine eggs, corn and ½ cup reserved corn liquid in a large bowl; add cream-style corn, milk, butter, onion, salt and pepper. Lightly stir in saltines and cheese. Spray an 8"x8" casserole dish with non-stick vegetable spray. Spoon in mixture and bake, covered, at 350 degrees for 50 minutes. Uncover and bake 10 more minutes until set. Let stand for 5 minutes before serving. Serves 8 to 10.

*Lori Hobscheidt*
*Washington, IA*

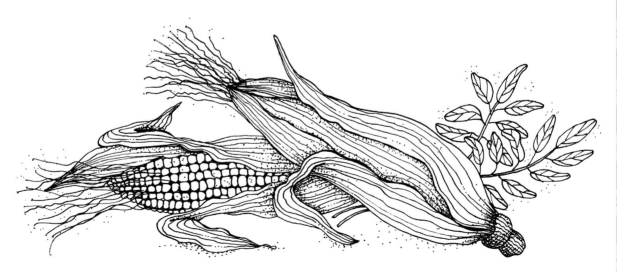

## Mom's Squash Casserole

*Loosely cover the casserole with aluminum foil halfway through the baking time so that the crackers don't over-brown.*

1½ lbs. zucchini, sliced
1½ lbs. yellow squash, sliced
1 onion, chopped
1 egg, beaten
½ t. salt
¼ t. pepper
½ c. butter, melted and divided
2 c. round buttery crackers, crushed

Cook zucchini and squash in boiling salted water until tender, about 12 to 15 minutes; drain and mash. Add onion, egg, salt, pepper and half of melted butter. Pour mixture into a greased 13"x9" baking dish. Sprinkle with cracker crumbs; drizzle with remaining butter. Bake, uncovered, at 350 degrees for one hour. Serves 10 to 12.

*Cheryl Donnelly*
*Arvada, CO*

## Golden Onions

*A warm, tasty side that goes especially well with beef roasts.*

¾ c. butter, melted and divided
6 onions, sliced
10¾-oz. can cream of chicken soup
1 c. milk
¼ t. salt
¼ t. pepper
3 c. shredded Swiss cheese
6 slices bread

Combine ½ cup butter and onions in a large skillet over medium heat. Cook, stirring frequently, for 15 minutes, or until tender. Pour into a greased 2-quart baking pan; set aside. Combine soup, milk, salt and pepper; spoon over onions. Sprinkle with cheese and set aside. Brush remaining butter over bread slices; arrange on top of onion mixture. Bake at 350 degrees for 25 to 30 minutes, until golden. Serves 6 to 8.

*Marie Warner*
*Jennings, FL*

### freezer friendly!
What's one of the many advantages of making side-dish casseroles? They can be made ahead and frozen for busy weeknights. Just be sure to wrap them carefully in plastic wrap and aluminum foil.

Mom's Squash Casserole

Squash Puff

## Squash Puff

*Mandarin oranges make this a unique side.*

2 10-oz. pkgs. frozen cooked winter squash,
 thawed
½ c. brown sugar, packed
⅓ c. butter, melted
½ c. light cream
½ c. mandarin oranges
1 t. salt
½ t. cinnamon
½ t. nutmeg
1 egg, beaten
1½ c. mini marshmallows
¼ c. finely chopped pecans
⅓ c. honey

Mix together squash, brown sugar, butter, cream, oranges, salt, cinnamon, nutmeg and egg; pour into a 3-quart casserole dish. Bake, uncovered, at 375 degrees for 25 minutes. Remove from oven; sprinkle with marshmallows and pecans and drizzle with honey. Return to oven for 10 more minutes. Serves 6 to 8.

*Catherine Kellogg*
*Orlando, FL*

### simple swap
Butternut squash can be used in place of pumpkin in some recipes. Try adding it to pies, soups and risotto. It has a sweeter flavor and is less watery.

## Pecan-Butternut Squash Bake

⅓ c. butter, softened
¾ c. sugar
2 eggs
5-oz. can evaporated milk
1 t. vanilla extract
¼ t. cinnamon
2 c. butternut squash, cooked and mashed

Beat together butter and sugar in a large bowl with an electric mixer at medium speed. Beat in eggs, milk, vanilla and cinnamon. Add squash and mix well. Pour into a lightly greased 11"x 8" baking pan. Bake, uncovered, at 350 degrees for 45 minutes, or until set. Sprinkle with Crunchy Topping and bake for 5 to 10 more minutes. May be served hot or cold. Serves 4 to 6.

### Crunchy Topping:
½ c. crispy rice cereal
¼ c. sugar
¼ c. chopped pecans
2 T. butter, melted

Combine all ingredients in a bowl; mix well.

*Lisa Cameron*
*Twin Falls, ID*

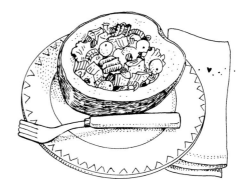

## Scalloped Zucchini

*We own a farm and raise veggies, so we always have plenty of zucchini. I have come up with different ways to cook it, and my family loves this recipe. Choose small and medium zucchini...they're more tender than the really big ones.*

4 to 5 zucchini, sliced
1 onion, sliced
2 c. pasteurized process cheese spread, sliced
1 sleeve round buttery crackers, crushed
½ c. butter, sliced

Layer half each of zucchini, onion and cheese slices in a buttered 13"x9" baking pan. Repeat layering. Top with crackers and dot with butter. Bake, uncovered, at 325 degrees until tender, about 40 minutes. Serves 8 to 10.

*Liz Gatewood*
*Madison, IN*

### pretty pantry!
Homemade preserves are beautiful when displayed in an old-fashioned corner cupboard. Bright red tomatoes, green pickles, and golden corn are particularly nice.

## Summery Herbed Tomato Pie

*A refrigerated pie crust makes this one quick-to-fix dish.*

9-inch pie crust
3 to 4 tomatoes, sliced
½ c. fresh chives, chopped
2 T. fresh basil, chopped
salt and pepper to taste
2 c. shredded mozzarella cheese
½ c. mayonnaise
Garnish: additional fresh chives and basil, chopped

Press pie crust into a 9" pie plate. Bake at 425 degrees for 5 minutes. Reduce oven to 400 degrees. Arrange tomato slices in crust; sprinkle with chives, basil, salt and pepper. Combine cheese and mayonnaise; spread over tomatoes. Bake at 400 degrees for 35 minutes. Garnish with additional chives and basil. Serves 8 to 10.

*Janice O'Brien*
*Warrenton, VA*

Summery Herbed
Tomato Pie

Ginger Ale Baked Apples

## Tomato Pudding

*This recipe came from an old restaurant in Toledo called the Tally Ho and was handed down from my grandma. It's delicious, sweet and savory all at the same time.*

1 c. brown sugar, packed
10¾-oz. can tomato purée
¼ c. water
1 t. salt
4 c. fresh bread cubes
½ c. butter, melted

Combine brown sugar, tomato purée, water and salt in a small saucepan. Bring to a boil over medium heat for about 5 minutes. Toss together bread cubes and melted butter in a large bowl. Stir in tomato mixture, mixing well. Spread in a lightly greased 2-quart casserole dish. Bake, covered, at 350 degrees for 45 minutes. Uncover and bake 15 more minutes. Serves 8 to 10.

*Laura Hoevener*
*Milford, OH*

## Ginger Ale Baked Apples

*A yummy fall dessert or after-the-game snack!*

4 baking apples
¼ c. golden raisins, divided
4 t. brown sugar, packed and divided
½ c. ginger ale

Core apples but do not cut through bottoms. Place apples in an ungreased 8"x8" baking pan. Spoon one tablespoon raisins and one teaspoon brown sugar into center of each apple. Pour ginger ale over apples. Bake, uncovered, at 350 degrees, basting occasionally, for 45 minutes, or until apples are tender. Serve warm or cold. Serves 4.

*Judy Lange*
*Imperial, PA*

## Prize-Winning Pineapple Cheddar Bake

*This recipe has been in my family for a very long time, and I even won 2nd place when I entered it in a Dairy Council contest. My family always requests it when we have our May family reunion.*

2 20-oz. cans pineapple tidbits, drained
¾ c. all-purpose flour
1 c. sugar
8-oz. pkg. shredded Cheddar cheese
¾ c. margarine, melted
1 sleeve round buttery crackers, crushed

Spread pineapple into a greased 2-quart casserole. Mix together flour, sugar and cheese; add to pineapple, stirring well. Combine margarine and cracker crumbs; spread over pineapple mixture. Bake, covered, at 350 degrees for 30 minutes. Serve hot or cold. Serves 8.

*Marta May*
*Anderson, IN*

## Tried & True Apple Casserole

*Whenever I would fry apples, they turned out like applesauce...until a friend said, "I have a recipe you will love." She was right...I've been using it ever since, and it never fails! This is a great potluck dish.*

8 to 10 tart apples, cored, peeled and halved
½ c. sugar
1 T. all-purpose flour
½ t. cinnamon
¼ t. nutmeg
2 T. butter, diced
Optional: golden raisins, chopped walnuts

Place apples in a greased 2-quart casserole dish; set aside. Mix together dry ingredients; sprinkle over apples. Dot with butter. Sprinkle with raisins and walnuts, if desired. Cover and bake at 350 degrees for 45 minutes to one hour. Serves 6 to 8.

*Gerry Donnella*
*Boston, VA*

### first come, first served!

For the best selection, plan to be at the farmers' market first thing in the morning. Bring along a roomy shoulder bag or basket so that it's easy to tote all your goodies.

Tried & True
Apple Casserole

Candied Sweet Potatoes

## Candied Sweet Potatoes

*We love this clever way to fix an old favorite by using an oven roasting bag. There's no messy, sticky clean-up…just toss away the bag!*

¼ c. all-purpose flour
4 sweet potatoes, peeled and thinly sliced
⅓ c. brown sugar, packed
¼ c. margarine, sliced
2 T. maple-flavored pancake syrup
¼ t. nutmeg

Shake flour in a large oven bag; arrange bag in a 13"x9" baking pan. Toss sweet potatoes with remaining ingredients to blend; arrange in an even layer inside bag. Close bag with provided nylon tie; cut six ½-inch slits in top. Bake at 350 degrees for 45 minutes. Serves 6 to 8.

*Chris Revennaugh*
*Mentor, OH*

## Scalloped Pineapple

*A friend shared this recipe when we were invited to her house for a hot dog roast. Now it's a favorite for family gatherings.*

3 eggs
2 c. sugar
1 c. butter, melted
¾ c. milk
20-oz. can pineapple chunks, drained
8 slices white bread, torn

Beat together eggs and sugar in a large bowl; stir in remaining ingredients in order given. Pour into a greased 11"x7" baking pan. Bake, uncovered, at 350 degrees for 40 minutes. Serves 6 to 8.

*Dollie Isaacson*
*Danville, IL*

## Twice-Baked Sweet Potatoes

*My father and I love this side dish…it's like eating dessert!*

2 sweet potatoes, halved lengthwise
¼ c. Neufchâtel or cream cheese, cubed
2 T. milk
1 T. brown sugar, packed
¼ t. cinnamon
¼ c. chopped pecans

Place sweet potatoes cut-side down in an aluminum foil-lined 9"x9" baking pan. Bake, uncovered, at 425 degrees for 25 to 30 minutes, until tender and potatoes are pulling away from potato skins. Scoop potato pulp into a bowl, leaving ¼-inch-thick potato shells. Arrange potato shells in pan; set aside. Add cheese, milk, brown sugar and cinnamon to potato pulp; mash until blended. Spoon potato mixture into shells; top with pecans. Bake, uncovered, for 8 minutes, or until potatoes are heated through and nuts are toasted. Serves 4.

*Tina Goodpasture*
*Meadowview, VA*

# Easy Ranch Potatoes

*These crispy potato puffs are scrumptious and oh-so easy to fix for a busy-night supper.*

¼ c. olive oil
2 .4-oz. pkgs. ranch salad dressing mix
32-oz. pkg. frozen potato puffs, thawed

Combine oil and salad dressing mix in a large bowl; stir well. Add potato puffs and toss to coat. Arrange potatoes in a single layer on an ungreased 15"x10" jelly-roll pan. Bake, uncovered, at 450 degrees for 30 to 35 minutes, stirring every 10 minutes, until potatoes are crisp and golden. Serves 6 to 8.

*Jennie Gist*
*Gooseberry Patch*


# Old-Fashioned Scalloped Potatoes

*Takes a little longer to fix...but it's worth it!*

2 T. all-purpose flour
1 t. salt
¼ t. pepper
4 c. potatoes, peeled and thinly sliced
⅔ c. sweet onion, thinly sliced
2 T. butter, sliced
1½ c. milk
paprika to taste

Mix together flour, salt and pepper in a small bowl; set aside. Layer half each of potatoes, onion, flour mixture and butter in a greased 2-quart casserole dish. Repeat layering with remaining potatoes, onion, flour mixture and butter. Set aside. Heat milk just to boiling and pour over top; sprinkle with paprika. Bake, covered, at 375 degrees for 45 minutes. Uncover and bake 10 more minutes. Serves 8.

*Vickie*
*Gooseberry Patch*


# Nannie Raue's Sweet Potato Pone

6 c. sweet potatoes, peeled and grated
1⅓ c. sugar
½ c. all-purpose flour
1 t. cinnamon
1 t. nutmeg
1 to 1¼ c. evaporated milk, divided
1 egg, beaten
6 T. butter, melted
1 t. vanilla extract
Optional: gingersnap cookies, crumbled

Combine sweet potatoes, sugar, flour, cinnamon and nutmeg in a large bowl. Add one cup evaporated milk; mix well. Stir in egg, blending well. Add butter and vanilla. Pour into a lightly greased 13"x9" baking pan. Bake, uncovered, at 350 degrees for 1½ hours, stirring frequently. Add more milk if dry. Sprinkle with crumbled gingersnap cookies, if desired. Cut into squares; serve hot or cold. Serves 8 to 10.

*Mary Rabon*
*Mobile, AL*


## sweet potato fries

Sweet potato fries are deliciously different! Slice sweet potatoes into strips or wedges, toss with olive oil and place on a baking sheet. Bake at 400 degrees for 20 to 40 minutes, until tender, turning once. Sprinkle with a little cinnamon-sugar for added sweetness or chili powder for a spicy kick.

Nannie Raue's Sweet
Potato Pone

Paula's Twice-Baked Potatoes

## Paula's Twice-Baked Potatoes

*Top with a dollop of sour cream and a sprinkle of snipped fresh chives…heavenly!*

6 russet baking potatoes
¼ c. butter
½ c. milk
1 onion, finely chopped
6 slices bacon, crisply cooked and crumbled
1 t. salt
½ t. pepper
1½ c. shredded Cheddar cheese, divided
Optional: fresh chives, sour cream, extra cheese, extra bacon

Bake potatoes at 375 degrees for one hour, or until tender. Cool. Cut a thin slice off top of each potato and scoop out insides, leaving a thin shell. Mash potato with butter in a mixing bowl; blend in milk, onion, bacon, salt, pepper and one cup cheese. Spoon mixture into potato shells; place on a lightly greased baking sheet. Bake at 375 degrees for 25 minutes. Top with remaining cheese; bake 5 more minutes, or until cheese melts. Serve with desired toppings. Serves 6.

*Paula Smith*
*Ottawa, IL*

## Grandpa Jim's Potatoes

8 to 10 potatoes, peeled, cooked and mashed
12-oz. pkg. bacon, crisply cooked and crumbled
8-oz. pkg. shredded Cheddar cheese
1¼ c. ranch salad dressing

Mix all ingredients together in a large bowl and spoon into a lightly greased 13"x9" baking pan. Bake, uncovered, at 375 degrees for 30 minutes, or until heated through. Serves 12 to 15.

*JoAnn Houghtby*
*Farmington, MN*

"After my grandma passed away, my grandpa learned to make coffee and cook for himself. It was just so adorable to see this 80-year-old man learning these skills for himself. This is a recipe that he was especially proud of...and it is SO good! He made it for our church potluck, and it was a hit. I was so happy to go with him and see the twinkle in his eye." —JoAnn

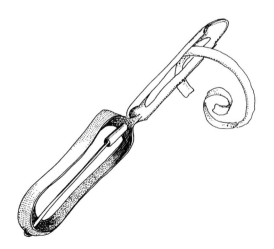

## Potluck Potato Bake

32-oz. pkg. frozen diced potatoes, thawed
16-oz. container sour cream
1 onion, chopped
8-oz. pkg. shredded Cheddar cheese
10¾-oz. can cream of celery soup
¾ c. butter, melted and divided
2 c. corn flake cereal, crushed

Stir together potatoes, sour cream, onion, cheese, soup and ¼ cup butter in a large bowl. Spoon into a lightly greased 13"x9" baking pan. Toss together cereal and remaining butter in a medium bowl; spread over potato mixture. Bake, covered, at 350 degrees for one hour and 15 minutes. Uncover and bake for 15 more minutes. Serves 16 to 20.

*Trisha Donley*
*Pinedale, WY*

## Aunt Annie's Macaroni & Cheese

*This recipe was my Great-Aunt Annie's. She was such a sweet and loving person; I know she would want me to share this recipe that has become one of my favorites through the years.*

16-oz. pkg. elbow macaroni, cooked
16-oz. pkg. shredded Cheddar cheese
10¾-oz. can cream of mushroom soup
1 c. mayonnaise
4-oz. jar chopped pimentos, drained
¼ c. onion, chopped
¼ c. green pepper, chopped
¼ c. butter, softened
10 to 12 saltine crackers, crushed

Mix together all ingredients except crackers in a large bowl. Spread in a greased 13"x9" baking pan. Sprinkle with cracker crumbs. Bake, uncovered, at 325 degrees for 25 minutes. Serves 8 to 10.

*Elaine Philyaw*
*Coosada, AL*

Aunt Annie's
Macaroni & Cheese

Mom's Macaroni & Cheese

## Mom's Macaroni & Cheese

8-oz. pkg. elbow macaroni, uncooked
1 c. milk
5-oz. can evaporated milk
⅓ c. water
3 T. butter
3 T. all-purpose flour
½ t. salt
1 T. dried, minced onion
1½ c. shredded sharp Cheddar cheese, divided

Cook macaroni according to package instructions; drain. Combine milk, evaporated milk and water; set aside. Melt butter in a medium saucepan over medium heat. Add flour and salt, whisking until blended. Add onion and evaporated milk mixture, stirring well to avoid lumps. Add one cup cheese. Simmer until cheese melts and sauce is thickened, stirring frequently. Stir in macaroni. Pour into a lightly greased 8"x8" baking pan. Top with remaining cheese and bake, uncovered, at 350 degrees for 30 minutes, or until bubbly and lightly golden. Serves 4 to 6.

*Jenny Newman*
*Goodyear, AZ*

## Beefy Mushroom Rice

*This recipe brings back special memories of my grandma & grandpa...I used to help them make it when I was growing up. Now it's a favorite of my own family.*

16-oz. pkg. long-cooking rice, uncooked
2 10¾-oz. cans French onion soup
2 10½-oz. cans beef broth
1¼ c. water
4-oz. can sliced mushrooms, drained
1 c. butter, sliced
Optional: 2 10¾-oz. cans cream of
    mushroom soup

Combine rice, French onion soup, broth and water in an ungreased 13"x9" baking pan. Add mushrooms. Arrange butter evenly over top. Bake, covered, at 325 degrees for about one hour, until rice is tender. If creamier rice is desired, stir in cream of mushroom soup; heat through, about 15 to 20 minutes. Serves 8 to 10.

*Jennie Turner*
*La Vale, MD*

## Baked Spinach & Rice

*I find this casserole is just as tasty if I substitute 4 egg whites for the whole eggs and use a "light" cheese spread.*

2 c. cooked rice
10-oz. pkg. frozen spinach, cooked and well drained
8-oz. pkg. pasteurized process cheese spread,
    cubed
⅓ c. onion, chopped
⅓ c. red pepper, chopped
3 eggs, beaten
⅛ t. pepper
Optional: ¼ lb. turkey bacon, crisply cooked
    and crumbled

Combine all ingredients in a bowl; mix well. Spread in a greased 10"x6" baking pan; smooth top with a spatula. Bake, uncovered, at 350 degrees for 30 minutes. Let stand for 5 minutes; cut into squares. Serves 8 to 10.

*Elena Smith*
*Seaside, CA*

Mushroom & Orzo Casserole

# Mushroom & Orzo Casserole

*An easy-to-make side with lots of spicy goodness.*

8-oz. pkg. orzo pasta, cooked
½ c. margarine, softened
1½-oz. pkg. onion soup mix
8-oz pkg. sliced mushrooms
¼ c. fresh parsley, chopped

Combine orzo, margarine, soup mix and mushrooms in a bowl. Spoon into a 2-quart casserole dish; cover and bake at 375 degrees for 30 minutes. Uncover and bake 10 more minutes. Stir in parsley. Serves 6.

*Laurie Gross*
*Thousand Oaks, CA*

# Cornbread-Biscuit Dressing

*Bake up your favorite packaged cornbread and biscuit mixes to make this tasty stuffing.*

4 c. cornbread crumbs
4 c. biscuit crumbs
6 stalks celery, chopped
1 onion, chopped
⅓ c. butter, melted
1 T. dried parsley
1 t. dried sage
1 t. salt
1 t. pepper
2½ c. chicken or turkey broth
½ c. milk

Spread cornbread and biscuit crumbs on an ungreased baking sheet. Bake at 300 degrees for 15 minutes, or until crumbs are toasted, stirring twice. Set aside. Sauté celery and onion in butter over medium heat until tender; remove from heat. Combine celery and crumb mixtures with seasonings in a large bowl. Stir in broth and milk; stir to mix. Spoon into a greased 13"x9" baking pan. Bake, uncovered, at 350 degrees for one hour, or until golden. Serves 10.

*Jennifer Kann*
*Dayton, OH*

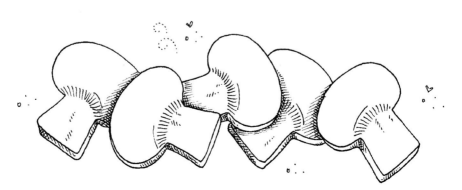

Wild Rice Stuffing

# Wild Rice Stuffing

*Dates and crunchy almonds make this stuffing recipe special!*

1⅓ c. wild rice, uncooked
2 T. butter
2 c. onion, chopped
1 c. carrots, peeled and chopped
1 c. green pepper, chopped
6 c. herb-seasoned stuffing mix
3 c. chicken broth
10-oz. pkg. dates, chopped
1 c. slivered almonds
½ c. fresh parsley, chopped
1½ t. dried rosemary
1½ t. dried thyme
1½ t. dried sage

Prepare rice according to package directions; set aside. Combine butter, onion, carrots and pepper in a medium skillet over medium-high heat and sauté until onion is tender; remove from heat. Blend in remaining ingredients; stir in rice. Spoon stuffing into a greased 3-quart casserole dish. Bake, covered, at 325 degrees for 45 minutes. Uncover and bake 15 more minutes. Serves 10 to 12.

Strawberry Layer Cake
(page 257)

Chocolate Pound Cake
(page 271)

Comforting Southern Cake
(page 262)

Black-Bottom Cupcakes
(page 276)

# FAVORITE CAKES
# & CUPCAKES

*Yummy baked goods to ensure every
meal has a sweet ending*

# Double-Chocolate Mousse Cake

16-oz. pkg. semi-sweet chocolate chips
2 c. butter
1 c. half-and-half
1 c. sugar
1 T. vanilla extract
½ t. salt
8 eggs, beaten
Garnish: whipped topping, strawberries

Combine all ingredients except eggs and garnish in a heavy saucepan. Cook over low heat until chocolate chips melt, stirring frequently. Cool to room temperature; fold in eggs. Pour chocolate mixture into a greased 9"x3" springform pan with bottom lined with parchment paper. Bake at 350 degrees for 45 minutes, or until firm. Cool to room temperature. Spread Chocolate Topping on top of cooled cake. Chill, covered, 4 hours, or until firm; carefully remove pan. Cut into slices and garnish with whipped topping and strawberries before serving. Serves 10.

## Chocolate Topping:
1 c. chocolate chips
2 T. butter
2 T. corn syrup
3 T. half-and-half

Combine chocolate chips, butter and corn syrup in top of a double boiler; cook over medium heat until chocolate and butter melt, stirring to blend. Remove from heat. Add half-and-half, stirring until smooth.

*Jessica Jones*
*York, PA*

Double-Chocolate
Mousse Cake

# Chocolate Gooey Cake

*A creamy, caramel, chocolatey cake that's perfect for sharing at potlucks and family dinners.*

18¼-oz. pkg. German chocolate cake mix
14-oz. can sweetened condensed milk
12-oz. jar caramel ice cream topping
8-oz. container frozen whipped topping, thawed
3 1.4-oz. chocolate-covered toffee candy bars, crushed

Prepare cake according to package directions; bake in a greased 13"x9" baking pan. While cake is still warm, poke holes about ½ inch apart with a wooden spoon handle. Pour condensed milk over cake; let stand for a few minutes and drizzle with caramel topping. Spread with whipped topping; sprinkle with crushed candy. Refrigerate 2 hours to overnight before serving; keep refrigerated. Serves 16.

*Jennie Gist*
*Gooseberry Patch*

## gorgeous garnish

Decorate cakes and trifles with a sparkling bunch of sugared grapes…it's easier than it looks, and it's so pretty on a dessert buffet. Brush grapes with light corn syrup and then sprinkle generously with sanding sugar and let dry.

# Mocha Cake

*We have this cake at all of our get-togethers…it's always the first dessert to disappear!*

2 c. all-purpose flour
2 c. sugar
¾ c. baking cocoa
2 t. baking soda
1 t. baking powder
2 eggs, beaten
1 c. milk
1 c. coffee, brewed and cooled
½ c. oil

Sift together flour, sugar, cocoa, baking soda and baking powder in a large bowl. Add eggs, milk, coffee and oil; mix well. Pour into a greased and floured 13"x9" baking pan. Bake at 350 degrees for 25 to 30 minutes. Cool completely; spread Frosting over top. Serves 10 to 12.

## Frosting:
¼ c. sugar
¼ c. shortening
1¼ T. all-purpose flour
¼ c. milk

Beat sugar, shortening and flour with an electric mixer at medium speed. Gradually add milk; beat until smooth and creamy.

*Nicole Belgio*
*Shamokin, PA*

# Three-Layer Chocolate Cake

1 c. butter, softened
1¾ c. sugar
3 eggs
1 T. vanilla extract
2¼ c. all-purpose flour
1 c. baking cocoa
1½ t. baking powder
1 t. baking soda
¼ t. salt
1¾ c. milk

Beat butter in a large bowl with an electric mixer at medium speed until creamy. Gradually add sugar, beating well after each addition. Add eggs, one at a time, beating until blended after each addition. Add vanilla, beating until blended. Sift together flour and remaining ingredients except milk in a separate bowl. Add flour mixture to butter mixture alternately with milk, beginning and ending with flour mixture, beating until blended after each addition. Pour batter into 3 greased 9" round cake pans. Bake at 350 degrees for 25 to 30 minutes, until a toothpick inserted in center comes out clean. Cool in pans on a wire rack 10 minutes. Remove from pans and cool on wire racks one hour, or until completely cool. Spread Fudge Frosting on top and sides of cake. Serves 12.

## Fudge Frosting:
1 c. butter, softened
4 c. powdered sugar, divided
½ c. baking cocoa
4 to 5 T. milk
2 t. vanilla extract

Beat butter in a bowl with an electric mixer at medium speed until fluffy; gradually add 2 cups powdered sugar and cocoa and beat at medium speed until combined. Gradually add milk and remaining powdered sugar, beating at low speed after each addition until blended. Stir in vanilla.

*Pam Vienneau*
*Derby, CT*

# Chocolate-Peanut Butter Marble Cake

*I baked this cake for my son because he's fond of both peanut butter and chocolate. When I combined them just for fun, the cake came out very well...it's warm and yummy!*

1 c. all-purpose flour
1 c. sugar
1 t. baking powder
½ t. salt
1 c. semi-sweet chocolate chips, melted and cooled slightly
½ c. butter
5 T. canola oil
2 eggs, beaten
1 t. vanilla extract
1 c. peanut butter chips, melted
Optional: chocolate frosting

Mix flour, sugar, baking powder and salt in a large bowl; set aside. Combine melted chocolate chips, butter, oil, eggs and vanilla in a separate bowl; beat together. Add chocolate mixture to flour mixture; beat with an electric mixer at medium speed for 3 minutes. Pour batter into a greased 8" round cake pan or 8"x8" baking pan. Add spoonfuls of melted peanut butter chips on top of batter; swirl through batter with a table knife. Bake at 350 degrees for 40 minutes, or until a toothpick inserted in center comes out clean. Frost cake with chocolate frosting, if desired. Serves 8.

*Aqsa Masood*
*Ontario, Canada*

# Cocoa & Coffee Sheet Cake

2 c. all-purpose flour
2 c. sugar
1 c. butter
1 c. brewed coffee
¼ c. baking cocoa
2 eggs, beaten
½ c. buttermilk
1 t. baking soda
1 t. cinnamon
1 t. vanilla extract

Combine flour and sugar in a large bowl; set aside. Combine butter, coffee and cocoa in a saucepan; bring to a boil. Slowly stir butter mixture into flour mixture. Batter will resemble fudge. Let cool 3 minutes. Stir in eggs and remaining ingredients, mixing until well blended. Pour batter into a greased and floured 13"x9" baking pan. Bake at 350 degrees for 30 to 35 minutes. Pour Chocolate-Pecan Frosting over cake immediately after removing cake from oven. Allow frosting to set before cutting cake. Serves 24.

## Chocolate-Pecan Frosting:

¼ c. baking cocoa
6 T. milk
½ c. butter
16-oz. pkg. powdered sugar
½ c. chopped pecans
1 t. vanilla extract

Combine cocoa, milk and butter in a saucepan; bring to a boil. Add powdered sugar, pecans and vanilla, stirring well. Use immediately.

*Patricia Ivey*
*Lamar, AR*

# Orange-Peach Dump Cake

*A different flavor combination for this trusty dessert.*

18¼-oz. pkg. orange supreme cake mix
21-oz. can peach pie filling, chopped
½ c. sour cream
2 eggs

Combine all ingredients in an ungreased 13"x9" baking pan. Mix with a fork until well blended; smooth top. Bake at 350 degrees for 40 to 45 minutes. Serves 8 to 10.

*Elizabeth Wenk*
*Cuyahoga Falls, OH*

# Chocolate Spice Cake

18¼-oz. German chocolate cake mix
1½ t. cinnamon
3 eggs, lightly beaten
21-oz. can raisin pie filling

Combine cake mix and cinnamon in a large bowl; mix well. Add eggs and pie filling, stirring just until dry ingredients are moistened. Pour mixture into a greased 10" tube pan or 10-cup Bundt® pan. Bake at 350 degrees for 55 minutes to one hour, until a toothpick inserted in center comes out clean. Cool completely in pan on a wire rack. Serves 8 to 10.

*Judy Kelly*
*Saint Charles, MO*

# Fresh Strawberry Shortcake

*When time is short, use split biscuits, cubed angel food cake or waffles for a speedy version of strawberry shortcake.*

1 qt. strawberries, hulled and sliced
1 c. sugar, divided
2 c. all-purpose flour
4 t. baking powder
¼ t. salt
⅛ t. nutmeg
½ c. butter
½ c. milk
2 eggs, separated
2 c. sweetened whipped cream

Gently toss together strawberries and ½ cup sugar; chill. Combine flour, ¼ cup sugar, baking powder, salt and nutmeg in a large bowl; cut in butter with a pastry blender or fork until crumbly. Combine milk and egg yolks; mix well. Add to flour mixture, stirring just until moistened. Divide dough in half; pat into 2 greased 9" round cake pans. Beat egg whites in a small bowl at medium speed with an electric mixer until stiff peaks form; spread over dough. Sprinkle with remaining sugar. Bake at 300 degrees for 40 to 45 minutes, or until golden. Cool 10 minutes before removing from pan to a wire rack. Cool completely. Place one cake layer on a large serving plate; spread with half of whipped cream. Spoon half of strawberries over cream. Repeat layers. Serves 8.

*Nancy Ramsey*
*Delaware, OH*

Fresh Strawberry
Shortcake

Blueberry-Citrus Cake

## Blueberry-Citrus Cake

18¼-oz. pkg. lemon cake mix
1 c. water
½ c. plus 2 T. orange juice, divided
⅓ c. oil
3 eggs, beaten
1½ c. fresh or frozen blueberries
1 T. orange zest
1 T. lemon zest
1 c. powdered sugar
Garnish: lemon and orange zest

Beat cake mix, water, ½ cup orange juice, oil and eggs in a large bowl with an electric mixer at low speed for 30 seconds. Increase speed to medium; beat for 2 minutes. With a wooden spoon, gently fold in blueberries and zests. Pour batter into a greased and floured Bundt® pan. Bake at 350 degrees for 35 to 40 minutes, until a toothpick inserted in center comes out clean. Cool completely in pan on a wire rack. Remove from pan. Blend remaining orange juice and powdered sugar until smooth; drizzle over cake. Garnish with zests. Serves 10 to 12.

Sunny Lemon Cake

## Sunny Lemon Cake

1½ c. butter, softened
3 c. sugar
5 eggs
3 c. all-purpose flour
¾ c. lemon-lime soda
2 T. lemon extract
1 t. lemon zest
Optional: powdered sugar

Beat butter in a large bowl with an electric mixer at medium speed until creamy. Gradually add sugar, beating until light and fluffy. Add eggs, one at a time, beating well after each addition. Add flour, one cup at a time, beating well after each addition; add lemon-lime soda, lemon extract and lemon zest, beating well. Pour into a greased and floured 10" fluted pan. Bake at 350 degrees for one hour, or until a toothpick inserted in center comes out clean. Cool in pan on a wire rack 10 minutes; loosen sides of cake. Remove from pan and cool completely. Lightly sprinkle with powdered sugar, if desired. Serves 12.

*Leslie Stimel*
*Westerville, OH*

## Pineapple Upside-Down Cake

*An old favorite with a little twist. This doubly fresh-tasting cake has always been a hit at my office. Some like to say it's a good way to get your Vitamin C...really it's just an excuse to eat another slice!*

6 T. butter
1 c. brown sugar, packed
20-oz. can pineapple slices, drained
8 to 10 maraschino cherries
18¼-oz. pkg. yellow cake mix
3 eggs, beaten
⅓ c. oil
20-oz. can crushed pineapple, undrained
Garnish: whipped cream

Melt butter in a 13"x9" baking pan in a 350-degree oven. Remove pan from oven; sprinkle brown sugar over butter. Arrange pineapple slices in pan; fill in spaces with cherries and set aside. Combine dry cake mix, eggs, oil and crushed pineapple with its juice. Beat with an electric mixer on high speed for 2 minutes. Pour batter in pan over pineapple slices. Bake at 350 degrees for 40 minutes, or until a toothpick inserted in center comes out clean. Remove from oven; cool 10 to 15 minutes in pan. Place a serving platter onto pan and very carefully invert cake onto platter. Serve warm or at room temperature. Garnish with whipped cream. Serves 16.

*Cathy Clemons*
*Narrows, VA*

## Cranberry Swirl Cake

½ c. butter
1 c. sugar
2 eggs
1 t. almond extract
2 c. flour
1 t. baking powder
1 t. baking soda
½ t. salt
1 c. sour cream
8-oz. can whole-berry cranberry sauce
½ c. chopped pecans

Beat butter and sugar in a large bowl with an electric mixer at medium speed until light and fluffy. Add eggs, one at a time, beating well after each addition. Add extract and beat well. Combine flour, baking powder, baking soda and salt in a separate bowl, stirring to mix. Add flour mixture to butter mixture alternately with sour cream, beginning and ending with flour mixture, beating well after each addition. Spoon half of batter into a greased and floured 10" tube pan; spread cranberry sauce over top and add remaining batter. Sprinkle with pecans. Bake at 350 degrees for 50 to 55 minutes. Cool in pan on a wire rack 10 minutes; remove from pan and cool on a wire rack one hour, or until completely cool. Serves 8 to 10.

*Mariah Thompson*
*Smyrna, GA*

Cranberry Swirl Cake

Caramel-Glazed
Apple Cake

# Caramel-Glazed Apple Cake

*This made-from-scratch cake with its luscious glaze is irresistible! It's also easy to tote to holiday get-togethers or potlucks in its baking pan.*

1½ c. butter, softened
1 c. sugar
1 c. brown sugar, packed
3 eggs
3 c. all-purpose flour
2 t. cinnamon
1 t. baking soda
½ t. nutmeg
½ t. salt
5 Granny Smith apples, peeled, cored and diced
1¼ c. chopped pecans
2¼ t. vanilla extract

Beat butter and sugars in a large bowl with an electric mixer at medium-high speed until light and fluffy. Add eggs, one at a time, beating after each addition. Combine flour, cinnamon, baking soda, nutmeg and salt in a separate bowl. Gradually add flour mixture to butter mixture with a wooden spoon to form a very thick batter. Stir in remaining ingredients. Spoon batter into a greased and floured 13"x9" baking pan. Bake at 325 degrees for 50 minutes to one hour, until a toothpick inserted in center comes out clean. Cool cake in pan on a wire rack for at least 10 minutes. Poke holes all over surface of cake with a fork. Pour warm Caramel Glaze over cake. Serve warm or cooled. Serves 16.

# Caramel Glaze:
¼ c. butter
¼ c. sugar
¼ c. brown sugar, packed
⅛ t. salt
½ c. whipping cream

Melt butter in a saucepan over medium-low heat. Add sugars and salt. Cook, stirring frequently, for 2 minutes. Stir in cream and bring to a boil. Cook, stirring constantly, for 2 minutes.

*Brenda Smith*
*Delaware, OH*

# Coconut Fridge Cake

*Whenever I make this cake, I smile! This yummy recipe was given to me by one of my most favorite people in the whole world...my sister-in-law, Barb. Not only is it the yummiest cake ever, it makes me think of Barb and how lucky we are to have her in our family.*

18¼-oz. pkg. white cake mix
16-oz. container frozen whipped topping, thawed
8-oz. container sour cream
1 c. sweetened flaked coconut
1 c. sugar

Prepare cake mix according to package directions, baking in two 9" round baking pans. Cool; slice each layer horizontally in half to make 4 layers. To make frosting, blend remaining ingredients together well in a mixing bowl. Frost and stack layers on a cake plate; frost top and sides of cake with remaining frosting. Cover and refrigerate cake for one to 3 days before serving, as flavor improves over time. Serves 8 to 10.

*Jennifer Holcomb*
*Port Angeles, WA*

# Nana's Famous Coconut-Pineapple Cake

*The "secret" ingredient in this fabulous family favorite: lemon-lime soda.*

15¼-oz. can crushed pineapple in juice, undrained and divided
1½ c. butter, softened
3 c. sugar
5 eggs
½ c. lemon-lime soda
3 c. cake flour, sifted
1 t. lemon extract
1 t. vanilla extract
6-oz. pkg. frozen sweetened flaked coconut, thawed

Drain pineapple, reserving ¾ cup juice. Remove ¼ cup reserved juice for Cream Cheese Frosting and reserve crushed pineapple for Pineapple Filling. Beat butter in a large bowl at medium speed with an electric mixer until creamy; gradually add sugar, beating well. Add eggs, one at a time, beating until blended after each addition. Combine ½ cup reserved pineapple juice and lemon-lime soda. Add flour to butter mixture alternately with juice mixture, beginning and ending with flour. Beat at low speed until blended after each addition. Stir in extracts. Pour batter into 3 greased and floured 9" round cake pans lined with parchment paper. Bake at 350 degrees for 25 to 30 minutes, until a toothpick inserted in center comes out clean. Remove from pans immediately; cool on wire racks one hour. Spread ¾ cup Pineapple Filling between cake layers; spread remaining filling on top of cake. Spread Cream Cheese Frosting on sides of cake. Sprinkle top and sides of cake with coconut. Serves 10 to 12.

## Pineapple Filling:
2 c. sugar
¼ c. cornstarch
1 c. water
1 c. reserved crushed pineapple, drained

Stir together sugar and cornstarch in a medium saucepan. Stir in water and pineapple; cook over low heat, stirring occasionally, for 15 minutes, or until mixture is thickened. Let cool completely.

## Cream Cheese Frosting:
½ c. butter, softened
3-oz. pkg. cream cheese, softened
16-oz. pkg. powdered sugar, sifted
¼ c. reserved pineapple juice
1 tsp. vanilla extract

Beat butter and cream cheese at medium speed with an electric mixer until creamy. Gradually add powdered sugar, juice and vanilla; mix well.

Nana's Famous Coconut-Pineapple Cake

## Strawberry Layer Cake

6-oz. pkg. strawberry gelatin mix
½ c. hot water
16¼-oz. pkg. white cake mix
1 c. strawberries, hulled and chopped
2 T. all-purpose flour
4 eggs
Garnish: fresh strawberries

Dissolve dry gelatin mix in hot water in a large bowl; cool. Add dry cake mix, strawberries and flour; mix well. Add eggs, one at a time, beating slightly after each addition. Pour batter into 3 greased and floured 8" round cake pans. Bake at 350 degrees for 20 minutes, or until toothpick inserted in center comes out clean. Let cool one hour. Spread Strawberry Frosting between layers and on top and sides of cake. Garnish with strawberries. Serves 12.

### Strawberry Frosting:

¼ c. butter, softened
3¾ to 5 c. powdered sugar
⅓ c. strawberries, hulled and finely chopped

Blend together butter and powdered sugar, adding sugar to desired consistency. Add strawberries; blend thoroughly.

*Steven Wilson*
*Chesterfield, VA*

# Italian Cream Cake

2 c. sugar
½ c. butter, softened
½ c. shortening
½ c. buttermilk
2 c. all-purpose flour
1 t. baking soda
½ t. salt
5 eggs, separated
1 c. chopped pecans
2 c. sweetened flaked coconut

Beat sugar, butter, shortening and buttermilk in a large bowl with an electric mixer at medium speed until blended; set aside. Combine flour, baking soda and salt in a separate bowl, stirring to mix. Gradually add flour mixture and egg yolks to butter mixture, beating until well blended. Stir in pecans and coconut; set aside. Beat egg whites with clean beaters in a medium bowl with an electric mixer at high speed until stiff peaks form. Fold egg whites into batter and pour into 2 greased and floured 8" round cake pans. Bake at 350 degrees for 40 to 45 minutes, until a toothpick inserted in center comes out clean. Cool in pans on wire racks 10 minutes. Remove from pans and cool on wire racks one hour, or until completely cool. Spread Cream Cheese-Pecan Frosting between layers and on top and sides of cake. Serves 8 to 10.

## Cream Cheese-Pecan Frosting:

8-oz. pkg. cream cheese, softened
½ c. butter
1 t. vanilla extract
1 lb. powdered sugar
1 c. chopped pecans

Beat cream cheese, butter and vanilla in a large bowl with an electric mixer at medium speed until creamy. Gradually add powdered sugar, beating until fluffy after each addition. Stir in pecans until blended.

*Kim Schooler*
*Norman, OK*

# Lazy Daisy Cake

*My grandma used to make this cake. She loved to cook, and this recipe brings back all those memories of being in her kitchen.*

1¼ c. boiling water
1 c. long-cooking oats, uncooked
½ c. margarine, softened
1 c. sugar
1 c. brown sugar, packed
1 t. vanilla extract
2 eggs, beaten
1½ c. all-purpose flour
1 t. baking soda
¾ t. cinnamon
½ t. salt
¼ t. nutmeg

Pour water over oats; cover and let stand 20 minutes. Beat margarine with an electric mixer at medium speed until creamy; gradually add sugars and beat until fluffy. Add vanilla and eggs. Add oat mixture; mix well. Sift together flour, baking soda, cinnamon, salt and nutmeg; add to margarine mixture. Mix well. Pour batter into a greased and floured 9"x9" baking pan. Bake at 350 degrees for 50 to 55 minutes, until a toothpick inserted in center comes out clean. Spread Frosting on hot cake; broil until frosting is bubbly. Serves 8 to 10.

## Frosting:

¼ c. margarine, melted
½ c. brown sugar, packed
3 T. half-and-half
¾ c. sweetened flaked coconut
⅓ c. chopped nuts

Combine all ingredients in a bowl; mix well.

*Jennifer Lemon*
*Lexington, OH*

Italian Cream Cake

Old-Fashioned
Applesauce Cake

## Old-Fashioned Applesauce Cake

*Applesauce makes the cake moist and tender.*

2 c. sugar
½ c. shortening
2 eggs
1½ c. applesauce
½ c. water
2½ c. all-purpose flour
1½ t. baking soda
1½ t. salt
¼ t. baking powder
¾ t. cinnamon
½ t. ground cloves
½ t. allspice
½ c. chopped walnuts
Garnish: powdered sugar, whipped cream, cinnamon

Beat sugar and shortening with an electric mixer at medium speed; beat in eggs, applesauce and water. Gradually add flour, baking soda, salt, baking powder and spices. Mix thoroughly; stir in nuts. Pour into a greased and floured 13"x9" baking pan. Bake at 350 degrees for one hour, or until a toothpick inserted in center comes out clean; watch that edges don't get too dark. Garnish with powdered sugar, whipped cream and cinnamon. Serves 8 to 10.

*Gail Hageman*
*Albion, ME*

### egg advice!

Eggs work best in baking recipes when they're brought to room temperature first. If time is short, just slip the eggs carefully into a bowl of lukewarm water and let stand for 15 minutes...they'll warm right up.

## LaRae's Pumpkin Dump Cake

*A wonderful treat...don't wait for the holidays to enjoy it!*

29-oz. can pumpkin
12-oz. can evaporated milk
4 eggs
1½ c. sugar
1 t. cinnamon
1 t. ground ginger
1 t. ground cloves
½ t. salt
18¼-oz. pkg. yellow cake mix
1 c. butter, melted

Mix together pumpkin, milk, eggs, sugar, spices and salt with a whisk. Spread in a greased 13"x9" baking pan. Sprinkle dry cake mix over top; drizzle melted butter over all. Bake at 325 degrees for 1½ hours. Serves 8 to 10.

*Jennifer Lambrigger*
*Huntington Beach, CA*

## Butterscotch Picnic Cake

½ c. butter, softened
1 c. brown sugar, packed
3 eggs, beaten
1 t. vanilla extract
2 c. all-purpose flour
1 t. baking soda
1 t. salt
1½ c. buttermilk
1 c. quick-cooking oats, uncooked
6-oz. pkg. butterscotch chips
⅓ c. chopped walnuts

Beat butter and brown sugar in a bowl with an electric mixer at medium speed until light and fluffy. Add eggs, one at a time, beating after each addition. Add vanilla. Whisk together flour, baking soda and salt; add to butter mixture alternately with buttermilk, blending well after each addition. Beat at low speed until blended. Stir in oats. Pour into a greased 13"x9" baking pan. Combine butterscotch chips and nuts; sprinkle over top. Bake at 350 degrees for 30 to 35 minutes. Cool completely in pan on a wire rack. Serves 15 to 18.

*Cindy Neel*
*Gooseberry Patch*

### brown sugar fix
If a plastic bag of brown sugar has hardened, try this: add a dampened paper towel to the bag, close it and microwave for 20 seconds. Press out the lumps with your fingers. If that doesn't do the trick, microwave for another 10 seconds.

## Comforting Southern Cake

*A slice of this scrumptious cake will make you feel much better!*

18¼-oz. pkg. yellow cake mix
3.4-oz. pkg. vanilla-flavored instant pudding mix
4 eggs
½ c. cold water
½ c. oil
½ c. peach-flavored bourbon or orange juice
1½ c. chopped nuts
Garnish: powdered sugar

Beat all ingredients except nuts and powdered sugar in a large bowl with an electric mixer at medium speed for 3 minutes. Stir in nuts; pour batter into a greased and floured Bundt® pan. Bake at 325 degrees for one hour, or until a toothpick inserted in center comes out clean. While cake is still hot, poke holes all over with a toothpick; slowly pour Glaze over cake. Let cake cool in pan. Invert onto serving platter; garnish with powdered sugar. Serves 10 to 12.

### Glaze:
¼ c. butter
2 T. water
½ c. sugar
¼ c. peach-flavored bourbon or orange juice

Melt butter in a small saucepan over medium heat. Stir in water and sugar; boil for 3 minutes, stirring constantly. Remove from heat; stir in bourbon or orange juice.

*Vivian Nikanow-Kaszuba*
*Chicago, IL*

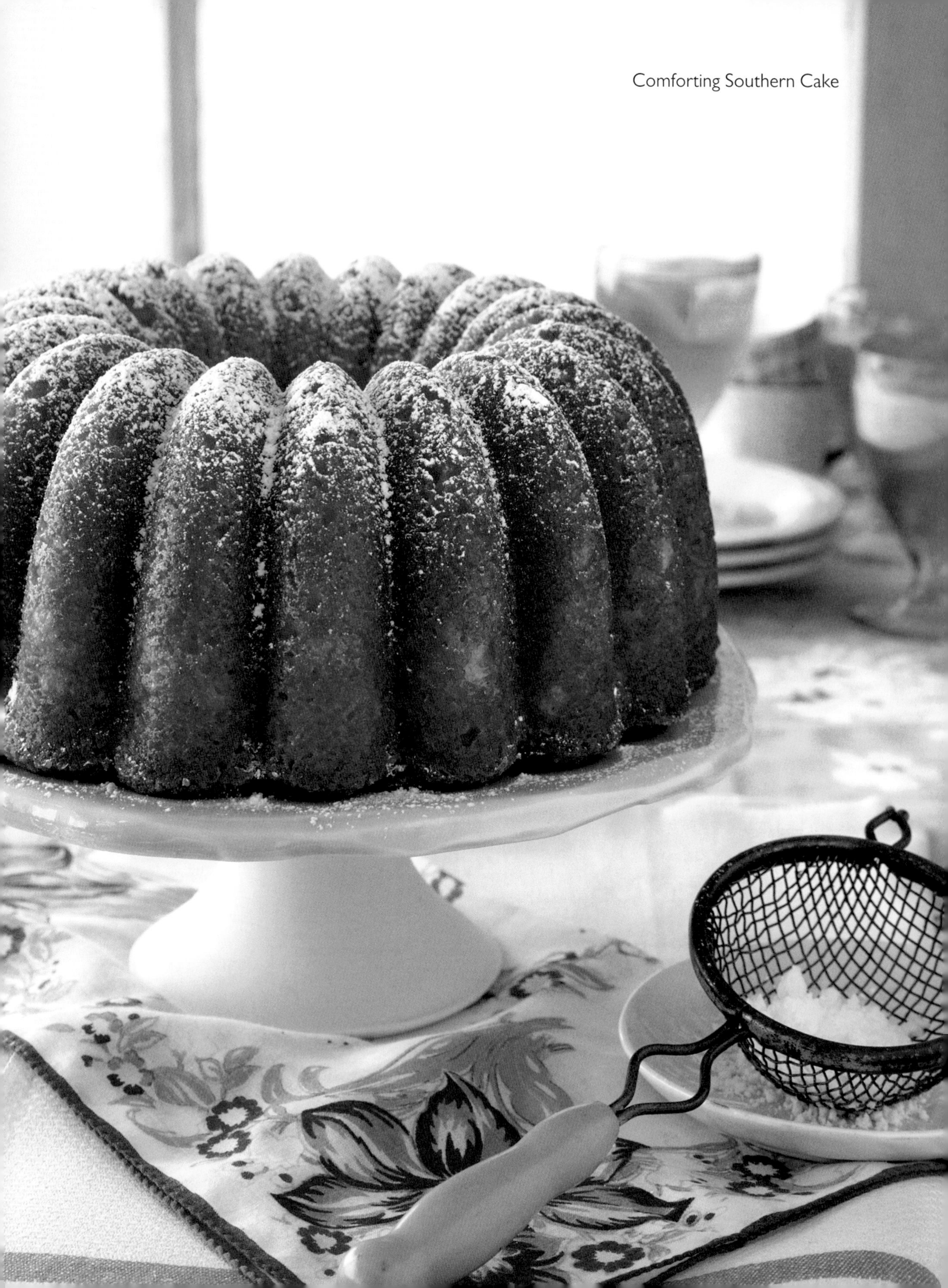
Comforting Southern Cake

Harvard Beet-
Spice Cake

## Harvard Beet-Spice Cake

15½-oz. jar Harvard beets
½ c. butter, softened
1¼ c. sugar
2 eggs
2¼ c. all-purpose flour
1 t. baking soda
2 t. apple pie spice
⅛ t. salt
1 c. chopped pecans
Garnish: powdered sugar

Place beets in a blender and process until puréed; set aside. Beat butter and sugar in a large bowl with an electric mixer at medium speed until light and fluffy. Add eggs, one at a time, beating just until blended after each addition. Sift together flour, baking soda, apple pie spice and salt in a separate bowl. Add flour mixture to butter mixture alternately with puréed beets, beginning and ending with flour mixture, beating at low speed just until blended after each addition. Fold in pecans. Pour batter into a greased and lightly floured 10-cup Bundt® pan. Bake at 350 degrees for 45 minutes, or until a toothpick inserted in center comes out clean. Cool in pan on a wire rack 30 minutes; remove from pan and cool completely on wire rack. Garnish with powdered sugar. Serves 8 to 10.

*Betty Wachowiak*
*Waukegan, IL*

# Homemade Gingerbread Cake

*Your entire home will smell delicious when you bake this cake. Don't skip the sauce...it's what takes this recipe over the top!*

2 c. all-purpose flour
2 t. ground ginger
1 t. cinnamon
1 t. nutmeg
1 t. baking powder
1 t. baking soda
½ t. salt
¼ t. ground cloves
½ c. butter, softened
½ c. sugar
1 c. molasses
1 c. buttermilk
1 egg, beaten
Garnish: whipped topping

Combine flour, ginger, cinnamon, nutmeg, baking powder, baking soda, salt and cloves in a large bowl. Beat butter and sugar in a separate large bowl with an electric mixer at medium speed until fluffy. Beat in molasses. Add flour mixture and buttermilk alternately to molasses mixture, beginning and ending with flour mixture. Beat at low speed after each addition until blended. Stir in egg. Spoon batter into a greased and floured 13"x9" baking pan. Bake at 350 degrees for 40 to 45 minutes, or until a toothpick inserted in center comes out clean. To serve, cut cake into squares; top with Warm Vanilla Sauce and garnish with whipped topping. Serves 12 to 15.

## Warm Vanilla Sauce:
1 c. brown sugar, packed
2 T. all-purpose flour
1 c. water
1 T. butter
½ t. vanilla extract
⅛ t. salt

Mix together sugar and flour in a saucepan. Add remaining ingredients; cook and stir over medium heat until thickened.

*Dee Ann Ice*
*Delaware, OH*

# Mix-in-a-Pan Nut Cake

*So simple to stir up…just right with a pot of coffee and a good friend.*

½ c. margarine
1¼ c. all-purpose flour
1 c. crushed pineapple with juice
1 c. sugar
1 c. chopped English walnuts
6-oz. jar strained carrot baby food
1 egg, beaten
2 t. cinnamon
1 t. baking soda
1 t. vanilla extract

Melt margarine in a 9"x9" baking pan. Gradually add remaining ingredients to pan; blend well. Bake at 325 degrees for 35 to 40 minutes. Serves 8 to 10.

*Phyllis Peters*
*Three Rivers, MI*

# Christmas Rainbow Cake

18¼-oz. pkg. moist white cake mix
3-oz. pkg. raspberry gelatin mix
2 c. boiling water, divided
3-oz. pkg. lime gelatin mix
12-oz. container frozen whipped topping, thawed

Prepare cake mix and bake in 2 greased 8" round cake pans, according to package directions. Cool in pans 10 minutes; remove from pans and cool completely on wire racks. Clean pans and return cake layers, top sides up, to pans; prick each layer with a fork every half-inch. Combine raspberry gelatin mix and one cup boiling water in a small bowl, stirring until gelatin dissolves; pour raspberry gelatin over one cake layer. Combine lime gelatin mix and remaining one cup boiling water in a separate small bowl, stirring until gelatin dissolves; pour lime gelatin over second cake layer. Chill layers 3 to 4 hours. Dip one cake pan into a pan of warm water to loosen cake; invert onto a plate and remove pan. Spread one cup whipped topping on top of layer. Dip second cake pan into warm water, invert on top of first layer and remove pan. Spread remaining topping on top and sides of cake. Serves 6 to 8.

*Karen Whitby*
*Charlotte, VT*

Christmas Rainbow Cake

# Candied Fruitcake

*My friend, Gerry, shared this recipe with me in the early 1960s. These fruitcakes are nearly all fruit and nuts with just enough batter to hold them together.*

3 7½-oz. pkgs. pitted dates, chopped
16-oz. pkg. candied pineapple, chopped
16-oz. pkg. whole candied cherries
2 c. all-purpose flour
2 t. baking powder
½ t. salt
4 eggs, beaten
1 c. sugar
2 16-oz. pkgs. pecan halves

Combine dates, pineapple and cherries in a large bowl. Stir together flour, baking powder and salt in a second bowl; pour onto fruit mixture. Mix well with hands; separate pieces so that all are well coated. Blend eggs in another bowl with a hand mixer until frothy; gradually blend in sugar. Add to fruit mixture; mix well with a large spoon. Add pecans; mix with hands until evenly distributed and coated with batter. Grease two 9" springform pans or two 9"x5" loaf pans; line with parchment paper cut to fit and then grease paper. Spread mixture in pans; press mixture down with hands; rearrange pieces of fruit and nuts as necessary to fill up any empty spaces. Bake at 275 degrees for 1¼ to 1½ hours; tops will look dry when done. Remove from oven; cool for 5 minutes on wire racks; turn out onto racks, carefully peel off paper and cool thoroughly. Store loosely wrapped. Makes 2 cakes.

*Marie Needham*
*Columbus, OH*

# Hot Milk Cake

*We serve this versatile cake often at our family restaurant. It's good either with chocolate frosting or as strawberry shortcake.*

4 eggs, beaten
2 c. sugar
2¼ c. all-purpose flour
2¼ t. baking powder
1 t. vanilla extract
1¼ c. milk
10 T. butter, sliced

Beat eggs and sugar together with an electric mixer at medium speed until fluffy; set aside. Combine flour and baking powder in a large bowl; add to egg mixture along with vanilla. Beat until smooth; set aside. Heat milk and butter in a saucepan over low heat until butter melts; stir into egg mixture. Pour into a greased 13"x9" baking pan; bake at 350 degrees for 30 to 35 minutes. Serves 8 to 10.

*Darlene Hartzler*
*Marshallville, OH*

## Caitlin's Famous Sour Cream Cake

*I share this recipe in memory of Caitlin Hammeran, the daughter of a dear friend. A wonderful young lady, she loved cooking. This was one of her favorite recipes.*

1 c. butter, softened
1¼ c. sugar
2 eggs, beaten
1 c. sour cream
1 t. vanilla extract
2 c. cake flour, sifted
1 t. baking powder
½ t. baking soda
Garnish: powdered sugar

Beat butter and sugar in a bowl with an electric mixer at medium speed. Add eggs, sour cream and vanilla. Add flour, baking powder and baking soda; mix well. Place half of batter into a greased tube pan. Sprinkle with Topping; add remaining batter. Bake at 375 degrees for 40 minutes, or until a toothpick inserted in center comes out clean. Cool in pan for one hour. Invert onto a serving platter; garnish with powdered sugar before serving. Serves 10 to 12.

### Topping:
½ c. chopped pecans or walnuts
½ t. cinnamon
2 T. sugar

Combine all ingredients in a small bowl.

*Wendy Lee Paffenroth*
*Pine Island, NY*

## Sunshine Angel Food Cake

6 eggs, separated
⅜ t. salt, divided
½ t. cream of tartar
1 t. vanilla extract
1½ c. sugar, divided
1¼ c. all-purpose flour, divided
¼ c. cold water
1 t. baking powder
½ t. lemon extract

Beat egg whites in a bowl with an electric mixer at medium speed until foamy. Add ¼ teaspoon salt, cream of tartar and vanilla; beat at high speed until stiff peaks form. Mix in ¾ cup sugar and ½ cup flour; pour batter into an ungreased 10" tube pan. Beat egg yolks in a separate large bowl until lemon colored. Add water, baking powder, lemon extract and remaining salt, sugar and flour; mix well. Carefully fold in yolk mixture. Bake at 350 degrees for 50 minutes to one hour, until toothpick inserted in center comes out clean. Run a knife around cake to loosen edges. Invert pan on wire rack and let cool one hour, until completely cool. Serves 10.

> *easy breakfast!*
> Toast slices of Eggnog Pound Cake for a perfect breakfast treat on holiday mornings. The kids will love it!

Eggnog Pound Cake

# Eggnog Pound Cake

1 c. butter, softened
3 c. sugar
6 eggs, beaten
3 c. all-purpose flour
1 c. eggnog
1 t. lemon extract
1 t. vanilla extract
1 t. coconut extract
1 c. sweetened flaked coconut
Optional: powdered sugar

Beat butter in a large bowl with an electric mixer at medium speed until creamy. Gradually add sugar, beating until fluffy after each addition.

Add eggs, one at a time, beating just until blended. Add flour to butter mixture alternately with eggnog, beginning and ending with flour, beating at low speed just until blended. Stir in extracts and coconut. Pour into a greased and floured 10" tube pan. Bake at 325 degrees for 1½ hours, or until a toothpick inserted in center comes out clean. Cool in pan on a wire rack 10 minutes; remove from pan and cool completely. Lightly sprinkle with powdered sugar, if desired. Serves 12 to 14.

*Nancy Cohrs*
*Donna, TX*

Peanut Butter
Pound Cake

# Peanut Butter Pound Cake

*Delicious without the frosting, too!*

1 c. butter, softened
2 c. sugar
1 c. brown sugar, packed
½ c. creamy peanut butter
5 eggs
1 T. vanilla extract
3 c. cake flour
½ t. baking powder
½ t. salt
¼ t. baking soda
1 c. whipping cream or whole milk

Beat butter and sugar in a bowl with an electric mixer at medium speed. Add brown sugar and peanut butter; mix well. Add eggs, one at a time, beating after each addition; stir in vanilla. Sift together dry ingredients and add alternately with whipping cream or milk. Pour into a lightly greased and floured 10" tube pan. Bake at 325 degrees for one hour, or until a toothpick inserted in center comes out clean. Drizzle with Peanut Butter Frosting, if desired. Serves 10 to 12.

## Peanut Butter Frosting:
16-oz. pkg. powdered sugar
⅓ c. creamy peanut butter
¼ c. butter, softened
5 to 6 T. milk
⅛ t. salt

Combine all ingredients and blend until smooth.

*Charlotte Wolfe*
*Fort Lauderdale, FL*

# Miss Lizzie's Pound Cake

*This recipe came from a neighbor of my grandfather's back in the 1950s. I've been making it for 45 years and topping it with my mom's Caramel Frosting. I think you'll love it as much as I do!*

1 c. butter, softened
½ c. shortening
3 c. sugar
¼ t. salt
6 eggs
1 c. milk
1 t. imitation vanilla butter and nut flavoring
3 c. all-purpose flour

Beat butter and shortening with an electric mixer at medium speed; gradually add sugar and salt. Add eggs, one at a time, beating well after each addition; set aside. Mix together milk and flavoring; add to butter mixture alternately with flour. Spread into a greased and floured 10" tube pan. Bake at 325 degrees for one hour, until a toothpick inserted in center comes out clean. Remove from pan; cool completely before frosting with Caramel Frosting. Serves 8 to 10.

## Caramel Frosting:

1½ c. brown sugar, packed
½ c. sugar
½ c. butter
5-oz. can evaporated milk
1 t. vanilla extract

Combine all ingredients except vanilla in a saucepan over medium heat. Cook for 15 minutes, stirring constantly. Remove from heat; stir in vanilla. Immediately spread over cooled cake.

*Jody Brandes*
*Hartfield, VA*

# Chocolate Pound Cake

12-oz. pkg. milk chocolate chips
½ c. butter, softened
2 c. sugar
4 eggs
2 t. vanilla extract
1 c. buttermilk
2 T. water
2½ c. all-purpose flour
½ t. salt
¼ t. baking soda
Garnish: whipped cream, cocoa

Melt chocolate in a saucepan over low heat; remove from heat and set aside. Beat butter and sugar in a large bowl with an electric mixer at medium speed until light and fluffy. Add eggs, one at a time, beating well after each addition. Blend in melted chocolate and vanilla. Mix together buttermilk and water; set aside. Combine flour, salt and baking soda; add to chocolate mixture alternately with buttermilk mixture. Pour batter into a greased and floured Bundt® pan. Bake at 325 degrees for one hour and 20 minutes, or until a toothpick inserted in center comes out clean. Cool for 10 minutes; remove from pan to wire rack. Let cool one hour. Garnish with whipped cream and sprinkle with cocoa. Serves 12 to 16.

*Sandy Groezinger*
*Stockton, IL*

Chocolate Pound Cake

Too-Easy Toffee Cheesecake

# Too-Easy Toffee Cheesecake

*This simple cheesecake is a snap to pull together, yet it tastes like you spent hours in the kitchen!*

2 8-oz. pkgs. cream cheese, softened
⅔ c. brown sugar, packed
1 t. vanilla extract
2 eggs
1 c. chocolate-covered toffee baking bits, divided
9-inch graham cracker crust
Garnish: whipped topping

Beat cream cheese, brown sugar and vanilla in a bowl with an electric mixer on medium speed until blended. Add eggs, one at a time, beating after each addition. Stir in ¾ cup toffee bits; pour mixture into crust. Bake at 350 degrees for 35 to 40 minutes, until center is set. Sprinkle with remaining toffee bits while cheesecake is still warm. Cool; cover and refrigerate at least 3 hours. Garnish with whipped topping. Serves 6 to 8.

*Andrea Heyart*
*Aubrey, TX*

# Rhubarb Cream Cheesecake

*This recipe is a hit wherever I take it!*

1 c. plus 1 T. all-purpose flour, divided
1¼ c. sugar, divided
½ c. margarine, softened
3 c. rhubarb, cut in ½-inch pieces
12-oz. pkg. cream cheese
2 eggs, beaten

Mix together one cup flour, ¼ cup sugar and margarine; press into a 10" pie plate. Set aside. Combine rhubarb, ½ cup sugar and one tablespoon flour. Toss lightly and pour into crust. Bake at 375 degrees for 15 minutes. Beat cream cheese, remaining sugar and eggs with an electric mixer at medium speed until fluffy; pour over hot rhubarb mixture. Reduce oven to 350 degrees and bake for 30 more minutes, or until set. Add Topping; cut into squares. Serves 6 to 8.

## Topping:

8-oz. container sour cream
2 T. sugar
1 t. vanilla extract

Beat all ingredients in a large bowl with an electric mixer at medium speed until blended.

*Jenifer Bowser*
*Worthington, PA*

# Chocolate-Cappuccino Cheesecake

*This makes an absolutely delicious gift…if you can bear to give it away!*

1½ c. pecans, finely chopped
1½ c. chocolate wafer cookies, crushed
⅓ c. butter, melted
½ c. semi-sweet chocolate chips, melted

Combine pecans, cookies and butter; press into bottom and up sides of a greased 9" springform pan. Drizzle with chocolate; chill until chocolate is firm. Pour Filling into crust; bake at 300 degrees for one hour and 10 minutes. Cool completely. Cover and chill 8 hours. Spread Topping over cake. Remove sides of pan. Serves 12.

## Filling:

2 8-oz. pkgs. cream cheese, softened
1½ c. semi-sweet chocolate chips, melted and cooled
1 c. brown sugar, packed
4 eggs, beaten
1 c. sour cream
⅓ c. cold coffee
2 t. vanilla extract

Combine all ingredients; blend until smooth.

## Topping:

⅔ c. whipping cream
¼ c. sugar
½ c. semi-sweet chocolate chips

Heat whipping cream and sugar in a saucepan over low heat, whisking constantly. Add chocolate chips, whisking until smooth.

*Sandy Stacy*
*Medway, OH*

Chocolate-Cappuccino Cheesecake

Oma's Lemon Cheesecake

# Oma's Lemon Cheesecake

1½ c. all-purpose flour
2¼ c. sugar, divided
½ c. butter, softened
4 eggs, divided
1 T. milk
2 t. vanilla extract, divided
1 t. baking powder
½ t. salt
2 8-oz. pkgs. cream cheese, softened
16-oz. container sour cream, divided
zest of 1 lemon, divided
Garnish: fresh lemon slices

    Combine flour, ⅔ cup sugar, butter, 2 eggs, milk, one teaspoon vanilla, baking powder and salt in a large bowl; mix well. Press evenly into bottom and partially up sides of a lightly greased 9" round springform pan. For filling, beat cream cheese and 1⅓ cups sugar with an electric mixer until smooth. Beat in remaining eggs, one at a time, beating slightly after each addition; stir in one cup sour cream, remaining vanilla and ⅔ of lemon zest. Pour cream cheese filling into crust; bake at 325 degrees for one hour. Turn off oven; leave pan in oven for 15 minutes. For topping, mix together remaining sour cream, ¼ cup sugar and zest until smooth. Spread sour cream topping over filling. Set oven temperature to 325 degrees. Bake at 325 degrees for 15 more minutes. Cool on wire rack for one hour. Cover and chill 8 hours. Serves 12.

*Cora Wilfinger*
*Manitowoc, WI*

# Mixed-Up Cupcakes

*Yes, you really do frost these cupcakes before baking!*

⅓ c. butter, softened
1 c. sugar
2 eggs, separated and divided
½ c. milk
1 t. vanilla extract
1⅔ c. all-purpose flour
2 t. baking powder
½ t. salt
½ c. light brown sugar, packed
2 T. baking cocoa
¼ c. chopped pecans

    Beat butter and sugar in a bowl with an electric mixer at medium speed until smooth. Beat one egg, one yolk, milk and vanilla into butter mixture; mix well. Sift together flour, baking powder and salt; stir into butter mixture until smooth. Fill paper-lined muffin cups ½ full; set aside. Beat remaining egg white in a separate bowl with an electric mixer at high speed until stiff peaks form. Add brown sugar and cocoa to egg white; beat until well blended. Spoon a generous teaspoonful over each cupcake; sprinkle with pecans. Bake at 350 degrees for 20 minutes. Serves 12 to 15.

*Janie Saey*
*Wentzville, MO*

# Black-Bottom Cupcakes

*Chocolate and cream cheese...what a scrumptious combination!*

2 8-oz. pkgs. cream cheese, softened
2 eggs, beaten
2⅔ c. sugar, divided
1¼ t. salt, divided
1½ c. semi-sweet chocolate chips
3 c. all-purpose flour
2 c. water
⅔ c. oil
½ c. baking cocoa
2 T. vinegar
2 t. baking soda
2 t. vanilla extract

Combine cream cheese, eggs, ⅔ cup sugar, ¼ teaspoon salt and chocolate chips; mix well and set aside. Combine remaining 2 cups sugar, remaining one teaspoon salt and remaining ingredients in a large bowl; fill 24 paper-lined muffin cups ¾ full with chocolate batter. Top each with ¼ cup cream cheese mixture. Bake at 350 degrees for 25 to 30 minutes. Makes 2 dozen.

*Gretchen Brown*
*Forest Grove, OR*

# Chocolate-Zucchini Cupcakes

2 c. zucchini, shredded
3 eggs, beaten
2 c. sugar
¾ c. oil
2 t. vanilla extract
2 c. all-purpose flour
⅔ c. baking cocoa
1 t. salt
1 t. baking soda
½ t. baking powder
¾ c. milk chocolate chips

Stir together zucchini, eggs, sugar, oil and vanilla in a large bowl. Add remaining ingredients except chips; stir in chocolate chips. Fill 24 paper-lined muffin cups ⅔ full. Bake at 325 degrees for 25 minutes, or until a toothpick inserted in center comes out clean. Cool in pans on wire racks for 5 minutes. Remove from pans; cool completely. Frost with Peanut Butter Frosting. Makes 2 dozen.

## Peanut Butter Frosting:
½ c. creamy peanut butter
⅓ c. butter, softened
1 T. milk
½ t. vanilla extract
1½ c. powdered sugar

Beat all ingredients except sugar in a large bowl with an electric mixer at medium speed until smooth. Gradually beat in powdered sugar. Stir in a little more milk, if necessary, to reach desired consistency.

*Michelle Rooney*
*Sunbury, OH*

*"This recipe makes chocolate cupcakes so moist and delicious...no one will guess the secret ingredient is zucchini!"*

*—Michelle*

Black-Bottom Cupcakes

Grandma's Banana
Cupcakes

# Grandma's Banana Cupcakes

*You can drizzle jarred caramel sauce over the tops to make these yummy cupcakes extra special.*

½ c. butter, softened
1¾ c. sugar
2 eggs
2 c. all-purpose flour
1 t. baking powder
1 t. baking soda
¼ t. salt
1 c. buttermilk
2 bananas, mashed
1 t. vanilla extract
Garnish: 24 toasted pecan halves, sliced banana

Beat butter and sugar in a large bowl with an electric mixer at medium speed until light and fluffy. Add eggs, one at a time, beating after each addition. Combine flour, baking powder, baking soda and salt; add to batter alternately with buttermilk, beginning and ending with flour mixture. Beat at low speed after each addition until blended. Stir in bananas and vanilla. Fill paper-lined muffin cups ½ full. Bake at 350 degrees for 18 to 25 minutes, until a toothpick inserted in center comes out clean. Remove to wire racks to cool completely; frost with Cream Cheese Frosting. Store frosted cupcakes in an airtight container in refrigerator. Garnish each cupcake with a pecan half and banana slice before serving. Makes 1½ to 2 dozen.

## Cream Cheese Frosting:
8-oz. pkg. cream cheese, softened
½ c. butter, softened
1 t. vanilla extract
⅛ t. salt
16-oz. pkg. powdered sugar

Beat cream cheese, butter, vanilla and salt in a large bowl with an electric mixer at medium speed until creamy. Gradually add powdered sugar, beating until fluffy.

*Kelly Marcum*
*Rock Falls, IL*

# Flowerpot Cupcakes

*My children love to share these with their classmates for a special birthday treat.*

18¼-oz. pkg. favorite-flavor cake mix
20 flat-bottomed ice cream cones
16-oz. container favorite-flavor frosting
20 lollipops, unwrapped
20 spearmint candy leaves

Prepare cake mix according to package directions. Fill ice cream cones ¾ full. Arrange on ungreased baking sheets. Bake at 350 degrees for 18 to 20 minutes. Cool and frost cupcakes. Insert a lollipop into the center of each cupcake. Slice candy leaves in half; press one to each side of the lollipop stick to look like a flower leaf. Makes 20 cupcakes.

*JoAnna Nicoline-Haughey*
*Berwyn, PA*

Mom's Chocolate Malt Shoppe Pie (page 289)

Estelle's Baked Custard (page 312)

Coconut Cream Pie (page 299)

Brenda's Fruit Cup (page 304)

# HOMESTYLE PIES & COBBLERS

*These tasty treats are comfort food at its finest*

Perfect Pecan Pie

## Perfect Pecan Pie

*For a quick variation, try walnut halves in place of pecans.*

3 eggs, beaten
½ c. sugar
¼ t. salt
3 T. butter, melted
1 c. dark corn syrup
1 t. vanilla extract
2 c. pecan halves
9-inch refrigerated pie crust
Optional: vanilla ice cream

Whisk together eggs and next 5 ingredients until thoroughly blended. Stir in pecans. Fit pie crust into a 9" pie plate. Fold edges under and crimp. Pour filling into pie crust. Bake at 350 degrees on lower rack of oven for 40 minutes, or until pie is set, covering edges with aluminum foil after 15 minutes. Cool completely on a wire rack. Serve with vanilla ice cream, if desired. Serves 6.

## Tried & True Pie Dough

*My mother always makes about 13 to 15 pies during the holidays. This is the best dough and so very easy to work with.*

3½ c. all-purpose flour
2 c. shortening
1 T. sugar
1 egg, beaten
½ c. cold water
1 T. vinegar

Beat flour, shortening and sugar in a large bowl with an electric mixer. Combine remaining ingredients in a separate bowl. Add egg mixture to flour mixture; blend well. Divide dough into 3 balls; roll each out on a lightly floured surface. Makes 3 pie crusts.

*Sadie Phelan*
*Connellsville, PA*

Pecan Cheesecake Pie

## Pecan Cheesecake Pie

9-inch refrigerated pie crust
8-oz. pkg. cream cheese, softened
4 eggs, divided
¾ c. sugar, divided
2 t. vanilla extract, divided
¼ t. salt
1¼ c. chopped pecans
1 c. light corn syrup

Fit pie crust into a 9" pie plate. Fold edges under and crimp. Beat cream cheese, one egg, ½ cup sugar, one teaspoon vanilla and salt with an electric mixer at medium speed until smooth. Pour cream cheese mixture into pie crust; sprinkle evenly with chopped pecans. Whisk together corn syrup, remaining 3 eggs, ¼ cup sugar and one teaspoon vanilla; pour mixture over pecans. Place pie on a baking sheet. Bake at 350 degrees on lowest oven rack 50 to 55 minutes, until pie is set. Cool on a wire rack one hour or until completely cool. Serve immediately or cover and chill up to 2 days. Serves 8.

## Walnut Crunch Pumpkin Pie

*This brings back special memories of evenings spent shelling nuts with my mother. What a good time we would have…the jokes and laughter flew faster than the nutshells!*

16-oz. can pumpkin
12-oz. can evaporated milk
2 eggs
¾ c. brown sugar, packed
1½ t. cinnamon
½ t. ground ginger
½ t. nutmeg
½ t. salt
9-inch pie crust
Garnish: frozen whipped topping, thawed

Beat pumpkin, milk, eggs, brown sugar, spices and salt in a large bowl with an electric mixer at medium speed until well mixed. Fit crust into pie plate; pour pumpkin mixture into crust. Bake at 400 degrees for 40 minutes, or until a knife inserted one inch from edge comes out clean. Cool; sprinkle Walnut Topping evenly over pie. Turn on broiler. Place pie 5 to 7 inches below broiler and broil about 3 minutes, until topping is golden and sugar dissolved. Cool on wire rack; garnish with whipped topping. Serves 10.

### Walnut Topping:
1 c. chopped walnuts
¾ c. brown sugar, packed
4 T. butter, melted

Combine all ingredients in a small bowl; mix well.

*Judy Voster*
*Neenah, WI*

## Amish Sugar Cream Pie

*This is the best-tasting sugar cream pie I have ever had! A great change from the traditional pumpkin at Thanksgiving.*

2½ c. half-and-half
¾ c. sugar
½ t. salt
¼ c. brown sugar, packed
¼ c. cornstarch
½ c. butter, sliced
1 t. vanilla extract
10-inch pie crust, baked
cinnamon to taste

Mix half-and-half, sugar and salt in a saucepan over medium heat. Bring mixture just to a boil, until frothy. Stir occasionally. Combine brown sugar and cornstarch in another saucepan, whisking until smooth. Gradually whisk in hot half-and-half mixture until smooth. Add butter and return to heat. Cook, whisking constantly, until thick and mixture bubbles up in center. Add vanilla; stir. Pour into crust and sprinkle with cinnamon. Bake at 325 degrees for 20 minutes, or until pie is golden on top. Filling will be soft when removed from oven but will firm up as pie cools. Cool completely. Serves 10 to 12.

*Debra Manley*
*Bowling Green, OH*

# Sweet Potato Pie

¼ c. butter, softened
⅓ c. honey
⅛ t. salt
2 c. sweet potatoes, cooked and mashed
3 eggs, beaten
½ c. milk
1 t. vanilla extract
½ t. cinnamon
½ t. nutmeg
½ t. ground ginger
9-inch pie crust
Optional: 1 c. pecan halves

Beat butter, honey and salt in a large bowl with an electric mixer at medium speed until creamy. Combine sweet potatoes, eggs, milk, vanilla, cinnamon, nutmeg and ginger in a separate bowl, stirring well; add sweet potato mixture to butter mixture, stirring well. Pour into unbaked pie crust; top with pecan halves, if desired. Bake at 375 degrees for 50 to 55 minutes, until center is set. Cool completely on a wire rack. Store in refrigerator. Serves 8.

*Barb Kietzer*
*Niles, MI*

Sweet Potato Pie

## Grandma's Custard Pie

*This is a recipe that my grandma made on the farm and handed down to my mom and me. We love this pie...Grandma still does, too! If you wish, you can use two 8-inch pie crusts to make two shallower pies.*

4 eggs, beaten
½ c. sugar
1 t. vanilla extract
¼ t. salt
2½ c. milk
9-inch deep-dish pie crust
nutmeg to taste

Whisk eggs, sugar, vanilla and salt together in a bowl; beat well and set aside. Heat milk in a medium saucepan over medium-low heat just until bubbles form around the edge. Stir in egg mixture; pour into crust. Sprinkle nutmeg on top. Bake at 475 degrees for 5 minutes. Reduce heat to 425 degrees and bake for 15 to 20 more minutes, until top is golden. Let cool before slicing. Serves 6 to 8.

*Teena Hippensteel*
*Fort Wayne, IN*

## Chocolate Chess Pie

½ c. butter
1½ 1-oz. sqs. unsweetened baking chocolate, chopped
1 c. brown sugar, packed
½ c. sugar
2 eggs, beaten
1 T. milk
1 t. all-purpose flour
1 t. vanilla extract
9-inch refrigerated pie crust
Garnish: whipped cream, chocolate shavings

Melt butter and chocolate in a small saucepan over low heat; set aside. Combine sugars, eggs, milk, flour and vanilla in a medium bowl. Gradually add chocolate mixture, beating constantly. Fit pie crust into 9" pie plate according to package directions. Pour into pie crust; bake at 325 degrees for 40 to 45 minutes. Let cool before serving. Garnish with whipped cream and chocolate shavings. Serves 6 to 8.

*Heidi Jo McManaman*
*Grand Rapids, MI*

## Satin Slipper Pie

*What a cute name...and a yummy pie!*

20 marshmallows
½ c. milk
6 1.55-oz. milk chocolate candy bars
1 c. whipping cream
9-inch pie crust, baked
Garnish: toasted almonds

Combine marshmallows, milk and chocolate in a saucepan; heat until melted. Set aside to cool. Beat cream with an electric mixer at high speed until stiff peaks form; fold into chocolate mixture. Pour into pie crust; chill until firm. Garnish with toasted almonds. Serves 6 to 8.

*Pat Habiger*
*Spearville, KS*

Chocolate Chess Pie

Mom's Chocolate
Malt Shoppe Pie

# Mom's Chocolate Malt Shoppe Pie

*We're a family of chocoholics and also love chocolate malts, so my mom created this pie that combines our two favorite things.*

1-oz. pkg. sugar-free white chocolate instant
    pudding mix
4 to 5 t. chocolate malt powder
1 c. milk
8-oz. container frozen whipped topping, thawed
1½ c. malted milk balls, crushed and divided
9-inch chocolate cookie crust

Mix together pudding, malt powder and milk. Fold in ¾ of whipped topping and 1¼ cups crushed candy; spread in crust. Spread with remaining topping. Sprinkle with remaining candy; chill until set. Serves 8.

*Nancy Brush*
*Robinson, IL*

# Chocolate Buttermilk Pie

*My dad loved buttermilk…his favorite treat was leftover cornbread or crackers crumbled in a tall glass of buttermilk. Every time I see this pie recipe, I think of how much he would have loved a slice of it.*

1½ c. semi-sweet chocolate chips
1½ c. sugar
¼ c. all-purpose flour
½ t. salt
6 eggs, beaten
1 c. buttermilk
1½ T. vanilla extract
9-inch deep-dish pie crust
Garnish: whipped topping

Melt chocolate chips in a double boiler over low heat, stirring constantly; set aside. Mix together sugar, flour and salt in a medium bowl; set aside. Combine eggs, buttermilk and vanilla in a large bowl; add sugar mixture and whisk vigorously. Stir in melted chocolate with a rubber spatula. Pour all except one cup into pie crust; discard remaining batter. Bake at 325 degrees for one hour and 15 minutes to one hour and 25 minutes, until pie is crisp on top and a knife tip is inserted in center comes out with just a bit of moist chocolate on it. Remove from oven and cool completely; let stand for one hour before serving. Refrigerate if not serving immediately. Garnish with a dollop of whipped topping. Serves 8 to 10.

*Amy Hunt*
*Traphill, NC*

# Country Harvest Pie

*This pie looks and tastes amazing. The cranberries give it color and complement the sweet mellowness of the apples and pears. Everyone loves it!*

2  9-inch pie crusts
3 McIntosh apples, peeled, cored and thickly sliced
3 Bartlett pears, peeled, cored and sliced
¾ c. fresh cranberries
¾ c. sugar
3 T. all-purpose flour
¼ t. cinnamon
1 T. milk
2 t. butter, sliced
Optional: whipped cream or vanilla ice cream

Place one pie crust in a 9" pie plate; set aside. Combine apples, pears, cranberries and sugar in a large bowl; set aside. Mix together flour and cinnamon in a small bowl; combine with fruit mixture. Sprinkle milk over fruit mixture; stir well. Spoon into pie crust; dot with butter. Add top crust; crimp edges and cut several vents. Bake at 425 degrees for 15 minutes. Reduce oven to 350 degrees and bake for 35 to 45 more minutes, until apples are tender. Serve with whipped cream or ice cream, if desired. Serves 6 to 8.

*Janis Parr*
*Ontario, Canada*

---

### sweet offering!
For an oh-so pretty gift, top pies with an inverted pie plate and secure both together with a bandana.

---

# Cinnamon-Glazed Apple Pie

*This is one of those "must-haves" when the ladies at our church bring dessert to the men's chili cook-off in the fall.*

9-inch pie crust
1½ c. sour cream
14-oz. can sweetened condensed milk
¼ c. frozen apple juice concentrate, thawed
1 egg, beaten
1½ t. vanilla extract
¼ t. cinnamon
3 Granny Smith apples, peeled, cored and thinly sliced
2 T. butter

Place crust in a pie plate and bake at 375 degrees for 15 minutes. Blend together sour cream, sweetened condensed milk, apple juice, egg, vanilla and cinnamon until smooth. Pour into baked pie crust. Bake at 375 degrees for 30 minutes, or until center is set; cool. Cook apples in butter in a skillet over medium heat until apples are tender but still hold their shape. Arrange apples over pie filling; drizzle with Cinnamon Glaze. Serve warm or chilled. Store leftovers covered in refrigerator. Serves 8.

## Cinnamon Glaze:
¼ c. frozen apple juice concentrate, thawed
1 t. cornstarch
¼ t. cinnamon

Combine ingredients in a saucepan over low heat; blend well. Cook and stir until mixture is thickened.

*Elizabeth Blackstone*
*Racine, WI*

Sour Cream-Apple Pie

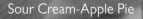

## Sour Cream-Apple Pie

9-inch refrigerated pie crust
2 c. Rome apples, peeled, cored and chopped
1 c. sugar, divided
⅓ c. plus 2 T. all-purpose flour, divided
¼ t. salt
1 c. sour cream
1 egg, beaten
1½ t. vanilla extract
1 T. cinnamon
2 T. butter

Place crust in a 9" pie plate; arrange apples in bottom of pie crust. Combine ⅔ cup sugar, 2 tablespoons flour and salt in a large bowl; stir to mix. Add sour cream, egg and vanilla; beat with an electric mixer at medium speed until smooth. Pour mixture over apples. Bake at 425 degrees for 15 minutes; reduce heat to 350 degrees and bake 30 more minutes. Combine cinnamon, butter, remaining flour and remaining sugar in a small bowl; sprinkle on top of pie. Increase heat to 400 degrees and bake 10 more minutes. Serves 8.

*Lois Vardaro*
*East Northport, NY*

Caramel-Banana Pie

## Pear Pie

4 pears, peeled, cored and thinly sliced
3 T. frozen orange juice concentrate, thawed
9-inch pie crust
¾ c. all-purpose flour
½ c. sugar
⅓ c. butter
2 t. cinnamon, divided
⅛ t. salt

Combine pears and orange juice in a large bowl and toss well; spoon pear mixture onto bottom of unbaked pie crust. Combine flour, sugar, butter, one teaspoon cinnamon and salt in a medium bowl. Mix until crumbly; sprinkle flour mixture over pear mixture. Sprinkle with remaining cinnamon. Bake at 400 degrees for 40 minutes, or until golden. Serves 8.

*Shirley Heinlein*
*Upper Arlington, OH*

## Caramel-Banana Pie

14-oz. can sweetened condensed milk
2 to 3 bananas, sliced
9-inch graham cracker pie crust
1 c. whipping cream
¼ c. powdered sugar
2 chocolate-covered toffee candy bars, chopped

Pour condensed milk into an 8" pie plate; cover with aluminum foil. Place covered pie plate in a shallow 2-quart casserole dish; pour hot water (110 to 115 degrees) to a depth of ¼-inch into casserole dish. Bake at 425 degrees for one hour and 20 minutes, or until milk is thick and caramel colored, adding more water to casserole dish if needed. Carefully remove casserole dish from oven; remove pie plate from casserole dish, uncover and set aside. Place bananas on bottom of graham cracker crust; pour caramelized milk over bananas. Cool 30 minutes. Beat cream in a medium bowl with an electric mixer at high speed until foamy; gradually add powdered sugar, continuing to beat until stiff peaks form. Spread whipped cream mixture over caramel layer. Chill at least 3 hours or overnight. Sprinkle with candy before serving. Serves 8.

*Dorthey Burgess*
*Mecosta, MI*

*consider having a pie night!*
Invite family and friends to bring their favorite pie to share. And don't forget copies of the recipes…someone's sure to ask!

People-Pleasin'
Peach Pie

## People-Pleasin' Peach Pie

2  9-inch pie crusts
8 c. peaches, peeled, pitted and sliced
2 t. lemon juice
1 t. vanilla extract
1 c. sugar
6 T. cornstarch
1 t. cinnamon
¼ t. nutmeg
¼ t. salt
4 T. butter, sliced
1 to 2 T. milk
Garnish: whipped cream

Line a 9" pie plate with one crust and set aside. Combine peaches, lemon juice and vanilla in a large bowl. Mix sugar, cornstarch, spices and salt in a separate bowl. Add sugar mixture to peach mixture; toss gently to coat. Spoon into pie crust; dot with butter. With a small cookie cutter, cut vents in remaining crust, reserving cut-outs. Place crust on top of pie; trim and seal edges. Brush milk over top crust and cut-outs; arrange cut-outs on crust. Cover edges loosely with aluminum foil. Bake at 400 degrees for 40 minutes. Remove foil and bake 10 to 15 more minutes, until crust is golden and filling is bubbly. Garnish with whipped cream. Serves 6 to 8.

*Kay Marone*
*Des Moines, IA*

# Green Tomato Pie

*You'll be surprised how much the tomatoes in this pie taste like apples.*

4 c. green tomatoes, peeled and sliced
1 T. lemon juice
1½ c. sugar
3 T. all-purpose flour
1 t. cinnamon
⅛ t. salt
2 9-inch pie crusts

Place tomatoes in a colander to drain; toss with lemon juice. Whisk together sugar, flour, cinnamon and salt; sprinkle over tomatoes and toss to coat. Place one crust in a 9" pie plate; spoon in filling. Top with remaining crust; flute edges and vent as desired. Bake at 450 degrees for 15 minutes; reduce oven temperature to 350 degrees and bake 45 more minutes or one hour. Serves 6 to 8.

*Abigail Bunce*
*Drain, OR*

Green Tomato Pie

# Heavenly Key Lime Pie

*This refreshing pie is wonderful. It's simple to make, and its sweet-tart flavor is always welcome after a hearty meal.*

14-oz. can sweetened condensed milk
3 egg yolks
2 t. Key lime zest
½ t. Key lime juice
9-inch graham cracker crust
1 c. whipping cream
2 T. powdered sugar
Garnish: Key lime slices

Whisk together condensed milk, egg yolks, lime zest and lime juice in a bowl until well blended. Pour into crust. Bake at 350 degrees for 15 minutes, or until set. Cool completely, about one hour; cover and chill one hour before serving. Beat cream with an electric mixer on high speed for 2 to 3 minutes, until soft peaks form. Gradually beat in powdered sugar. Garnish pie with whipped cream and slices of lime. Serves 6 to 8.

*Tina Goodpasture*
*Meadowview, VA*

# Hot Lemon Pie

*Being retired and spending our winters in Tucson, Arizona, we find ourselves with an overabundance of lemons. My husband loves this pie, and I love how easy it is to make!*

1 large lemon, unpeeled, cut into chunks
   and seeds removed
½ c. sugar
4 eggs
½ c. margarine, sliced
1 t. vanilla extract
9-inch pie crust
Garnish: whipped topping

Combine all ingredients except crust and topping in a blender. Blend until mixture is foamy but smooth. Pour into unbaked crust. Bake at 350 degrees for 40 minutes, or until filling is set. Serve warm or chilled. Garnish with whipped topping. Serves 6 to 8.

*Sharon Ostrem*
*Ankeny, IA*

Heavenly Key Lime Pie

Coconut Cream Pie

# Coconut Cream Pie

*I have such fond memories of when my dad's family would all get together to eat at a local restaurant. Their coconut cream pie was one of my favorites! This is my own version.*

2 c. milk
⅔ c. sugar
¼ c. cornstarch
¼ t. salt
3 egg yolks, beaten
1½ c. sweetened flaked coconut, divided
2 T. butter, softened
½ t. vanilla extract
9-inch pie crust, baked

Combine milk, sugar, cornstarch and salt in a large saucepan; cook over medium heat until thickened, stirring constantly. Remove from heat. Place egg yolks in a small bowl. Stir a small amount of hot milk mixture into egg yolks. Pour yolk mixture back into saucepan; simmer gently for 2 minutes. Stir in coconut, butter and vanilla. Pour into crust. Spread Meringue over hot pie filling; seal to edges. Bake at 350 degrees for 12 minutes, or until golden brown. Serves 8.

## Meringue:
4 egg whites
7-oz. jar marshmallow creme

Beat egg whites in a bowl with an electric mixer at high speed until stiff peaks form. Add marshmallow creme; beat for 2 minutes, or until well blended.

*Lauren Williams*
*Kewanee, MO*

# Chocolate Cobbler

*This is a treasured family recipe that has been passed down for many years…a rich, scrumptious treat for chocolate lovers!*

¾ c. margarine, melted
1½ c. self-rising flour
2½ c. sugar, divided
½ c. plus 1 T. baking cocoa, divided
¾ c. milk
1 t. vanilla extract
2¼ c. boiling water

Spread margarine in a 13"x9" glass baking pan; set aside. Combine flour, one cup sugar, 3 tablespoons cocoa, milk and vanilla; pour into pan. Mix together remaining sugar and cocoa; sprinkle over top. Pour boiling water over top; do not stir. Bake at 350 degrees for 40 to 45 minutes. Serves 12 to 14.

*Christy Bonner*
*Berry, AL*

Sweet Apple Tarts

## Sweet Apple Tarts

1 sheet frozen puff pastry, thawed
½ c. apricot jam
3 to 4 Granny Smith apples, peeled, cored and
  very thinly sliced
⅓ c. brown sugar, packed
½ t. cinnamon
½ c. pistachio nuts, chopped
Optional: vanilla ice cream

Roll pastry into a 12-inch square on a lightly floured surface. Cut pastry into nine 3-inch squares. Arrange squares on an ungreased baking sheet; pierce with a fork. Spoon jam evenly over each square; arrange apple slices over jam. Combine brown sugar and cinnamon in a small bowl; mix well. Sprinkle over apple slices. Bake at 400 degrees for 20 to 25 minutes, until pastry is golden and apples are crisp-tender. Sprinkle with nuts. Serve warm topped with scoops of ice cream, if desired. Serves 9.

*Jill Ball*
*Highland, UT*

---

*dress it up*
Sweet Apple Tarts is a delicious can't-fail recipe that's perfect for any occasion! To add flair, cut the pastry squares with a fluted pastry wheel for a pretty finish.

---

Easy Cherry Cobbler

## Easy Cherry Cobbler

*If they're available, use fresh-from-the-farm cherries for a special treat. Don't forget to pit them!*

15-oz. can tart red cherries
1 c. all-purpose flour
1¼ c. sugar, divided
1 c. milk
2 t. baking powder
⅛ t. salt
½ c. butter, melted
Optional: vanilla ice cream or whipped cream

Bring cherries with juice to a boil in a saucepan over medium heat; remove from heat. Mix flour, one cup sugar, milk, baking powder and salt in a medium bowl. Pour butter into 6 one-cup ramekins or into a 2-quart casserole dish; pour flour mixture over butter. Add cherries; do not stir. Sprinkle remaining sugar over top. Bake at 400 degrees for 20 to 30 minutes. Serve warm with ice cream or whipped cream, if desired. Serves 4 to 6.

*Melonie Klosterhoff*
*Fairbanks, AK*

## Buttermilk Pear Cobbler

*This recipe was inspired by my Grandmother Doris. She likely made a similar dessert on the farm in upstate New York when she was raising her children. It is a country cobbler topped with a lightly sweetened, soft buttermilk biscuit. Absolute comfort food!*

3 lbs. Anjou or Bosc pears, peeled, cored and
   sliced
⅓ c. brown sugar, packed
1 T. all-purpose flour
1 T. lemon juice
1 t. cinnamon
¼ t. nutmeg
¼ t. mace

Combine all ingredients in a large bowl; toss gently to coat pears. Spoon pear mixture into an 8"x8" baking pan coated with non-stick vegetable spray. Drop Biscuit Topping by heaping tablespoonfuls onto pear mixture. Bake at 350 degrees for 45 minutes, or until lightly golden and bubbly. Serves 8.

### Biscuit Topping:
1 c. all-purpose flour
1 T. baking powder
3 T. buttermilk
2 T. sugar
½ c. chilled butter
¾ c. milk

Mix together flour, baking powder, buttermilk and sugar in a bowl. Cut in butter with a pastry blender or fork until crumbly; add milk and mix well.

*Trysha Mapley*
*Palmer, AK*

## Apple-Gingerbread Cobbler

14½-oz. pkg. gingerbread cake mix, divided
¾ c. water
¼ c. brown sugar, packed
½ c. butter, divided
½ c. chopped pecans
2 21-oz. cans apple pie filling

Combine 2 cups gingerbread mix and water in a medium bowl; stir until smooth. Combine remaining gingerbread mix and brown sugar in a separate bowl, stirring to mix; cut in ¼ cup butter with a pastry blender or fork until mixture is crumbly. Stir in pecans; set aside. Combine pie filling and remaining butter in a large saucepan; cook over medium heat for 5 minutes, or until thoroughly heated, stirring often. Spoon apple mixture evenly into a lightly greased 11"x 7" baking pan. Spoon gingerbread mixture over apple mixture; sprinkle with pecan mixture. Bake at 375 degrees for 30 to 35 minutes, until center is set. Serves 8.

*Wendy Jacobs*
*Idaho Falls, ID*

### on hand à la mode!
Scoops of ice cream are perfect alongside warm apple dumplings, cobblers and pies. To make them ahead of time, simply scoop servings, arrange on a baking sheet and pop into the freezer. When frozen, store scoops in a freezer bag and then remove as many as needed at dessert time.

Apple-Gingerbread
Cobbler

## Brenda's Fruit Crisp

5 c. frozen peaches, apples or berries,
  thawed and juices reserved
2 to 4 T. sugar
½ c. long-cooking oats, uncooked
½ c. brown sugar, packed
¼ c. all-purpose flour
¼ t. nutmeg
¼ t. cinnamon
¼ t. vanilla extract
Optional: ¼ c. sweetened flaked coconut
¼ c. butter, diced
Optional: vanilla ice cream

Place fruit and juices in an ungreased 2-quart casserole dish; stir in sugar and set aside. Mix oats, brown sugar, flour, nutmeg, cinnamon and vanilla in a medium bowl. Stir in coconut, if desired. Add butter to oat mixture with a pastry blender or fork until mixture is crumbly. Sprinkle over fruit. Bake at 375 degrees for 30 to 35 minutes, until topping is golden and fruit is tender. Serve warm topped with ice cream, if desired. Serves 6.

Brenda's Fruit Crisp

## Graham Cracker Apple Crisp

*This dessert was a sweet tradition at our family's holiday dinners as well as at other times of the year. It's a little different, because it uses graham crackers in the topping instead of oats. It is the only kind of apple crisp Mom ever made for us...Grandma made it too.*

8 Granny Smith apples, peeled, cored and sliced
½ c. water
1¼ c. sugar, divided
1 c. graham cracker crumbs
½ c. all-purpose flour
1 t. cinnamon
⅛ t. salt
½ c. butter, melted

Arrange apple slices in a buttered 11"x7" baking pan. Use more or less apples depending on their size; pan should be nearly full to top but not heaping. Mix water and ½ cup sugar together; sprinkle over apples. Mix remaining ¾ cup sugar, graham cracker crumbs, flour, cinnamon and salt and sprinkle over apples. Drizzle melted butter evenly over topping. Bake at 450 degrees for 10 minutes; lower heat to 350 degrees and bake for 40 more minutes. Serves 8 to 10.

*Evie Prevo*
*Livermore, CA*

## Yummy Peach Dessert

*A tried & true sweet favorite that everyone loves.*

½ c. all-purpose flour
½ t. baking soda
½ t. salt
1 c. sugar
1 egg, beaten
16-oz. can sliced peaches, drained and chopped
½ c. brown sugar, packed
¼ c. chopped walnuts
Garnish: whipped cream

Sift together flour, baking soda and salt into a large bowl; add sugar. Stir in egg and peaches. Spread in a lightly greased 9"x9" baking dish. Sprinkle with brown sugar and walnuts. Bake at 350 degrees for one hour. Serve warm; garnish with whipped cream. Serves 12 to 14.

*Nina Roberts*
*Queensland, Australia*

Cherries Jubilee Crisp

# Cherries Jubilee Crisp

*I like to treat my family to a warm homemade dessert on weekends. This recipe makes just a few portions, so it's sized right for small families.*

16½-oz. can sweet cherries
2 T. orange liqueur or orange juice
2½ t. cornstarch
¼ c. quick-cooking oats, uncooked
6 T. all-purpose flour
¼ c. brown sugar, packed
¼ t. nutmeg
¼ c. cold butter, diced
Garnish: whipped cream, nutmeg

Combine undrained cherries, liqueur or juice and cornstarch in a saucepan. Cook and stir over medium heat about 2 minutes, until cornstarch dissolves and mixture is thickened. Pour into a lightly greased one-quart casserole dish; let cool for 10 minutes. Stir together oats, flour, brown sugar and nutmeg in a small bowl. Add butter; mix with a pastry blender or fork until crumbly. Sprinkle oat mixture over cherry mixture. Bake, uncovered, at 375 degrees for about 20 minutes, until topping is golden. Serve warm; garnish with whipped cream and a sprinkle of nutmeg. Serves 4.

*Jill Valentine*
*Jackson, TN*

# Mulberry Buckle

2 c. all-purpose flour
2½ t. baking powder
¼ t. salt
½ c. butter, softened
¾ c. sugar
1 egg, beaten
½ c. milk
2 c. mulberries

Stir together flour, baking powder and salt in a medium bowl; set aside. Beat butter and sugar in a bowl with an electric mixer at medium speed until light and fluffy. Add egg and beat well. Add flour mixture and milk alternately to egg mixture, beginning and ending with flour mixture. Beat at low speed after each addition until blended. Pour into a greased 9"x9" baking pan; top with mulberries and Crumb Topping. Bake at 350 degrees for 50 minutes to one hour, until golden. Serve warm. Serves 9.

## Crumb Topping:
½ c. all-purpose flour
½ c. sugar
½ t. cinnamon
¼ c. butter

Sift together flour, sugar and cinnamon. Cut in butter with a pastry blender or fork until crumbly.

*Mary Murray*
*Mount Vernon, OH*

## Blackberry Crumble

⅔ c. butter, softened
1½ c. quick-cooking oats, uncooked
1⅓ c. all-purpose flour
1 c. brown sugar, packed
½ t. baking soda
1 qt. blackberries
¾ c. sugar
3 T. cornstarch
⅛ t. salt
Optional: vanilla ice cream or whipped cream

Mix together butter, oats, flour, brown sugar and baking soda in a medium bowl with a pastry blender or fork until pea-sized crumbles form; set aside. Combine blackberries, sugar, cornstarch and salt in a large heavy saucepan. Gently mash some berries, leaving about half of them whole. Bring to a boil over medium-high heat, stirring constantly. Reduce heat to medium; cook until mixture thickens. Pour into a lightly greased 13"x9" glass baking pan; crumble topping over berries. Bake at 350 degrees for 30 minutes, or until lightly golden. Serve with ice cream or whipped cream, if desired. Serves 8 to 10.

*Marki Nordick*
*Meridian, ID*

"*My cousins and I used to pick blackberries in Grandma's backyard so she would bake us a crumble. The biggest, juiciest berries were always out of reach, so we had to climb on top of the old shed to get them. They were worth the work and the scratches from thorns!*"

—*Marki*

## Cherry-Pecan Bread Pudding

2-lb. loaf French bread, cubed
4 c. milk
2 c. half-and-half
¾ c. plus 2 T. sugar, divided
6 eggs, beaten
2 t. vanilla extract
½ t. cinnamon
½ c. dried tart cherries
½ c. chopped pecans
½ c. butter, melted

Spread bread cubes on a baking sheet; let dry overnight. Combine milk, half-and-half and 7 tablespoons sugar in a saucepan over low heat. Heat to 120 degrees on a candy thermometer; remove from heat. Whisk together eggs, vanilla, cinnamon and remaining sugar in a large bowl. Stir in cherries and pecans. Slowly whisk half of milk mixture into egg mixture; add remaining milk mixture. Stir in bread cubes; toss to mix and let stand for 5 minutes. Mix in butter; transfer mixture to a lightly greased 13"x9" baking pan. Bake at 350 degrees for 35 minutes, or until center is firm. Serve warm. Serves 8 to 10.

Cherry-Pecan
Bread Pudding

Chocolate
Bread Pudding

## Old-Fashioned Bread Pudding

*When the weather is cold outside, nothing brings the family in faster than the aroma of bread pudding baking in the oven.*

10 slices white bread, cubed
1/4 c. butter, melted
1/2 c. raisins
1 t. cinnamon
3/4 c. sugar
6 eggs, beaten
2 t. vanilla extract
1/2 t. salt
3 c. milk
1/8 t. nutmeg
Garnish: whipped topping

Combine bread cubes, butter, raisins and cinnamon. Mix well; spread in a lightly greased 2-quart casserole dish. Blend together sugar, eggs, vanilla and salt in a medium bowl until sugar is dissolved. Add milk; beat well. Pour over bread mixture; let stand for 5 minutes. Sprinkle with nutmeg. Bake, uncovered, at 375 degrees for 25 minutes. Cool slightly before serving. Garnish with dollops of whipped topping. Serves 8.

*Charlene McCain*
*Bakersfield, CA*

## Chocolate Bread Pudding

2 c. milk
6 slices white bread, crusts trimmed
1/2 c. sugar
1/3 c. baking cocoa
2 eggs, separated and divided
2 T. butter, melted
1 t. vanilla extract
1/2 c. semi-sweet chocolate chunks
Garnish: whipped cream, baking cocoa

Heat milk in a large saucepan just until tiny bubbles form; remove from heat. Cube bread and add to milk; stir until combined. Add sugar, cocoa and egg yolks; stir until well blended. Add butter and vanilla. Beat egg whites with an electric mixer at high speed until stiff peaks form; fold egg whites and chocolate chunks into chocolate mixture. Pour into 6 lightly greased custard cups; set cups in a large baking pan filled with one inch of hot water. Bake at 350 degrees for 40 to 45 minutes, until firm. Garnish each serving with a dollop of whipped cream and a dusting of cocoa. Serves 6.

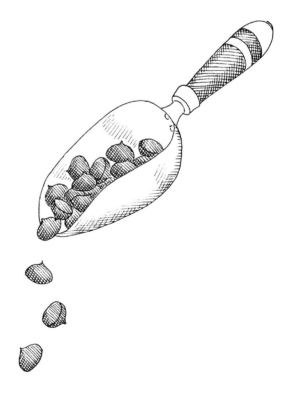

## Estelle's Baked Custard

6 eggs
6 c. milk
½ c. sugar
1½ t. vanilla extract
⅛ t. salt
Garnish: whipped cream, cinnamon or nutmeg

Whisk eggs until well beaten in a large bowl. Add milk, sugar, vanilla and salt; whisk well. Pour into 6 to 8 ungreased custard cups. Set cups in a rimmed baking pan. Pour an inch of hot water into baking pan. Bake at 325 degrees for one hour, or until a knife inserted in center comes out clean. Garnish with whipped cream, cinnamon or nutmeg. Cool at room temperature or in refrigerator 1½ to 2 hours before serving. Serves 6 to 8.

*Sharon Jones*
*Oklahoma City, OK*

*My grandmother Estelle made this custard for as long as I can remember, and now the secret has been passed down to me. It is one of my favorites...if you are a custard lover, you will love it, too!* —Sharon

## Pumpkin Custard Crunch

29-oz. can pumpkin
3 eggs, beaten
2 t. pumpkin pie spice
1 t. cinnamon
14-oz. can sweetened condensed milk
1 c. milk
2 t. vanilla extract

Combine pumpkin, eggs and spices, mixing well; stir in milks and vanilla. Pour into a greased 13"x9" baking pan; spoon Crunch Topping over pumpkin mixture. Bake at 350 degrees for 45 to 60 minutes, until a knife inserted in center comes out clean. Watch carefully so that topping doesn't burn. Serve warm. Serves 9 to 12.

### Crunch Topping:
3 c. quick-cooking oats, uncooked
1 c. brown sugar, packed
1 c. all-purpose flour
1 t. cinnamon
1 c. walnuts or pecans, crushed
1 c. butter or margarine, melted

Stir together oats, brown sugar, flour, cinnamon and nuts. Pour melted butter over top; toss to mix.

*Donna Borton*
*Columbus, OH*

Estelle's Baked Custard

Chocolate Pinwheels
(page 355)

Red Velvet Brownies
(page 345)

Cool Mint Chocolate
Swirls (page 317)

Gooey Toffee Scotchies
(page 339)

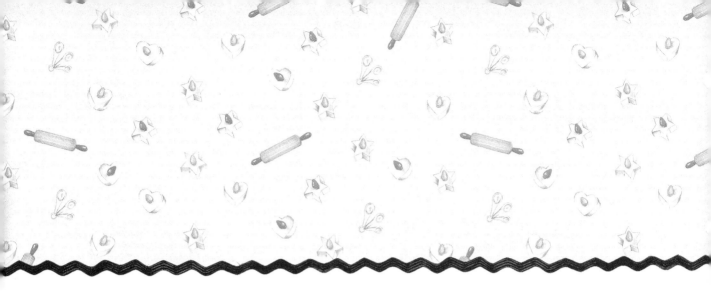

# WARM FROM THE OVEN

*Satisfy your sweet tooth with scrumptious cookies, bars & treats*

Cool Mint Chocolate Swirls

# Cool Mint Chocolate Swirls

¾ c. butter
1½ c. brown sugar, packed
2 T. water
12-oz. pkg. semi-sweet chocolate chips
2 eggs
2½ c. all-purpose flour
1¼ t. baking soda
½ t. salt
2 4.67-oz. pkgs. crème de menthe thins

Combine butter, brown sugar and water in a large saucepan; place over medium heat and cook, stirring occasionally, until butter melts and mixture is smooth. Remove from heat. Add chocolate chips, stirring until melted; cool 10 minutes. Pour chocolate mixture into a large bowl; add eggs, one at a time, stirring until well blended. Combine flour, baking soda and salt in a separate bowl, stirring to mix; add flour mixture to chocolate mixture, stirring well. Cover and chill one hour. Shape dough into walnut-size balls; place 2 inches apart on greased baking sheets. Bake at 350 degrees for 8 to 10 minutes, being careful not to overbake. Press one crème de menthe thin onto each warm cookie and let stand one minute; use back of a spoon to swirl softened thin over each cookie. Remove to wire racks to cool completely. Store in an airtight container. Makes 3 dozen.

*Regina Vining*
*Warwick, RI*

# Chocolate-Chocolate Chip Cookies

*Our favorite…be sure to serve with a big pitcher of icy cold milk!*

1 c. butter, softened
1 c. sugar
½ c. dark brown sugar, packed
1 t. vanilla extract
1 egg
⅓ c. baking cocoa
2 T. milk
1¾ c. all-purpose flour
¼ t. baking powder
1 c. chopped walnuts
6-oz. pkg. semi-sweet chocolate chips

Mix together butter, sugars and vanilla; beat in egg. Add cocoa and milk; set aside. Combine flour and baking powder; fold into butter mixture. Stir in nuts and chocolate chips. Form into balls by teaspoonfuls; place 2 inches apart on ungreased baking sheets. Bake at 350 degrees for 10 to 12 minutes. Cool for 5 minutes on baking sheets; remove to wire racks to cool completely. Makes 16 cookies.

*Rita Morgan*
*Pueblo, CO*

## Christmas Peppermint & Chocolate Meringues

*Use the ice pulse button on your blender to make quick work of crushing the candies.*

2 egg whites
1/8 t. cream of tartar
1/8 t. salt
3/4 c. sugar
2 c. mini semi-sweet chocolate chips
3 T. crushed peppermint candies
1/2 t. vanilla extract

Beat egg whites in a large bowl with an electric mixer at high speed until foamy. Add cream of tartar and salt, beating until mixed; gradually add sugar, one tablespoon at a time, beating well after each addition until stiff peaks form. Gently fold in remaining ingredients. Drop by teaspoonfuls 1½ inches apart onto greased baking sheets. Bake at 250 degrees for 40 minutes, or until dry. Remove to wire racks to cool completely. Store in an air-tight container. Makes 3 dozen.

*Peggy Cummings*
*Cibolo, TX*

### from cookies to snowmen
Turn meringue cookies into cute snowman faces simply by adding eyes, noses and mouths with mini chocolate chips and red cinnamon candies "glued on" with a bit of frosting.

## Chocolate Fudge Cookies

2 6-oz. pkgs. semi-sweet chocolate chips
1/4 c. butter
14-oz. can sweetened condensed milk
1 t. vanilla extract
1 c. all-purpose flour
1 c. chopped nuts

Combine chocolate chips, butter and condensed milk in a microwave-safe bowl; microwave on HIGH 2 to 3 minutes, until melted, stirring every 30 seconds. Add vanilla, flour and nuts. Drop by teaspoonfuls onto greased baking sheets. Bake at 350 degrees for 7 minutes. Remove to wire racks and cool completely. Makes 5 to 6 dozen.

*Karen Adams*
*Cincinnati, OH*

## Chewy Chocolate Chip Cookies

*Whenever I take these to family gatherings, everyone raves about them. The secret…use shortening rather than butter and don't bake them too long.*

3/4 c. shortening
1 c. sugar
1 c. brown sugar, packed
2 eggs
1 t. vanilla extract
2½ c. all-purpose flour
1 t. baking soda
1 t. salt
12-oz. pkg. semi-sweet chocolate chips
1/2 c. chopped nuts

Blend together shortening, sugars, eggs and vanilla. Add flour, baking soda and salt; mix well. Stir in chocolate chips and nuts. Drop by rounded tablespoonfuls onto ungreased baking sheets. Bake at 375 degrees for 10 to 12 minutes. Cool on a wire rack. Makes 4 to 5 dozen.

*Kathy Zimmerman*
*Burley, WA*

Christmas Peppermint &
Chocolate Meringues

## Grandma Sorensen's Sugar Cookies

*These cookies have been a family tradition as long as I can remember. Grandma, Mom, my aunt and cousins get together on the day after Thanksgiving to make them…one year we made more than 400 cookies!*

1½ c. sugar
1½ c. shortening
2 eggs, beaten
1 t. vanilla extract
2½ c. all-purpose flour
2 t. baking powder
¾ t. baking soda
8-oz. container sour cream
1 t. lemon or orange extract
favorite frosting

Combine all ingredients except frosting in a large bowl; mix well. Form into a ball; wrap with plastic wrap and chill in refrigerator for 2 days. Roll out dough to desired thickness on a lightly floured surface, working in a little more flour if needed to get desired consistency. Cut out using your favorite cookie cutters; arrange on ungreased baking sheets. Bake at 350 degrees for 10 to 12 minutes, until edges are golden. Let cool; frost as desired. Makes about 2 dozen.

*Jenny Newcomb*
*Arcadia, IN*

## Buttery Ricotta Cookies

½ c. butter, softened
¼ c. ricotta cheese
1 c. sugar
1 egg, beaten
1 t. vanilla extract
2 c. all-purpose flour
½ t. baking soda
½ t. salt

Beat butter and ricotta cheese in a large bowl with an electric mixer at medium speed until creamy. Gradually add sugar, beating until blended; stir in egg and vanilla. Add remaining ingredients, stirring to blend. Shape dough into one-inch balls and flatten slightly on greased baking sheets. Bake at 350 degrees for 10 minutes, or until edges are golden. Remove to wire racks to cool. Store in an airtight container. Makes about 2 dozen.

*April Hale*
*Kirkwood, NY*

## Powdered Sugar Sandies

1 c. butter, softened
1½ c. powdered sugar, divided
1 t. vanilla extract
2¼ c. all-purpose flour
¼ t. salt
Optional: ¾ c. chopped walnuts

Beat butter, ½ cup powdered sugar and vanilla in a large bowl with an electric mixer at medium speed until creamy. Gradually add flour, salt and nuts, if desired; mix well. Shape dough into one-inch balls and place on ungreased baking sheets. Bake at 400 degrees for 10 to 12 minutes. Place remaining powdered sugar in a bowl. Roll warm cookies in powdered sugar; let cool completely and roll again. Store in an airtight container. Makes 2 to 3 dozen.

*Holly Child*
*Parker, CO*

Powdered Sugar Sandies

Nanny's Shortbread
Chews

## Lacy Florentine Cookies

¾ c. quick-cooking oats, uncooked
¾ c. all-purpose flour
¾ c. sugar
1 t. cinnamon
½ t. baking soda
½ t. salt
1½ c. sliced almonds
½ c. plus 2 T. butter, melted
¼ c. half-and-half
¼ c. light corn syrup
1 t. vanilla extract
4 1-oz. sqs. semi-sweet baking chocolate, melted

Combine oats, flour, sugar, cinnamon, baking soda and salt in a large bowl, stirring to mix; add almonds and stir well. Add butter, half-and-half, corn syrup and vanilla, stirring until well blended. Drop by tablespoonfuls 3 inches apart onto aluminum foil-lined, greased baking sheets, with 6 cookies per sheet. Bake at 350 degrees for 7 to 9 minutes, one pan at a time on center rack, until edges are golden. Cool in pans 5 minutes; remove to wire racks to cool completely. Drizzle melted chocolate over cooled cookies. Store in an airtight container. Makes 4 dozen.

*Regina Vining*
*Warwick, RI*

*"These cookies are sweet and buttery... just like my Italian grandmother used to make."* —Regina

## Nanny's Shortbread Chews

½ c. butter, softened
1½ c. brown sugar, packed and divided
1 c. plus 2 T. all-purpose flour, divided
2 eggs, beaten
1 t. baking powder
1 t. vanilla extract
½ t. salt
1½ c. chopped dates or raisins
1 c. chopped walnuts or pecans

Mix together butter, ½ cup brown sugar and one cup flour in a bowl with a pastry blender or fork until crumbly. Press butter mixture into the bottom of a greased 13"x9" baking pan. Bake at 350 degrees for 8 to 10 minutes; remove from oven. Mix remaining brown sugar and flour, eggs, baking powder, vanilla and salt; blend well. Stir in dates or raisins and nuts; pour mixture over baked crust. Return to oven; bake 15 to 20 more minutes. Cool completely and cut into squares. Makes 2 dozen.

*Paula McFadden*
*Owensboro, KY*

## Almond Cream Spritz

1 c. butter, softened
3-oz. pkg. cream cheese, softened
½ c. sugar
½ t. almond extract
¼ t. vanilla extract
2 c. all-purpose flour
½ c. almonds, finely chopped

Beat butter and cream cheese in a large bowl with an electric mixer at medium speed until well blended. Add sugar and extracts; beat well. Stir in flour. Cover and chill dough 30 minutes, or until easy to handle. Place dough in a cookie press and press out cookies onto ungreased baking sheets; sprinkle with almonds. Bake at 375 degrees for 8 to 10 minutes, until edges are lightly golden; remove to wire racks to cool (be sure to let pans cool between batches…a warm pan will cause dough to soften and spread). Store in an airtight container. Makes 5 dozen.

*Lisa Johnson*
*Hallsville, TX*

## Sour Cream Drop Cookies

¾ c. butter, softened
1½ c. sugar
2 eggs, beaten
1 t. vanilla extract
½ t. lemon or orange extract
8-oz. container sour cream
3 c. all-purpose flour
1 t. baking powder
1 t. baking soda

Beat butter and sugar in a large bowl with an electric mixer at medium speed until fluffy. Add eggs, vanilla and lemon or orange extract; mix well. Fold in sour cream; set aside. Combine remaining ingredients in a separate bowl; gradually add to butter mixture. Drop by teaspoonfuls onto greased baking sheets. Bake at 350 degrees for 10 to 12 minutes. Remove to wire racks and cool completely. Store in an airtight container. Makes 3 dozen.

*Cheryl Bastian*
*Northumberland, PA*

Almond Cream Spritz

Snowcap Cookies

## Southern Oatmeal Cookies

*These are the best oatmeal cookies you'll ever taste.*
*They're great with a glass of cold milk.*

1 c. butter, softened
1 c. sugar
1 c. brown sugar, packed
2 eggs
1 t. vanilla extract
1½ c. all-purpose flour
1 t. baking soda
1 t. salt
3 c. long-cooking oats, uncooked
1 c. chopped walnuts or pecans

Beat butter and sugars in a large bowl with an electric mixer at medium speed until fluffy. Beat in eggs, one at a time, blending well after each addition. Add vanilla; set aside. Sift together flour, baking soda and salt. Fold flour mixture into butter mixture; stir in oats and nuts. Form rounded teaspoonfuls into balls and place on greased baking sheets 2 inches apart. Bake at 350 degrees for 5 to 7 minutes. Let stand on baking sheets for 4 to 5 minutes before removing to wire racks to cool completely. Store in an airtight container. Makes 4 dozen.

*Dawn Fannin*
*Ravenna, TX*

## Snowcap Cookies

¾ c. butter, softened
1 c. sugar
3 eggs
1 t. vanilla extract
6 1-oz. sqs. white baking chocolate, melted and
    cooled
3½ c. all-purpose flour
1 t. baking powder
1 t. salt
⅛ t. nutmeg
1½ c. chopped walnuts, toasted
Garnish: powdered sugar

Beat butter and sugar in a large bowl with an electric mixer at medium speed until light and fluffy; add eggs, one at a time, beating until blended after each addition. Stir in vanilla; add melted chocolate, beating 30 seconds. Combine flour, baking powder, salt and nutmeg in a separate bowl, stirring to mix; gradually add flour mixture to butter mixture, beating until blended. Fold in walnuts. Drop by tablespoonfuls onto greased baking sheets. Bake at 350 degrees for 10 to 12 minutes; remove to wire racks to cool completely. Garnish tops with powdered sugar. Store in an airtight container. Makes 3 to 4 dozen.

### snowcap in a snow cap
Wrap a batch of Snowcap Cookies in clear plastic wrap and tuck the package inside a woolly toboggan or stocking cap. Add a package of cocoa mix to help chase away the chills.

## Espresso Bean Cookies

*You can find chocolate-covered coffee beans in various package sizes at most coffee shops. One 6-ounce package equals about one cup.*

1 c. butter, softened
¾ c. brown sugar, packed
¼ c. sugar
2 eggs
1 t. vanilla extract
2¼ c. all-purpose flour
1 t. baking soda
1 t. salt
½ t. cinnamon
1 c. chopped almonds, toasted
1 c. chocolate-covered coffee beans
4 1.4-oz. toffee candy bars, chopped

Beat butter with an electric mixer at medium speed until creamy. Gradually add sugars, beating well after each addition. Add eggs, one at a time, beating until blended after each addition; add vanilla, and beat until blended. Combine flour, baking soda, salt and cinnamon in a separate bowl. Gradually add flour mixture to butter mixture, beating well. Stir in almonds, coffee beans and chopped candy bars. Cover and chill dough until firm. Drop by teaspoonfuls onto ungreased baking sheets. Bake at 350 degrees for 10 to 11 minutes, until golden. Cool on pans one minute; remove to wire racks to cool completely. Store in an airtight container. Makes 4 dozen.

*Kathy Grashoff*
*Fort Wayne, IN*

## Spicy Maple-Anise Snaps

1 c. butter, softened
1 c. sugar
1 c. dark brown sugar, packed
1 egg, beaten
1 t. maple extract
2½ c. all-purpose flour
1 T. ground anise seed
1 t. baking soda
1 t. cinnamon
¾ t. ground cloves
½ c. pecans, finely chopped

Beat butter and sugars in a large bowl with an electric mixer at medium speed until fluffy. Beat in egg and extract; set aside. Combine flour and remaining ingredients except pecans in a separate bowl; mix well. Gradually blend flour mixture into butter mixture; beat at low speed until blended. Add pecans and mix in well. Divide dough into 3 parts; form each into a log 8 inches long. Wrap tightly in wax paper; chill one hour, or until very firm. Remove one roll at a time from refrigerator and slice ¼-inch thick. Place one to 2 inches apart on parchment paper-lined baking sheets. Bake at 375 degrees for 10 to 12 minutes, until golden. Immediately remove cookies from baking sheets; cool completely on wire racks. Store in airtight containers. Flavors will improve over the next several days. Makes 7 dozen.

*Judy Gillham*
*Whittier, CA*

Espresso Bean Cookies

White Chocolate Cookies

## Ginger-Molasses Cookies

¾ c. butter, softened
1 c. brown sugar, packed
1 egg
⅓ c. molasses
2½ c. all-purpose flour
2 t. ground ginger
2 t. baking soda
1 t. cinnamon
½ t. salt
½ c. sugar

Beat butter and brown sugar in a large bowl with an electric mixer at medium speed until light and fluffy; add egg and molasses, beating until blended. Combine flour, ginger, soda, cinnamon and salt in a separate bowl, stirring to mix. Gradually add flour mixture to butter mixture, stirring just until blended. Chill dough one hour, or until firm. Place sugar in a shallow dish. Shape chilled dough into one-inch balls, roll in sugar and place on ungreased baking sheets. Bake at 350 degrees for 15 minutes, or until golden. Cool 2 minutes on pans; remove to wire racks to cool completely. Store in an airtight container. Makes 6 dozen.

*Lisa Sett*
*Thousand Oaks, CA*

## White Chocolate Cookies

1 c. butter, softened
¾ c. brown sugar, packed
½ c. sugar
1 egg
½ t. almond extract
2 c. all-purpose flour
1 t. baking soda
¼ t. cinnamon
¼ t. ground ginger
¼ t. salt
6-oz. pkg. white baking chocolate, chopped
1½ c. chopped pecans

Beat butter and sugars in a large bowl with an electric mixer at medium speed until smooth. Add egg and extract; beat well. Combine flour, baking soda, cinnamon, ginger and salt in a separate bowl, stirring to mix; add flour mixture to butter mixture, stirring well. Blend in chocolate and pecans. Drop by teaspoonfuls 2 inches apart onto greased baking sheets. Bake at 350 degrees for 10 to 12 minutes, until lightly golden. Remove to wire racks to cool. Store in an airtight container. Makes 5 dozen.

*Bunny Palmertree*
*Carrollton, MS*

## Maple Sugar Cookies

1 c. butter, softened
1¼ c. sugar
2 eggs
¼ c. maple syrup
1 T. vanilla extract
3 c. all-purpose flour
¾ t. baking powder
½ t. baking soda
½ t. salt

Beat butter and sugar in a large bowl with an electric mixer at medium speed until creamy. Add eggs, one at a time, beating well after each addition. Beat in syrup and vanilla. Combine flour, baking powder, baking soda and salt in a separate bowl, stirring to mix; gradually add flour mixture to butter mixture, stirring until blended. Cover and chill 2 hours. On a lightly floured surface, roll dough to ⅛-inch thickness; cut with a 2½-inch cookie cutter dipped in flour. Place cookies one inch apart on ungreased baking sheets. Bake at 350 degrees for 8 to 10 minutes, until golden. Remove to wire racks to cool completely. Store in an airtight container. Makes 3 dozen.

*Michelle Crabtree*
*Lee's Summit, MO*

## Butterscotch Gingerbread Cookies

½ c. butter, softened
½ c. brown sugar, packed
3.5-oz. pkg. cook & serve butterscotch
    pudding mix
1 egg, beaten
1½ c. all-purpose flour
1½ t. ground ginger
1 t. cinnamon
½ t. baking soda

Beat butter, brown sugar and pudding mix in a large bowl with an electric mixer at medium speed until light and fluffy; add egg and beat well. Combine flour, ginger, cinnamon and baking soda in a separate bowl, stirring to mix. Gradually stir flour mixture into butter mixture, mixing until blended. Chill 30 minutes. Roll dough in batches to ¼-inch thickness on a floured surface; cut with cookie cutters as desired. Place on a greased baking sheet and bake at 350 degrees for 8 to 10 minutes, until golden. Remove to a wire rack to cool completely. Store in an airtight container. Makes about one dozen.

*Amy Butcher*
*Columbus, GA*

### a clever tip
Take two gift bags the same size but different colors and cut through the middle of each. Swap halves and glue together, overlapping edges by ½ inch. Glue a strip of wide ribbon around each bag to hide the seam...you'll have two clever boutique bags for giving cookies!

Maple Sugar Cookies

# Nellie's Persimmon Cookies

*A ripe persimmon should be soft to the touch and yield between ½ to ¾ cup of pulp.*

1 persimmon
1 c. butter, softened
1 c. brown sugar, packed
1 c. sugar
2 eggs, beaten
2½ c. all-purpose flour
½ t. baking soda
1 c. chopped pecans

Rinse persimmon under cold water; pat dry. Using a small sharp knife, make an X-shaped cut in the pointed end. Pull back sections of peel from cut end; discard seeds, peel and stem end. Process pulp in food processor or blender until smooth.

Reserve ½ cup persimmon pulp purée; save any remaining pulp purée for another use. Beat butter and sugars in a large bowl with an electric mixer at medium speed until light and fluffy. Beat in eggs and persimmon pulp. Combine flour and baking soda in a separate bowl, stirring to mix; gradually add flour mixture to butter mixture, beating until blended. Fold in pecans; cover and chill one hour. Drop by teaspoonfuls onto ungreased baking sheets. Press each cookie with a fork dipped in warm water. Bake at 350 degrees for 10 minutes, or until golden. Remove to wire racks to cool. Store in an airtight container. Makes 6 dozen.

*Dorothy Ames*
*Lerna, IL*

Nellie's Persimmon Cookies

## Dazzling Neapolitan Cookies

1 c. butter, softened
1 c. sugar
1 egg
1 t. vanilla extract
2½ c. all-purpose flour
1½ t. baking powder
½ t. salt
1-oz. sq. baking chocolate, melted
⅓ c. chopped pecans
¼ c. chopped candied cherries, diced
2 drops red food coloring
⅓ c. sweetened flaked coconut
½ t. almond extract

Beat butter and sugar in a large bowl with an electric mixer at medium speed until light and fluffy; add egg and vanilla, beating until blended. Gradually beat in flour, baking powder and salt. Divide dough into thirds and place each third in a separate bowl. Stir chocolate and pecans into one third, cherries and food coloring into another third and coconut and almond extract into remaining third. Line an 8"x8" baking pan with plastic wrap, allowing 2 to 4 inches to extend over sides; press chocolate mixture evenly into bottom of pan. Add coconut mixture and then cherry mixture, gently pressing each layer; cover and chill 8 hours. Using plastic wrap as handles, lift dough from pan; cut into 5 equal sections. Carefully cut each section into ⅛ inch-thick slices; place on ungreased baking sheets. Bake at 375 degrees for 8 to 10 minutes, until golden; remove to wire racks to cool. Store in an airtight container. Makes 8 dozen.

## Key Lime Bites

¾ c. butter, softened
1 c. powdered sugar, divided
zest of 2 limes
2 T. lime juice
1 T. vanilla extract
1¾ c. plus 2 T. all-purpose flour
2 T. cornstarch
½ t. salt

Beat butter and ⅓ cup powdered sugar in a large bowl with an electric mixer at medium speed until fluffy. Add zest, lime juice and vanilla; beat until blended. Whisk together flour, cornstarch and salt in a separate bowl; add flour mixture to butter mixture, stirring until combined. Shape dough into a log and chill one hour. Cut log into ⅛-inch-thick slices; place on parchment-lined baking sheets. Bake at 350 degrees for 12 to 14 minutes, until golden. Remove to wire racks and cool one minute. Place remaining powdered sugar in a large plastic bag; add warm cookies and toss gently to coat. Return to wire racks to cool completely. Store in an airtight container. Makes 2 dozen.

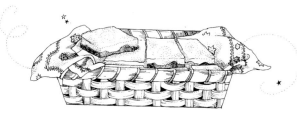

Cherry-Cardamom
Cookies

## Cherry-Cardamom Cookies

6-oz. jar maraschino cherries, drained and diced
2⅓ c. plus 2 T. all-purpose flour, divided
1 t. baking powder
1 t. cardamom
½ t. baking soda
½ c. butter, softened
1 c. sugar
3-oz. pkg. cream cheese, softened
1 egg
2 T. buttermilk
1 t. almond extract
Garnish: powdered sugar

Combine cherries and 2 tablespoons flour in a small bowl. Toss to mix; set aside. Combine remaining flour, baking powder, cardamom and baking soda in a medium bowl, stirring to mix. Beat butter, sugar and cream cheese in a large bowl with an electric mixer at medium speed until fluffy. Add egg, buttermilk and almond extract; beat until blended. Gradually add flour mixture to butter mixture, beating just until moistened; fold in cherry mixture. Chill for one hour. Shape dough into one-inch balls; place on ungreased baking sheets. Bake at 350 degrees for 12 to 14 minutes; remove to wire racks to cool completely. Garnish with powdered sugar. Store in an airtight container. Makes about 3 dozen.

*Holly Child*
*Parker, CO*

# Orangey-Ginger Cookie Sticks

1¾ c. cake flour
⅔ c. almonds
2 t. ground ginger
1 t. baking powder
1 c. butter, softened
1 c. brown sugar, packed
6 T. plus 2 t. sugar, divided
2 T. orange zest
2 egg yolks, divided and beaten
½ t. vanilla extract
⅔ c. pistachios, finely chopped

Combine cake flour, almonds, ginger and baking powder in a food processor; process until finely ground. Combine butter, brown sugar and 6 tablespoons sugar in a large bowl. Beat with an electric mixer at medium speed until light and fluffy. Add zest, one egg yolk and vanilla; beat well. Add ground almond mixture, stirring just until blended. Stir in pistachios. Divide dough in half. Using floured hands, roll each half into a ½-inch-thick log on a lightly floured surface. Place logs 4 inches apart on a greased and floured baking sheet. Cover with plastic wrap and chill one hour. Brush logs with remaining egg yolk; sprinkle with remaining 2 teaspoons sugar. Bake at 350 degrees for 30 minutes, or until deep golden and firm to the touch; cool 10 minutes. Reduce oven temperature to 300 degrees. Using a serrated knife, cut logs crosswise into ½-inch-thick slices. Place sliced-side down on same baking sheet. Bake at 300 degrees for 12 minutes, or until golden. Turn over; bake 12 more minutes, or until golden. Remove to wire racks to cool completely. Store in an airtight container. Makes 1½ dozen.

*Carrie O'Shea*
*Marina Del Ray, CA*

Orangey-Ginger
Cookie Sticks

Lemon-Macadamia Cookies

## Lemon-Macadamia Cookies

*One of my daughters, Lisa, loves macadamia nuts, and I love lemon; so I combined our favorite flavors to create these scrumptious cookies.*

¾ c. butter, softened
1 c. sugar
1 c. brown sugar, packed
2 eggs
3.4-oz. pkg. instant lemon pudding mix
2¼ c. all-purpose flour
2 t. lemon zest
1 t. baking soda
¼ t. salt
1 t. lemon extract
1 c. macadamia nuts, coarsely chopped
½ c. toffee baking bits

Beat butter and sugars in a large bowl with an electric mixer at medium speed until light and fluffy. Add eggs, one at a time, beating until blended after each addition. Combine dry pudding mix, flour, zest, baking soda, and salt in a separate bowl. Slowly add pudding mixture to butter mixture. Add extract; beat until combined. Stir in nuts and toffee bits. Drop by rounded tablespoonfuls onto ungreased baking sheets 2 inches apart. Bake at 350 degrees for 10 to 12 minutes, until lightly golden around edges. Cool cookies on baking sheets for 2 minutes. Remove to wire racks to cool completely. Store in an airtight container. Makes 4 dozen.

*Brenda Melancon*
*Gonzales, LA*

## Chocolatey Chewy Brownies

1 c. butter, softened
2 c. sugar
4 eggs, beaten
1 c. all-purpose flour
1 c. chopped walnuts
4 1-oz. sqs. unsweetened baking chocolate, melted
1 t. vanilla extract

Beat butter and sugar in a bowl with an electric mixer at medium speed until creamy. Beat in eggs, mixing well. Stir in remaining ingredients. Pour into a greased and floured 13"x9" baking pan. Bake at 350 degrees for 30 minutes. Cool; cut into squares. Makes 1½ to 2 dozen.

*Jacklyn Akey*
*Merrill, WI*

Grandma's Special Cookies

Gooey Toffee Scotchies

## Gooey Toffee Scotchies

18¼-oz. pkg. yellow cake mix
½ c. brown sugar, packed
½ c. butter, melted and slightly cooled
2 eggs, beaten
1 c. cashews, chopped
8-oz. pkg. toffee baking bits

Beat dry cake mix, brown sugar, butter and eggs in a bowl with an electric mixer at medium speed for one minute. Stir in cashews. Press mixture into bottom of a greased 15"x10" jelly-roll pan; sprinkle with toffee bits. Bake at 350 degrees for 15 to 20 minutes, until a toothpick inserted in center comes out clean. Cool in pan and cut into bars or triangles. To serve, drizzle with warm Toffee Sauce. Makes about 2½ dozen.

## Toffee Sauce:

¾ c. plus 1 T. dark brown sugar, packed
2 T. dark corn syrup
6 T. butter
⅔ c. whipping cream

Bring sugar, syrup and butter to a boil in a saucepan over medium heat. Cook for 2 minutes. Carefully stir in cream and simmer for 2 more minutes, or until sauce thickens. Keep warm.

*Rhonda Reeder*
*Ellicott City, MD*

# Brown Sugar Brownies

⅔ c. butter, softened
2¼ c. brown sugar, packed
4 eggs
1 t. vanilla extract
2 c. all-purpose flour
2 t. baking powder
1 t. salt
12-oz. pkg. semi-sweet chocolate chips

Beat butter and brown sugar in a large bowl with an electric mixer at medium speed until light and fluffy. Beat in eggs, one at a time, just until blended. Beat in vanilla. Combine flour, baking powder and salt in a separate bowl; gradually add flour mixture to butter mixture, stirring until blended. Stir in chocolate chips; spoon batter into a greased 13"x9" baking pan. Bake at 350 degrees for 35 to 40 minutes, until a toothpick inserted in center comes out with a few moist crumbs. Cool completely in pan on a wire rack. Cut into squares. Store in an airtight container. Makes 1½ dozen.

*Diana Pindell*
*Wooster, OH*

Brown Sugar Brownies

## Double-Dark Chocolate Brownies

1½ c. butter, melted
3 c. sugar
2 t. chocolate or vanilla extract
1 t. almond extract
6 eggs, beaten
1½ c. all-purpose flour
1 c. baking cocoa
1½ t. baking powder
1 t. salt
1 c. semi-sweet chocolate chips

Combine melted butter, sugar and extracts in a large bowl; stir well. Add eggs and beat well with spoon. Combine flour, cocoa, baking powder and salt in a separate bowl. Gradually add flour mixture to butter mixture, beating until well blended. Add chocolate chips and stir well. Spread batter evenly in a greased 13"x9" glass baking dish. Bake at 350 degrees for 30 to 40 minutes, until a toothpick inserted in center comes out clean. Cool completely in pan on a wire rack; cut into bars. Store in an airtight container. Makes 1½ dozen.

*Terri Lotz-Ganley*
*South Euclid, OH*

Chocolate Crunch Brownies

## Chocolate Crunch Brownies

1 c. butter, softened
2 c. sugar
4 eggs
2 t. vanilla extract
1 c. all-purpose flour
6 T. baking cocoa
½ t. salt
7-oz. jar marshmallow creme
1 c. creamy peanut butter
2 c. semi-sweet chocolate chips
3 c. crispy rice cereal

Beat butter and sugar in a large bowl with an electric mixer at medium speed until creamy. Add eggs, one at a time, beating until blended after each addition. Add vanilla. Combine flour, cocoa and salt in a separate bowl; whisk to mix. Gradually add flour mixture to butter mixture. Spread batter into a lightly greased 13"x9" baking pan. Bake at 350 degrees for 35 to 40 minutes, until a toothpick inserted in center comes out with a few moist crumbs. Cool completely in pan on a wire rack. Spread marshmallow creme over brownies. Combine peanut butter and chocolate chips in a saucepan; heat over low heat, stirring constantly, until melted and smooth. Remove from heat; stir in cereal. Spread peanut butter mixture over marshmallow layer and chill until firm. Cut into bars and store in an airtight container in the refrigerator. Makes about 2½ dozen.

*Lisa Willard*
*Dunwoody, GA*

## Chocolate-Mint Candy Brownies

1½ c. butter, melted
3 c. sugar
2 t. vanilla extract
5 eggs, beaten
1 c. all-purpose flour
1 c. baking cocoa
1 t. baking powder
1 t. salt
24 chocolate-covered mint patties, unwrapped
Garnish: chocolate-covered mint patties, chopped

Combine butter, sugar and vanilla in a large bowl; stir to mix. Add eggs and blend well. Combine flour, cocoa, baking powder and salt in a separate bowl. Gradually add flour mixture to butter mixture; stir until blended. Reserve 2 cups of batter; spread remaining batter in a greased 13"x9" baking pan. Place chocolate-covered mint patties over batter in a single layer; spread reserved batter over patties. Bake at 350 degrees for 50 to 55 minutes, until brownies begin to pull away from sides of pan. Cool completely in pan on a wire rack before cutting. Garnish with chopped chocolate-covered mint patties. Store in an airtight container. Makes 3 dozen.

*Summer Staib*
*Broomfield, CO*

## Peppermint Bark Brownies

20-oz. pkg. fudge brownie mix
12-oz. pkg. white chocolate chips
2 t. butter
1½ c. candy canes, crushed

Prepare and bake brownie mix in a lightly greased 13"x9" baking pan according to package directions. Cool completely in pan on a wire rack. Combine chocolate chips and butter in a saucepan; heat over low heat until melted, stirring constantly with a rubber spatula. Spread chocolate mixture over brownies; sprinkle with crushed candy. Let stand 30 minutes, or until frosting hardens. Cut into squares; store in an airtight container. Makes 2 dozen.

*Angie Biggin*
*Lyons, IL*

### round is nice!
Need a clever way to give a gift of brownies? Cut the brownies with a round cookie cutter. Stack them inside a wide-mouth glass jar, layered with circles of parchment paper or colorful tissue paper.

Chocolate-Mint Candy Brownies

Red Velvet Brownies

# Red Velvet Brownies

4-oz. bittersweet chocolate baking bar, chopped
¾ c. butter
2 c. sugar
4 eggs
1½ c. all-purpose flour
1-oz. bottle red liquid food coloring
1½ t. baking powder
1 t. vanilla extract
⅛ t. salt
Optional: chopped pecans

Line bottom and sides of a 9½"x9½" baking pan with aluminum foil, allowing 2 to 4 inches to extend over sides; lightly grease foil. Microwave chocolate and butter in a large microwave-safe bowl on high 1½ to 2 minutes, until melted and smooth, stirring at 30-second intervals. Add sugar, whisking to blend. Add eggs, one at a time, whisking after each addition until just blended. Gently stir in flour and remaining ingredients except pecans. Pour mixture into pan. Bake at 350 degrees for 44 to 48 minutes, until a toothpick inserted in center comes out with a few moist crumbs. Cool completely in pan on a wire rack. Spread with Cream Cheese Frosting; cut into bars. Top with chopped pecans, if desired. Store in refrigerator in an airtight container. Serves 16.

## Cream Cheese Frosting:

8-oz. pkg. cream cheese, softened
3 T. butter, softened
1½ c. powdered sugar
⅛ t. salt
1 t. vanilla extract

Beat cream cheese and butter in a large bowl with an electric mixer at medium speed until creamy. Gradually add powdered sugar and salt, beating until blended. Stir in vanilla.

*Barbara Girlardo*
*Pittsburgh, PA*

# Fudgy Cream Cheese Brownies

⅔ c. butter
4 to 5 T. baking cocoa
6 eggs, divided
2 t. vanilla extract, divided
1¼ c. plus 2 T. all-purpose flour, divided
1 t. baking powder
½ t. salt
¾ c. chopped walnuts
8-oz. pkg. cream cheese, softened
½ c. sugar

Combine butter and cocoa in a large saucepan; heat over medium heat until butter melts, stirring often. Remove from heat and cool 5 minutes. Add 4 eggs, one at a time, beating well after each addition. Stir in 1 teaspoon vanilla. Combine 1¼ cups flour, baking powder and salt in a bowl. Gradually add flour mixture to cocoa mixture; fold in nuts. Spread batter into a greased 13"x9" baking pan; set aside. Beat cream cheese and sugar in a separate bowl with an electric mixer at medium speed until creamy. Add remaining eggs, 2 tablespoons flour and one teaspoon vanilla; mix until blended. Spread cream cheese mixture evenly over cocoa mixture in pan; swirl with a knife. Bake at 350 degrees for 35 to 40 minutes, until a toothpick inserted in center comes out clean and edges pull away from sides of pan. Cool completely in pan on a wire rack; cut into bars. Store in an airtight container in refrigerator. Makes one dozen.

*Wendy Ross*
*Boulder Junction, WI*

German Apple Streusel Kuchen

# Grandma Gray's Spice-Nut Bars

1½ c. all-purpose flour
½ t. baking powder
½ t. baking soda
½ t. salt
½ t. cinnamon
¼ t. nutmeg
⅛ t. ground cloves
¼ c. butter, softened
1 c. brown sugar, packed
1 egg, beaten
½ c. plus 1 T. hot coffee, divided
½ c. raisins
½ c. chopped walnuts
½ c. powdered sugar

Combine flour, baking powder, baking soda, salt, cinnamon, nutmeg and cloves in a large bowl; mix. Beat butter, brown sugar and egg in a separate large bowl with an electric mixer at medium speed until blended. Add ½ cup coffee and beat well; stir in raisins and walnuts. Gradually add flour mixture to butter mixture. Pour into a greased 13"x9" baking pan. Bake at 350 degrees for 20 to 25 minutes, until golden. Combine powdered sugar and remaining coffee in a small bowl; stir well. Immediately spread glaze over warm bars. Cool in pan on a wire rack and cut into bars. Makes 2 dozen.

*Kelly Wood*
*Salem, OH*

*This recipe belonged to my great-grandmother on my mother's side. Mother made these cookie bars every Christmas... we always gobbled them up immediately. The aromatic spices of cinnamon, nutmeg and cloves remind me of the holidays.*

*—Kelly*

# German Apple Streusel Kuchen

16-oz. loaf frozen bread dough, thawed
4 Granny Smith apples, peeled, cored and
    thinly sliced
¾ c. plus ⅓ c. sugar, divided
1 t. cinnamon
1 T. vanilla extract
¼ c. sliced almonds
1¼ c. all-purpose flour
¼ c. butter, melted

Let dough rise according to package directions. Spread dough in a greased 16"x11" baking sheet. Cover dough with plastic wrap and let rise in a warm place (85 degrees), free from drafts, 20 to 25 minutes, until double in size. Mix apples, ¾ cup sugar, cinnamon and vanilla; spread apple mixture evenly over dough. Sprinkle with almonds. Combine flour, butter and remaining sugar in a separate bowl; mix until crumbly and spread evenly over apple layer. Bake at 375 degrees for 25 minutes, or until a toothpick inserted in center comes out clean. Cool completely in pan on a wire rack; cut into squares. Makes 2 dozen.

*Karin Anderson*
*Hillsboro, OH*

# Apple-Cheddar Bars

1 c. brown sugar, packed
2 eggs
3 c. apples, peeled, cored and chopped
1 c. all-purpose flour
2 t. baking powder
1 t. salt
1 c. shredded Cheddar cheese
¾ c. chopped nuts
¼ c. sweetened flaked coconut

Combine sugar and eggs in a large bowl; stir well. Fold in apples. Combine flour, baking powder and salt in a separate bowl, stirring to mix. Add cheese, nuts and coconut to flour mixture, stirring to mix. Gradually add flour mixture to apple mixture, stirring just until combined. Spread batter in a greased and floured 13"x9" baking pan. Bake at 375 degrees for 20 to 25 minutes, until a toothpick inserted in center comes out clean. Let cool in pan on a wire rack for 10 minutes; cut into bars. Makes 2 to 3 dozen.

*Marie Stewart*
*Pensacola, FL*

Apple-Cheddar Bars

## Teresa's Tasty Apricot Bars

½ c. butter, softened
1 c. all-purpose flour
1 t. baking powder
1 egg, beaten
1 T. milk
¾ c. apricot preserves

Beat butter, flour and baking powder in a large bowl with an electric mixer at medium speed until blended. Stir in egg and milk. Press into a lightly greased 9"x9" baking pan; spread preserves over top and set aside. Prepare Coconut Topping and spread over preserves. Bake at 350 degrees for 25 to 30 minutes, until a toothpick inserted in center comes out clean. Cool completely in pan on a wire rack. Cut into bars. Makes one dozen.

## Coconut Topping:

¼ c. butter, softened
1 c. sugar
1 egg, beaten
1 t. vanilla extract
1 c. sweetened flaked coconut

Combine butter and sugar in a bowl, stirring until blended. Add egg and vanilla; stir well. Add coconut and stir until well blended.

*Teresa Stiegelmeyer*
*Indianapolis, IN*

Teresa's Tasty
Apricot Bars

# Applesauce Spice Bars

⅔ c. brown sugar, packed
1 c. all purpose flour
1 t. baking soda
½ t. salt
1 t. pumpkin pie spice
1 c. applesauce
¼ c. butter, softened
1 egg
Optional: 1 c. raisins

Combine all ingredients and raisins, if desired, in a large bowl; mix thoroughly. Spread batter in a lightly greased 13"x9" baking pan. Bake at 350 degrees for 25 minutes, or until a toothpick inserted in center comes out clean. Cool completely in pan on a wire rack; frost with Browned Butter Frosting. Cut into 3"x1" bars. Makes 2½ to 3 dozen.

## Browned Butter Frosting:

3 T. butter
1½ c. powdered sugar
1 to 1½ T. milk
1 t. vanilla extract

Melt butter in a medium saucepan over medium heat until light brown in color; remove from heat. Blend in remaining ingredients; beat with an electric mixer at medium speed until frosting is smooth and spreading consistency.

*Barbara Wise*
*Jamestown, OH*

# Choco-Berry Goodie Bars

3 c. quick-cooking oats, uncooked
14-oz. can sweetened condensed milk
1 c. sweetened flaked coconut
1 c. sliced almonds
1 c. mini semi-sweet chocolate chips
½ c. sweetened dried cranberries
2 T. butter, melted

Combine all ingredients in a large bowl; use your hands to mix well. Press into a greased 13"x9" baking pan. Bake at 350 degrees for 20 to 25 minutes, until edges are golden. Cool 5 minutes; slice into squares and cool completely. Store in an airtight container. Makes 2 dozen.

*Brenda Smith*
*Delaware, OH*

## switch things up!

It's so easy to change these yummy Choco-Berry Goodie Bars to suit your family's taste…try using chopped walnuts or pecans instead of almonds and chopped, dried apricots or pineapple instead of cranberries.

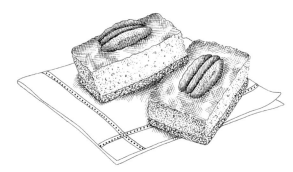

Coconut-Pecan Fudge Bars

Chocolate Chip Cheesecake Squares

# Coconut-Pecan Fudge Bars

15.25-oz. pkg. chocolate fudge cake mix
15-oz. container coconut-pecan frosting
1 c. applesauce
1 egg, beaten
Garnish: powdered sugar

Combine all ingredients except powdered sugar in a large bowl and mix well; spread in a lightly greased 13"x9" baking pan. Bake at 350 degrees for 30 to 32 minutes, until a toothpick inserted in center comes out clean. Cool for one hour; cut into 2-inch squares. Garnish with powdered sugar. Makes 2 dozen.

*Linda Nichols*
*Wintersville, OH*

# Chocolate Chip Cheesecake Squares

*Everyone loves this easy-to-make cheesecake. When I take it to potlucks, there are never any leftovers! Put the cookie dough in the freezer for 15 minutes before slicing...it makes it so much easier to slice!*

2  18-oz. tubes refrigerated chocolate chip cookie dough, sliced ¼-inch thick and divided
2 c. sugar
3 eggs, beaten
2  8-oz. pkgs. cream cheese, softened

Arrange half of cookie dough slices in a greased 13"x9" baking pan; press together to form crust and set aside. Combine sugar, eggs and cream cheese; beat until smooth. Spread over sliced cookies. Arrange remaining cookie dough slices over cream cheese mixture. Bake at 350 degrees for 45 minutes to one hour, until golden. Cut into squares or circles. Serves 15.

*Cindy Windle*
*White Hall, AR*

Sweet Raspberry-
Oat Bars

# Sweet Raspberry-Oat Bars

½ c. butter
1 c. brown sugar, packed
1½ c. all-purpose flour
½ t. baking soda
½ t. salt
1½ c. long-cooking oats, uncooked
¼ c. water
⅔ c. seedless raspberry jam
1 t. lemon juice

Beat butter and brown sugar in a large bowl with an electric mixer at medium speed until light and fluffy. Combine flour, baking soda and salt in a separate bowl; stir to mix. Add flour mixture into butter mixture, stirring to blend. Add oats and water; mix until crumbly. Firmly pat half of oat mixture into bottom of a greased 13"x9" baking pan. Combine jam and lemon juice in a small bowl; stir to blend. Spread jam mixture over oat mixture. Sprinkle remaining oat mixture over top. Bake at 350 degrees for 25 minutes, or until a toothpick inserted in center comes out clean. Cool completely in pan on a wire rack; cut into bars. Makes 2½ dozen.

Kathleen Sturm
Corona, CA

# Lemon Chess Bars

*These delicious bars freeze well...keep some on hand to serve to unexpected guests!*

½ c. butter or margarine, softened
1 c. plus 2 T. all-purpose flour,
    sifted and divided
¼ c. powdered sugar
2 eggs
1 c. sugar
zest of 1 lemon
3 T. lemon juice
additional powdered sugar

Place butter or margarine in a bowl and beat with an electric mixer at medium speed until fluffy. Add one cup flour and ¼ cup powdered sugar and beat well; spoon into an ungreased 8"x8" pan and press firmly. Bake at 325 degrees for 20 minutes. Meanwhile, combine eggs, sugar, remaining 2 tablespoons flour, lemon zest and lemon juice in a bowl and mix well; pour over baked bottom layer. Bake 25 more minutes, or until center is set. Cool. Sprinkle with powdered sugar. Cut into bars. Makes 16 bars.

Lemon Chess Bars

## Hello Dolly Bars

*My sister began making these in the late 1970s. Every time I need a little pick-me-up, I make these. My sister is no longer with us, but these wonderful treats hold some very special memories for me, which I've passed down to my children and now my grandson.*

½ c. margarine
1 c. graham cracker crumbs
1 c. sweetened flaked coconut
6-oz. semi-sweet chocolate chips
6-oz. butterscotch chips
14-oz. can sweetened condensed milk
1 c. chopped pecans

Mix together margarine and graham cracker crumbs; press into a lightly greased 9"x9" baking pan. Layer with coconut, chocolate chips and butterscotch chips. Pour condensed milk over top; sprinkle with pecans. Bake at 350 degrees for 25 to 30 minutes. Let cool; cut into bars. Makes 12 to 16 bars.

*Marilyn Morel*
*Keene, NH*

# Homemade Graham Crackers

½ c. butter
¾ c. brown sugar, packed
1 t. vanilla extract
2 c. whole-wheat flour
1 c. all-purpose flour
1 t. baking powder
½ t. baking soda
⅛ t. salt
¾ c. milk
cinnamon to taste

Beat butter and brown sugar in a large bowl with an electric mixer at medium speed until fluffy; add vanilla and beat until blended. Combine flours, baking powder, baking soda and salt in a separate bowl, stirring to mix. Gradually add flour mixture to butter mixture alternately with milk, beginning and ending with flour mixture, beating after each addition. Cover dough and chill one hour, or until firm. Roll dough to ⅛-inch thickness on a lightly floured surface; cut into 2-inch rectangles and sprinkle with cinnamon. Place crackers ½ inch apart on greased baking sheets. Bake at 350 degrees for 10 to 12 minutes, until edges are golden. Remove to wire racks to cool. Sprinkle with cinnamon. Store in an airtight container. Makes 4 dozen.

Homemade Graham Crackers

Chocolate Pinwheels

Beth's Caramel Corn

## Chocolate Pinwheels

1 11-oz. tube refrigerated bread sticks
¾ c. semi-sweet chocolate chips
¼ c. butter, melted
½ c. sugar

Unroll bread sticks and cut them in half. Press chocolate chips in a single row along top of each bread stick half; roll up into a pinwheel. Arrange pinwheels on a parchment paper-lined baking sheet. Brush with melted butter; sprinkle with sugar. Bake at 350 degrees for 10 to 12 minutes, until golden. Makes 16 pinwheels.

*Lisa Ashton*
*Aston, PA*

## Beth's Caramel Corn

16 c. popped popcorn
1 c. butter
1⅔ c. brown sugar, packed
½ c. corn syrup
1 t. salt
½ t. baking soda
1 t. vanilla extract

Spray a roasting pan with non-stick vegetable spray. Place popcorn in pan; set aside. Melt butter in a large heavy saucepan over medium heat; stir in brown sugar, corn syrup and salt. Bring to a boil, stirring constantly. Stop stirring; continue to boil for exactly 5 minutes. Remove from heat; stir in baking soda and vanilla. Gradually pour hot mixture over popcorn; mix well. Cover and bake at 250 degrees for one hour, stirring every 15 minutes. Spread on parchment paper and cool completely. Break apart; store in an airtight container. Serves 12.

*Beth Hershey*
*Denver, PA*

# menus for all occasions

## Brunch Time
### Serves 8

*Mocha Muffins (page 12)*

*Tangy Cranberry Breakfast Cake (page 24)*

*Sausage & Cherry Tart with Walnuts
(page 30)*

*Creamy Crab Bake (page 33)*

*Oven-Fried Bacon Potatoes (page 42)*

## Neighborhood Cookout
### Serves 8

*Becky's BBQ Beef for a Crowd (page 88)*

*Cheryl's Country-Style Ribs (page 97)*

*The Best-Yet Buffalo Wings (page 118)*

*Aunt Karen's Baked Beans (page 206)*

*Tangy Corn Casserole (page 218)*

*People-Pleasin' Peach Pie (page 294)*

*double recipe

## Kid's Dinner
Serves 6

*Cheeseburger & Fries Casserole (page 131)*

*Mom's Macaroni & Cheese (page 239)*

*Chocolate Crunch Brownies (page 341)*

## Weeknight Meal
Serves 6

*Mama's Meatloaf (page 91)*

*Quick & Easy Parmesan Asparagus (page 205)*

*Easy Ranch Potatoes (page 232)*

*Chewy Chocolate Chip Cookies (page 318)*

## Mediterranean Feast

Serves 6 to 8

*Stuffed Eggplant Boats (page 125)

Greek Pizza (page 126)

Mediterranean Baked Fish (page 102)

Roasted Cauliflower (page 217)

Oma's Lemon Cheesecake (page 275)

## Cookie Exchange

Serves 16

Cool Mint Chocolate Swirls (page 317)

Almond Cream Spritz (page 324)

Espresso Bean Cookies (page 328)

Orangey-Ginger Cookie Sticks (page 337)

hot tea

*double recipe

## Sunday Lunch

Serves 4 to 6

*Sunday Baked Chicken (page 105)*

*Mile-High Buttermilk Biscuits (page 65)*

*Green Beans Supreme (page 210)*

*Blackberry Crumble (page 308)*

## Dinner Party

Serves 6

*Rosemary & Onion Bread (page 52)*

*Peppered Beef in Parsley Crust (page 88)*

*Zesty Horseradish Carrots (page 214)*

*tossed salad*

*Double-Chocolate Mousse Cake (page 244)*

## Fiesta Night

Serves 6 to 8

*South-of-the-Border Chicken (page 106)

Mexican Casserole (page 134)

Texas Corn & Green Chile Casserole
(page 160)

Chocolate Bread Pudding (page 311)

## Fall Feast

Serves 8

Hazelnut-Raisin Cornbread (page 57)

Tuscan Pork Loin (page 99)

*Pecan-Butternut Squash Bake (page 223)

Cinnamon-Glazed Apple Pie (page 290)

*double recipe

## A Taste of Louisiana

Serves 4

Cajun Crab Casserole *(page 158)*

Cajun Seafood Fettuccine *(page 193)*

Zesty Creole Bake *(page 197)*

Cornbread *(page 57)*

Perfect Pecan Pie *(page 283)*

## Summer Luncheon

Serves 6 to 8

Summery Herbed Tomato Pie *(page 224)*

Classic Quiche Lorraine *(page 35)*

Cherry-Cardamom Cookies *(page 336)*

*lemonade*

# METRIC EQUIVALENTS

The recipes that appear in this cookbook use the standard U.S. method for measuring liquid and dry or solid ingredients (teaspoons, tablespoons, and cups). The information in the following charts is provided to help cooks outside the United States successfully use these recipes. All equivalents are approximate.

## METRIC EQUIVALENTS FOR DIFFERENT TYPES OF INGREDIENTS

A standard cup measure of a dry or solid ingredient will vary in weight depending on the type of ingredient. A standard cup of liquid is the same volume for any type of liquid. Use the following chart when converting standard cup measures to grams (weight) or milliliters (volume).

| Standard Cup | Fine Powder (ex. flour) | Grain (ex. rice) | Granular (ex. sugar) | Liquid Solids (ex. butter) | Liquid (ex. milk) |
|---|---|---|---|---|---|
| 1 | 140 g | 150 g | 190 g | 200 g | 240 ml |
| ¾ | 105 g | 113 g | 143 g | 150 g | 180 ml |
| ⅔ | 93 g | 100 g | 125 g | 133 g | 160 ml |
| ½ | 70 g | 75 g | 95 g | 100 g | 120 ml |
| ⅓ | 47 g | 50 g | 63 g | 67 g | 80 ml |
| ¼ | 35 g | 38 g | 48 g | 50 g | 60 ml |
| ⅛ | 18 g | 19 g | 24 g | 25 g | 30 ml |

## USEFUL EQUIVALENTS FOR LIQUID INGREDIENTS BY VOLUME

| | | | | |
|---|---|---|---|---|
| ¼ tsp | = | | | 1 ml |
| ½ tsp | = | | | 2 ml |
| 1 tsp | = | | | 5 ml |
| 3 tsp | = 1 Tbsp | = ½ fl oz | = | 15 ml |
| | 2 Tbsp = ⅛ cup | = 1 fl oz | = | 30 ml |
| | 4 Tbsp = ¼ cup | = 2 fl oz | = | 60 ml |
| | 5⅓ Tbsp = ⅓ cup | = 3 fl oz | = | 80 ml |
| | 8 Tbsp = ½ cup | = 4 fl oz | = | 120 ml |
| | 10⅔ Tbsp = ⅔ cup | = 5 fl oz | = | 160 ml |
| | 12 Tbsp = ¾ cup | = 6 fl oz | = | 180 ml |
| | 16 Tbsp = 1 cup | = 8 fl oz | = | 240 ml |
| 1 pt | = 2 cups | = 16 fl oz | = | 480 ml |
| 1 qt | = 4 cups | = 32 fl oz | = | 960 ml |
| | | 33 fl oz | = 1000 ml | = 1 liter |

## USEFUL EQUIVALENTS FOR DRY INGREDIENTS BY WEIGHT

(To convert ounces to grams, multiply the number of ounces by 30.)

| | | | | |
|---|---|---|---|---|
| 1 oz | = | 1/16 lb | = | 30 g |
| 4 oz | = | ¼ lb | = | 120 g |
| 8 oz | = | ½ lb | = | 240 g |
| 12 oz | = | ¾ lb | = | 360 g |
| 16 oz | = | 1 lb | = | 480 g |

## USEFUL EQUIVALENTS FOR LENGTH

(To convert inches to centimeters, multiply the number of inches by 2.5.)

| | | | |
|---|---|---|---|
| 1 in = | | = | 2.5 cm |
| 6 in = ½ ft | | = | 15 cm |
| 12 in = 1 ft | | = | 30 cm |
| 36 in = 3 ft | = 1 yd | = | 90 cm |
| 40 in = | | = 100 cm | = 1 meter |

## USEFUL EQUIVALENTS FOR COOKING/OVEN TEMPERATURES

| | Fahrenheit | Celsius | Gas Mark |
|---|---|---|---|
| Freeze Water | 32° F | 0° C | |
| Room Temperature | 68° F | 20° C | |
| Boil Water | 212° F | 100° C | |
| Bake | 325° F | 160° C | 3 |
| | 350° F | 180° C | 4 |
| | 375° F | 190° C | 5 |
| | 400° F | 200° C | 6 |
| | 425° F | 220° C | 7 |
| | 450° F | 230° C | 8 |
| Broil | | | Grill |

# index

Butterfly Yeast Rolls (page 68)

## breads

Angel Biscuits, 58

Anytime Cheesy Biscuits, 61

Auntie Kay Kay's Sticky Buns, 16

Boston Brown Bread, 49

Brown Sugar Muffins, 11

Butterfly Yeast Rolls, 68

Butter-Rum Muffins, 15

Champion Banana Bread, 75

Cheddar Biscuits, 58

Cheese-Stuffed Biscuits, 57

Cheesy Batter Bread, 55

Chocolate-Cherry Cream Scones, 83

Chocolatey Banana Muffins, 12

Cornbread, 57

Country Biscuits Supreme, 61

Cranberry-Orange Scones, 83

Cranberry-Pecan-Coconut Loaf, 78

Cranberry Upside-Down Muffins, 14

Cream Biscuits, 65

Creamy Cinnamon Rolls, 19

Dilly Bread, 50

Emma's Gingerbread Muffins, 15

Garden Path Herbal Bread, 52

Garlic Bubble Bread, 52

Golden Raisin Buns, 73

Grandma Hilda's Sweet Biscuits, 66

Grandma Retha's Rhubarb
    Muffins, 12

Grandma's Irish Soda Bread, 72

Gran-Gran's Sweet Bread, 77

Hazelnut-Raisin Cornbread, 57

Holiday Eggnog Bread, 77

Honey Koek Loaf, 77

Honey-Wheat Bread, 49

Italian Bread, 49

Jane's Sweet Bubble Bread, 80

Kathy's Bacon Popovers, 52

Last Hurrah of Summer Peach
    Bread, 80

Marie's Yeast Rolls, 71

Mary's Sweet Corn Cake, 54

Mile-High Buttermilk Biscuits, 65

Mini Butterscotch Drop Scones, 81

Mini Cheddar Loaves, 54

Mocha Muffins, 12

Mom's Orange Bow Knots, 16

Mom's Raisin Bread, 75

Mother's Rolls, 69

No-Knead Oatmeal Bread, 48

Old-Fashioned Icebox Rolls, 69

Orange-Glazed Chocolate Rolls, 66

Peach Cobbler Muffins, 11

Peppery Biscuit Sticks, 62

Pizza Dough, 126

Rosemary & Onion Bread, 52

Stone-Ground Corn Rolls, 71

Sunday Dinner Potato Rolls, 72

Supreme Caramel Apple Rolls, 19

Sweet Potato Biscuits, 62

That Yummy Bread, 50

Velvet Pumpkin Bread, 78

## breakfast

Bacon & Chile Quiche, 36

Best-Ever Breakfast Bars, 45

Blueberry & Cream Cheese Strata, 30

Breakfast Pie, 38

Brown Sugar Baked Oatmeal, 42

Cherry Streusel Coffee Cake, 25

Classic Quiche Lorraine, 35

Country-Style Breakfast Pizza, 38

Cozy Breakfast Casserole, 33

Crab, Corn & Pepper Frittata, 37

Cream Cheese Danish, 21

Creamy Crab Bake, 33

Dutch Puffed Apple Pancake, 23

Esther's Delicious Breakfast Treat, 29

Finnish Pancakes, 23

Glorious Cheese Grits, 42

Haystack Eggs, 40

Herbed Sausage Quiche, 35

Make-Ahead Pumpkin Pie French
    Toast, 20

Mom's Texas Hash, 41

Niles Coffee Cake, 26

Orange-Walnut Brunch Cake, 25

Oven-Fried Bacon Potatoes, 42

Overnight Blueberry French Toast, 20

Pumpkin Biscotti, 44

Sausage Balls, 41

Sausage & Cherry Tart with
    Walnuts, 30

Simply Scrumptious Frittata, 36

Summer Swiss Quiche, 34

Sweet Blintz Soufflé, 29

Sweet & Spicy Bacon, 41

Tangy Cranberry Breakfast Cake, 24

Trudy's Cherry Coffee Cake, 26

Walnut-Maple Streusel Cake, 27

Yummy Brunch Strata, 32

## cakes & cupcakes

Black-Bottom Cupcakes, 276

Blueberry-Citrus Cake, 251

Butterscotch Picnic Cake, 262

Caitlin's Famous Sour Cream
    Cake, 268

Candied Fruitcake, 267

Caramel-Glazed Apple Cake, 255

Chocolate-Cappuccino
    Cheesecake, 273

Chocolate Gooey Cake, 245

Chocolate-Peanut Butter Marble
    Cake, 247

Chocolate Pound Cake, 271

Chocolate Spice Cake, 248

Chocolate-Zucchini Cupcakes, 276

Christmas Rainbow Cake, 266

Cocoa & Coffee Sheet Cake, 248

Coconut Fridge Cake, 255

Comforting Southern Cake, 262

Cranberry Swirl Cake, 252

Double-Chocolate Mousse
    Cake, 244

Eggnog Pound Cake, 269

Flowerpot Cupcakes, 279

Fresh Strawberry Shortcake, 249

Grandma's Banana Cupcakes, 279

Harvard Beet-Spice Cake, 264

Homemade Gingerbread Cake, 265

Hot Milk Cake, 267

Italian Cream Cake, 258

LaRae's Pumpkin Dump Cake, 261

Lazy Daisy Cake, 258

Miss Lizzie's Pound Cake, 271

Mixed-Up Cupcakes, 275

Mix-in-a-Pan Nut Cake, 265

Mocha Cake, 245

Nana's Famous Coconut-Pineapple
    Cake, 256

Old-Fashioned Applesauce Cake, 261

Oma's Lemon Cheesecake, 275

Orange-Peach Dump Cake, 248

Peanut Butter Pound Cake, 270

Pineapple Upside-Down Cake, 252

Rhubarb Cream Cheesecake, 272

Strawberry Layer Cake, 257

Sunny Lemon Cake, 251

Sunshine Angel Food Cake, 268

Three-Layer Chocolate Cake, 247

Too-Easy Toffee Cheesecake, 272

Oma's Lemon Cheesecake
(page 275)

## cookies & bars

Almond Cream Spritz, 324

Apple-Cheddar Bars, 347

Applesauce Spice Bars, 349

Brown Sugar Brownies, 340

Butterscotch Gingerbread
    Cookies, 332

Buttery Ricotta Cookies, 320

Cherry-Cardamom Cookies, 336

Chewy Chocolate Chip Cookies, 318

Choco-Berry Goodie Bars, 349

Chocolate Chip Cheesecake
    Squares, 350

Chocolate-Chocolate Chip
    Cookies, 317

Chocolate Crunch Brownies, 341

Chocolate Fudge Cookies, 318

Chocolate-Mint Candy Brownies, 342

Chocolatey Chewy Brownies, 338

Christmas Peppermint & Chocolate
    Meringues, 318

Coconut-Pecan Fudge Bars, 350

Cool Mint Chocolate Swirls, 317
Dazzling Neapolitan Cookies, 335
Double-Dark Chocolate
    Brownies, 341
Espresso Bean Cookies, 328
Fudgy Cream Cheese Brownies, 345
German Apple Streusel Kuchen, 346
Ginger-Molasses Cookies, 331
Gooey Toffee Scotchies, 339
Grandma Gray's Spice-Nut Bars, 346
Grandma Sorensen's Sugar
    Cookies, 320
Hello Dolly Bars, 353
Key Lime Bites, 335
Lacy Florentine Cookies, 323
Lemon Chess Bars, 352
Lemon-Macadamia Cookies, 338
Maple Sugar Cookies, 332
Nanny's Shortbread Chews, 323
Nellie's Persimmon Cookies, 334
Orangey-Ginger Cookie Sticks, 337
Peppermint Bark Brownies, 342
Powdered Sugar Sandies, 320
Red Velvet Brownies, 345
Snowcap Cookies, 327
Sour Cream Drop Cookies, 324
Southern Oatmeal Cookies, 327
Spicy Maple-Anise Snaps, 328
Sweet Raspberry-Oat Bars, 351
Teresa's Tasty Apricot Bars, 348
White Chocolate Cookies, 331

## desserts

Apple-Gingerbread Cobbler, 302
Beth's Caramel Corn, 355
Blackberry Crumble, 308
Brenda's Fruit Crisp, 304
Buttermilk Pear Cobbler, 302
Cherries Jubilee Crisp, 307
Cherry-Pecan Bread Pudding, 308
Chocolate Bread Pudding, 311
Chocolate Cobbler, 299
Chocolate Pinwheels, 355
Easy Cherry Cobbler, 301
Estelle's Baked Custard, 312

Graham Cracker Apple Crisp, 305
Homemade Graham Crackers, 354
Mulberry Buckle, 307
Old-Fashioned Bread Pudding, 311
Pumpkin Custard Crunch, 312
Yummy Peach Dessert, 305

## entrées

Aunt B's Chicken Tetrazzini, 183
Baked Crumbed Haddock, 101
Baked Ham in Peach Sauce, 94
Baked Potatoes & Chicken Sauce, 121
Balsamic Rosemary Chicken, 102
Becky's BBQ Beef for a Crowd, 88
Beef Brisket in a Bag, 87
Beefy Cheddar Bake, 169
Beefy Chow Mein Noodle
    Casserole, 134
Beefy Spinach Casserole, 132
Black Bean Casserole, 160
Boycott-Your-Grill Beef Kabobs, 90
Broccoli-Chicken Lasagna, 180
Brown Sugar Ham, 94
Brunswick Chicken Bake, 187
Buttermilk Baked Chicken, 105
Cajun Crab Casserole, 158
Cajun Seafood Fettucine, 193
Cheeseburger & Fries Casserole, 131
Cheesy Beef & Bacon Burger
    Meatloaf, 93
Cheesy Chicken Enchiladas, 189
Cheesy Chicken & Mac, 180
Cheesy Sausage-Potato Casserole, 137
Cheryl's Country-Style Ribs, 97
Chicken à la Kym, 109
Chicken-Cashew Casserole, 147
Chicken Kiev, 110
Chicken Lasagna with Roasted Red
    Pepper Sauce, 181
Chicken Mozzarella, 106
Chicken Noodle Casserole, 148
Chicken Parmigiana Casserole, 144
Chicken Spaghetti Deluxe, 183
Chicken Tex-Mex Bake, 184
Chicken-Zucchini Bake, 186

Chilly-Day Chicken Pot Pie, 189
Company Baked Ziti, 175
Cornbread-Topped Barbecue
    Beef, 166
Crab-Stuffed Eggplant, 193
Cream Cheese Enchiladas, 169
Deep South Chicken &
    Dumplings, 121
Delicious Drumsticks, 117
Dijon Salmon Bake, 198
Divine Casserole, 131
Easy Baked Chicken, 105
Easy Beef Burgundy, 86
Easy Mexican Bake, 198
Eggplant Parmesan, 199
Family Swiss Steak, 88
Farmers' Market Casserole, 160
Flat Meatballs & Gravy, 93
Florence's Meatball Surprise, 172
Garlicky Chicken Casserole, 151
Glazed Lemon Chicken, 110
Gram Walker's Smothered
    Chicken, 113
Grandma Great's Chicken
    Casserole, 144
Grandma Knorberg's Pork Chop
    Casserole, 138

Oodles of Noodles
Casserole (page 148)

Gran's Rosemary Roast Chicken, 117
Grecian Chicken, 109
Greek Pizza, 126
Ham & Cauliflower Casserole, 143
Ham-It-Up Casserole, 141
Hashbrown-Pork Chop Casserole, 138
Hearty Ham & Potato Casserole, 143
Hearty Pierogi Casserole, 137
He-Man Casserole, 143
Herbed Seafood Casserole, 155
Hobo Dinner, 165
Homemade Cheese Pizza, 126
Homemade Turkey Pot Pie, 191
Honey & Brown Sugar Meatloaf, 90
Hot Tamale Casserole, 152
Italian Zucchini Casserole, 161
Linda's Spring Greens Pizza, 125
Make-Ahead Faux Lasagna, 176
Mama's Meatloaf, 91
Mama's Scrumptious Roast Beef, 87
Mary's Heavenly Chicken, 109
Mediterranean Baked Fish, 102
Mexican Casserole, 134
Mile-High Pork Chop Casserole, 141
Mock Oyster Casserole, 156
Newlywed Pork Chops, 98
One-Dish Chicken & Gravy, 184
One-Dish Reuben Dinner, 166
Oodles of Noodles Casserole, 148
Orange-Pecan Cornish Hens, 122
Oven-Baked Ragout, 176
Oven Chicken Cordon Bleu, 107
Overnight Scalloped Turkey, 190
Pantry Casserole, 133
Party Ham Casserole, 142
Party Paella Casserole, 156
Penne with Sausage & Cheese, 178
Peppered Beef in Parsley Crust, 88
Pizzeria Sausage Supper, 179
Polynesian Chicken, 113
Potato Puff & Ground Beef
    Casserole, 134
Ravioli Taco Bake, 175
Renae's Taco Bake, 173
Roast Chicken Dijon, 114
Roast Chicken & Vegetables, 114

Rooster Pie, 187
Rotini-Tuna Casserole, 159
Saucy Pork Chop Scallop, 179
Savory Salisbury Steak, 93
Seafood Bisque Casserole, 155
Shrimply Divine Casserole, 159
Sour Cream Noodle Bake, 190
Southern-Style Shrimp & Rice, 197
South-of-the-Border Chicken, 106
Southwestern Turkey Casserole, 151
Spaghetti Pie, 170
Spicy Pork Packets, 97
Spicy Sausage & Chicken Creole, 118
Stuffed Cabbage Casserole, 132
Stuffed Eggplant Boats, 125
Sunday Baked Chicken, 105
Swiss Seafood Lasagna, 194
Tamale Pot Pie, 165
Texas Corn & Green Chile
    Casserole, 160
Texas Two-Step Casserole, 147
The Best-Yet Buffalo Wings, 118
3-Bean & Ham Casserole, 141
3-Cheese Spinach Rigatoni, 200
Tomato-Basil Pasta Bake, 200
Top-Prize Chicken Casserole, 145
Tuna Noodle Supreme, 194
Turkey, Almond & Wild Rice
    Casserole, 152

Turkey-Spinach Quiche, 122
Tuscan Pork Loin, 99
Unstuffed Pork Chops, 101
Use Your Noodle Casserole, 148
Veggie-Chicken Bake, 186
Western Pork Chops, 98
Wild Rice Hot Dish, 170
Zesty Creole Bake, 197
Zippy Chili Casserole, 147

## frostings, fillings & toppings

Biscuit Topping, 302
Browned Butter Frosting, 349
Caramel Frosting, 271
Caramel Glaze, 255
Chocolate-Pecan Frosting, 248
Chocolate Topping, 244
Cinnamon Glaze, 290
Coconut Topping, 348
Cranberry Topping, 14
Cream Cheese Frosting, 256, 279, 345
Cream Cheese-Pecan Frosting, 258
Crumb Topping, 307
Crunch Topping, 312
Crunchy Topping, 223
Filling, 273
Frosting, 245, 258

Cherry-Pecan Bread Pudding (page 308)

Spicy Carrot French Fries
(page 214)

Fudge Frosting, 247

Glaze, 25, 66, 80, 262

Herb Filling, 50

Meringue, 299

Orange Frosting, 16

Peanut Butter Frosting, 270, 276

Pineapple Filling, 256

Strawberry Frosting, 257

Toffee Sauce, 339

Topping, 11, 24, 214, 268, 272, 273

Walnut Filling, 27

Walnut Topping, 284

Warm Vanilla Sauce, 265

## pies & pastries

Amish Sugar Cream Pie, 284

Caramel-Banana Pie, 293

Chocolate Buttermilk Pie, 289

Chocolate Chess Pie, 286

Cinnamon-Glazed Apple Pie, 290

Coconut Cream Pie, 299

Country Harvest Pie, 290

Grandma's Custard Pie, 286

Green Tomato Pie, 295

Heavenly Key Lime Pie, 296

Hot Lemon Pie, 296

Mom's Chocolate Malt Shoppe
    Pie, 289

Pear Pie, 293

Pecan Cheesecake Pie, 283

People-Pleasin' Peach Pie, 294

Perfect Pecan Pie, 283

Satin Slipper Pie, 286

Sour Cream-Apple Pie, 291

Sweet Apple Tarts, 301

Sweet Potato Pie, 285

Tried & True Pie Dough, 283

Walnut Crunch Pumpkin Pie, 284

## sauces

Barbecue Sauce, 97

Roasted Red Pepper Sauce, 181

Supreme Sauce, 121

## side dishes

Asparagus Casserole, 205

Aunt Annie's Macaroni & Cheese, 236

Aunt Karen's Baked Beans, 206

Baked Hominy & Cheese, 209

Baked Spinach & Rice, 239

Beefy Mushroom Rice, 239

Cabbage Pudding, 210

Candied Sweet Potatoes, 231

Corn & Onion Casserole, 219

Cornbread-Biscuit Dressing, 240

Creamy Cabbage Bake, 213

Dumplings, 121

Easy Ranch Potatoes, 232

Ginger Ale Baked Apples, 227

Golden Onions, 220

Grandpa Jim's Potatoes, 235

Green Bean Bundles, 213

Green Beans Supreme, 210

Herbed Veggie-Cheese Casserole, 217

Kansas Scalloped Corn, 219

Kielbasa Bean Pot, 209

Mom's Macaroni & Cheese, 239

Mom's Squash Casserole, 220

Mushroom & Orzo Casserole, 240

Nannie Raue's Sweet Potato
    Pone, 232

Oh-So-Hot Banana Peppers, 206

Old-Fashioned Scalloped Potatoes, 232

Patty's Broccoli & Swiss
    Casserole, 217

Paula's Twice-Baked Potatoes, 235

Pecan-Butternut Squash Bake, 223

Potluck Potato Bake, 236

Prize-Winning Pineapple Cheddar
    Bake, 228

Quick & Easy Parmesan
    Asparagus, 205

Roasted Cauliflower, 217

Sage Stuffing, 114

Scalloped Pineapple, 231

Scalloped Zucchini, 224

Spicy Carrot French Fries, 214

Squash Puff, 223

Summery Herbed Tomato Pie, 224

Tangy Corn Casserole, 218

Tomato Pudding, 227

Tried & True Apple Casserole, 228

Twice-Baked Sweet Potatoes, 231

Wild Rice Stuffing, 241

Zesty Horseradish Carrots, 214

# BIG BOOK OF
# COUNTRY BAKING

©2013 by Gooseberry Patch
2500 Farmers Dr., #110, Columbus, Ohio 43235
1-800-854-6673, **gooseberrypatch.com**

©2013 by Time Home Entertainment Inc.
135 West 50th Street, New York, NY 10020

ISBN-13: 978-0-8487-4224-9
ISBN-10: 0-8487-4224-9
Library of Congress Control Number: 2013938918
Printed in the United States of America
First Printing 2013

**Oxmoor House**
Editorial Director: Leah McLaughlin
Creative Director: Felicity Keane
Brand Manager: Vanessa Tiongson
Senior Editor: Rebecca Brennan
Managing Editor: Rebecca Benton

**Gooseberry Patch Big Book of Country Baking**
Editor: Susan Ray
Art Director: Claire Cormany
Project Editor: Lacie Pinyan
Assistant Designer: Allison Sperando Potter
Director, Test Kitchen: Elizabeth Tyler Austin
Recipe Developers and Testers: Wendy Ball, R.D.; Victoria E. Cox;
    Tamara Goldis; Stefanie Maloney; Callie Nash; Karen Rankin;
    Leah Van Deren
Recipe Editor: Alyson Moreland Haynes
Food Stylists: Margaret Monroe Dickey, Catherine Crowell Steele
Photography Director: Jim Bathie
Senior Photographer: Hélène Dujardin
Senior Photo Stylist: Kay E. Clarke
Photo Stylist: Mindi Shapiro Levine
Assistant Photo Stylist: Mary Louise Menendez
Senior Production Manager: Greg A. Amason
Associate Production Manager: Kimberly Marshall

**Contributors**
Editor: Julia Sayers
Compositors: Carol Damsky, Frances Gunnells
Copy Editors: Adrienne Davis, Rhonda Lee Lother
Indexer: Mary Ann Laurens
Interns: Megan Branagh, Susan Kemp, Sara Lyon, Staley McIlwain,
    Jeffrey Preis, Maria Sanders
Photographer: Beau Gustafson
Photo Stylists: Mary Clayton Carl, Missie Crawford,
    Caitlin Van Horn

**Time Home Entertainment Inc.**
Publisher: Jim Childs
Vice President, Brand and Digital Strategy: Steven Sandonato
Executive Director, Marketing Services: Carol Pittard
Executive Director, Retail & Special Sales: Tom Mifsud
Director, Bookazine Development & Marketing: Laura Adam
Executive Publishing Director: Joy Butts
Associate Publishing Director: Megan Pearlman
Finance Director: Glenn Buonocore
Associate General Counsel: Helen Wan

To order additional publications, call 1-800-765-6400.
To search, savor, and share thousands of recipes,
visit **myrecipes.com**

Front Cover (from left to right, top to bottom): Mama's Meatloaf, page 91; Anytime Cheesy Biscuits, page 61; People-Pleasin' Peach Pie, page 294; Simply Scrumptious Frittata, page 36; Paula's Twice-Baked Potatoes, page 235; Strawberry Layer Cake, page 257
Page 1: Orange-Glazed Chocolate Rolls, page 66
Back Cover (from left to right, top to bottom): Aunt Annie's Macaroni & Cheese, page 236; Hello Dolly Bars, page 353; Gran's Rosemary Roast Chicken, page 117; Oodles of Noodles Casserole, page 148; Espresso Bean Cookies, page 328